Before You Invest
Read
PENNY STOCKS

"You might make a buck or two in trading the penny stocks. This book will tell you a great deal about how to do it."
—*The Stock Market Magazine*

"It has set a high standard for any to follow.... [McWilliams] writes with a very lively style that makes even an explanation of the most technical points relatively easy reading."
—*The National OTC Stock Journal*

"An articulate and intelligent author"
—*Financial Analysts Journal*

Bruce G. McWilliams is a former editor and chief writer for *The Denver Stock Exchange,* the *Wall Street Journal* of the Rocky Mountain over-the-counter securities market. A veteran investor in penny stocks, he charts the progress of his portfolio in Philadelphia, where he's taking an advanced degree from the Wharton School of Business.

PENNY STOCKS

How the Small Investor Can Make Large Profits in the Penny Market

Bruce G. McWilliams

WARNER BOOKS

A Warner Communications Company

To Erna Studinski, my grandmother,
who gave me so much but was unable
to see this work in its final form,
and to Maurine Gordon

A CAVEAT: I am not an SEC-registered investment adviser. Nothing in this book should be construed as investment advice in reference to a particular security. I currently own and have owned several of the securities mentioned in the book. As I make clear in the study, the past performance of these stocks is not an indicator of their future direction.

Warner Books Edition

This Warner Books edition is published by arrangement with Doubleday & Company, Inc., 245 Park Avenue, New York, New York 10167.

Warner Books, Inc., 666 Fifth Avenue, New York, NY 10103

W A Warner Communications Company

Printed in the United States of America

First Warner printing: February 1984
10 9 8 7 6 5 4 3 2 1

Library of Congress Cataloging in Publication Data

McWilliams, Bruce G.
    Penny stocks.

    Includes bibliographical references and index.
    1. Speculation. 2. Stocks. 3. Venture capital.
I. Title.
[HG6041.M39   1984]   332.63'22   83-16971
ISBN 0-446-38010-5 (USA) (pbk.)
ISBN 0-446-38011-3 (Canada) (pbk.)

Preface to the Paperback Edition

Since the original edition was first written, the penny stock market has undergone a roller-coaster ride. As was to be expected, when the big-league stocks on the New York Exchange recovered in August 1982, the penny stock market exploded. At this writing, the market enjoys breathtaking exhilaration as stock prices reach new highs. But in the interim, between the boom of 1980 and 1982, there was a period of rough sledding in the market. Many investors lost considerable sums, some of the penny stock firms went belly-up, and several of the brokerage houses that specialize in these stocks suffered. But, as seasoned investors realize, this was and is to be expected. As I make clear in the book you are about to read, there are no guarantees. In fact, since the original writing, some of the firms mentioned in the text have gone bankrupt. Yet others have soared to new heights as their managers proved to the market that they had the staying power and the ability to manage the firm.

The ground rules for investing in the market remain the same: Research the company before buying the stock and understand the market mechanics. The book you have in your hands remains a powerful tool for accomplishing these objectives.

Philadelphia
July 1983

Contents

"I turned $500 into $18,000 in a year's time, through the penny stock market."

Beth Cooke, airlines reservation clerk

PART ONE

GROUND RULES

1

Penny Fortunes

What's the small investor to do these days? Gold has lost its glimmer; residential real estate, the financial salvation of middle Americans during the 1970s, has collapsed; and bank passbook savings accounts have become an insult to anyone of intelligence. Even money market funds offer only dim promise of keeping pace with inflation.

In the fiscally confusing 1980s, penny stocks shine through as one of the few ways an investor with only modest resources can reap big profits. These securities, priced less than $5 (and many between 10 cents and $1) surge forward much more rapidly than do their higher-priced major exchange counterparts. Gains of between 300% and 1,000% in less than two years are not unusual.

An investment portfolio in the "pennies" can be started with as little as $500, and can grow manyfold when carefully managed. The terrain of the market is treacherous, though, and after months of careful prospecting your penny stock investment could turn out to be just a dry hole.

On the other hand, it could prove to be a gusher. This book's aim is to guide new and seasoned investors alike through the landscape of the lower-priced realm of the Over the Counter (OTC) stock market. We'll explain some of the market verbiage that often scares away the uninitiated and suggest strategies for successful maneuvering in the marketplace—i.e., making money. But as with any potentially lucrative venture it takes time, hard work, and, of course, a modicum of luck. You can be assured

that the time you invest in reading this book will greatly improve
your odds.

Penny stocks have been called, by some, venture stocks. Most
penny stock companies are young companies, still in their corporate infancy. An investment in such a company is a risk, a venture. One investor started with a mere $500 in a 10-cent venture
capital stock and in just five years parlayed his gains to over
$100,000. This is what makes the market special: it allows those
without a fortune to make a fortune. By comparison, if that same
investor had sunk the $500 into a New York Stock Exchange se-
curity, he'd be lucky to have made 50% on his money. Most
likely, though, he could not have found a broker willing to accept
his relatively minuscule investment. Brokers dealing in New York
Stock Exchange stocks usually require an investment in the thousands and grumble about anything smaller. Well, the great majority of Americans just don't have $10,000 sitting around idle. If
you invest that money you sacrifice crucial liquidity, rainy-day
money, or the kids' college funds. On the other hand, many
Americans do have $500 available—the generally accepted mini-
mum for making a small venture stock investment.

At a recent gathering of potential investors, J. Daniel Bell,
president of one of the leading venture stock houses (J. Daniel
Bell & Company), dubbed the venture stock market "the people's
market." He noted that "this little market has reached out and
touched people." The engaging Mr. Bell went on to say, "Penny
stocks are fun. If you're involved in a humdrum day at work and
you want the excitement of taking a gamble, then they may be the
right investment for you."[1]

The trade-off between investing in New York Stock Exchange
stocks and venture stocks is between risk and potential reward. If
you buy ten shares of AT&T, it's a pretty safe bet that this bed-
rock of American business isn't going to go under and you will
eventually make a little money. By comparison, if you invest in a
10-cent oil and gas stock, you might end up with nothing when
the young company files for bankruptcy—or you might end up
with a 1,000% gain when the stock nudges $1.10. Both have hap-
pened. New York Stock Exchange stocks trudge along a rather
predictable course. Venture stocks pinball around with incredible
velocity.

VENTURE STOCK ROOTS

Denver and the Rocky Mountain region have emerged as one of the chief centers of these low-priced venture stocks even though the seeds of the market were planted halfway around the world. The 1973 OPEC oil embargo sparked a number of consequences. First, of course, the joint action of the major oil producers forced the price of a barrel of crude petroleum into upward spiral. This cooled slightly in 1981 with the alleged oil glut, but no evidence exists today that oil prices will plummet on a long-term basis.

Because of OPEC's actions, the inadequacy of domestic energy sources was indelibly etched into modern American history. The nation began a frenzied drive to uncover domestic energy resources. Coal, uranium, and geothermal energy have all been discussed but there has been relatively little action: oil and gas still remain at the top of the energy menu. This drive for internal energy stems less from the patriotic imperative than from the changed economic realities. President Reagan, in one of his first official moves, began deregulating oil prices. Exploring for riskier and harder-to-find energy could now be justified because of higher prices. Denver, the center of the Rocky Mountain states and the nearest major city to the Overthrust Belt, was the logical financial center for this drive.*

The second major catalyst behind the growth and development of the venture capital stock market was the eroding purchasing power of the dollar. In the 1970s, middle Americans wrung their hands in despair as the value of their dollars was halved and then quartered. Up until the last few years of the decade, real estate was one of the few avenues for middle Americans to shield their precious dollars. No longer, though. *The Wall Street Journal* reported in August 1981 that home prices have suffered "the worst inflation-adjusted drop . . . since World War II, and perhaps . . . the first actual decline since the Great Depression."[2] A passbook savings account earning 5½% interest, altogether satis-

---

* The Overthrust Belt is a geological formation containing oil and gas deposits similar in magnitude to the Alaskan oil find. The Belt runs from the Canadian border of Montana down to Mexico. Because of recent advances in petroleum recovery methods, the enormous quantities of energy resources buried within the ground are now recoverable.

factory in the 1960s, became a losing proposition in the 1970s. Small investors became stymied as passbook accounts shrank on a monthly basis with the release of the latest Consumer Price Index (CPI).

Thus, the catalysts for the skyrocketing of venture stocks were in place several years ago: rising energy costs, a domestic energy drive, shrinking dollars, and millions of disgruntled investors holding on to these dollars, a rapidly depreciating resource.

CAUSE AND EFFECT

The confluence of these forces is typified by Paul Hoovler and his energy company, Chaparral Resources, Inc. Just a little before the OPEC embargo, Hoovler was working in Denver. An experienced oil-field hand, he had been finding oil and gas for other men all of his life. Finally, in 1973, Hoovler's entrepreneurial spirit took wing and he opened his own firm, Chaparral.

No bank would even talk to Hoovler: he did not have enough tangible assets with which to collateralize a loan. As you'll soon see, drilling for oil is very much akin to prospecting for gold: it takes money, a lot of it. And after all the money is spent, there's no assurance of finding a revenue-generating asset. So Chaparral went to the public market and sold stock for 10 cents per share. The time was March 1973. Hoovler told me he had a hard time digging up enough people willing to invest in his company. Granted, an investment in Chaparral was fraught with all sorts of risk, but what an investment those lucky people made! Hoovler could have run off with the money or he could have drilled all dry holes. This group of early investors had only Hoovler's past experience as an oil finder on which to base their investment decision. The company had not been in operation very long, so past earnings were irrelevant. Let's say you made a $500 investment in Chaparral and bought 5,000 shares. By June 1981, those shares had a market value of $90,000. The annual rate of return on this investment amounts to an almost inconceivable 91%.*

The flip side of this story is that with their $500 investments,

---

* Chaparral's stock underwent a 1:10 reverse split in September 1978, a 4:1 split in January 1981, and a 2:1 split in May 1981. Accordingly, the 500 shares at the June 1981 date would have been, in actuality, 4,000 shares. The bid price in early June was $22.50 per share.

venture stock supporters provided Hoovler with the opportunity to drill for oil and gas. He's made some mistakes along the way, no doubt. Like the time his first well in Wyoming burst into flames. It took twenty-eight days and the famed oil-field firefighter Red Adair's efforts to quench the blaze. The story goes down in the annals of U.S. petroleum history as one of the largest oil well fires ever.

The fire, while certainly disrupting Chaparral, didn't send the company up in smoke—though Hoovler became a bit more cautious from then on. Chaparral kept pushing ahead, taking smaller risks to develop a sizable oil and gas revenue stream. Hoovler wanted to make sure that the next time he went out on a limb the safety net was firmly attached. Then, in 1978, Hoovler was ready once again to go after "the big carrot"—a tremendous producer. He planned to drill a wildcat well in the Madden gas field of Wyoming where he'd already acquired considerable geologic experience. When an operator drills in an area without any proven oil or gas reserves, this is called a wildcat or exploratory well. In contrast, a developmental drilling takes place in an already-established oil or gas pool. Wildcat wells are very risky and development wells less so.

Chaparral began drilling this well in Wyoming in the hope of finding natural gas. They drilled to 10,000 feet and discovered no commercially feasible quantities of gas. Hoovler, however, was sure there was gas in this ground. He just wasn't sure where, so Chaparral continued to drill. Keep in mind that each foot drilled is more expensive than the last one. At 18,000 feet—nearly three and one-half miles under the earth's surface—nothing tremendous had been uncovered. His engineers and accountants told him, "Paul, we can't afford this; we really haven't found anything yet and we've got to stop." Undaunted, Hoovler continued to drill. Never mind that no well in the Rockies had ever been drilled that deep, he was going to find natural gas.

After 342 days of drilling and when the company was nearly broke, Chaparral ceased drilling operations on Halloween of 1979. At nearly 21,000 feet, Hoovler had found gas. In fact, Hoovler found lots of gas—approximately 11 billion cubic feet of the stuff.

The story of Chaparral Resources is both typical of the venture oil and gas stock market and atypical. Founded in 1972, the company is one of the older regional energy firms adorning Denver's Seventeenth Street (called by western enthusiasts the Wall Street of the West). On the other hand, the average annual appreciation of 91% on investment isn't that far out of line with potential gains in the market. And it's been small investors like yourself who have fueled this high-powered market.

OTC GUSHER

Drilling an oil well is an expensive venture. On the one hand, if the drilling hits, as Chaparral's did, it can prove to be a bonanza. On the other hand, dry hole drillings are a frequent occurrence. Energy prospectors need tremendous sums of capital in order to discover that one producing well. This is where the venture stock market comes in. Over the last four years more than $600,000,000—nearly two thirds of a billion dollars—in venture capital has been raised by independent energy companies and others in the Rocky Mountain securities market. This money is raised exclusively via the Over the Counter (OTC) market.

You may be thinking that Chaparral is one of those stock investments you always hear your friends talking about but can never seem to find. Similar comments were probably made about such stocks as Xerox and Polaroid in earlier times. But for oil and gas stocks, this isn't necessarily the case. A look at all oil and gas issues emanating from the Denver market between 1968 and 1979 showed the growth of these stocks to be 1,825%. If a $500 investment had been made in each of the seventy-two energy issues for a total investment of $36,000, that portfolio could have been sold on November 30, 1980, for $693,156.[8] Only one of the companies went out of business, while the remaining seventy-one stocks were selling well above their offering price. How does that return compare with the money you have languishing in a savings account? Or even in a supposedly high-yielding money market fund?

After all these reports of tremendous success, a word of caution is called for. Oil and gas venture stocks have done exceedingly well in the past. This does not mean they'll continue to jog the same upward path. Indeed, both Big Board and start-up energy company stocks slid sideways and downward during the softening of the oil market in 1981. Further, while the long-term growth picture is bright, this doesn't mean there won't be major dips. If you should need to pull out your investment, there's no guarantee that it won't be at a loss. The penny stock market is quite speculative and therefore quite risky. In other words, don't bet the rent money on venture stocks. The risk and reward potential in this market will be discussed at considerable length in the third chapter.

HIGH-TECH WAVE AND GOLDEN GLIMMER

Energy development, while a driving force, isn't the only source of this stock market dynamite. Start-up high technology and mining firms also have found the market a bonanza. Companies with such futuristic names as Sci-Pro, Ultrak, and Staodynamics, among others, have been capitalized by offering stock priced at $1 or less. Investors reap huge gains when these companies actually begin producing their specialized products. Medical firms on the cutting edge of new health technologies often find that a financial booster shot from the market gives them the get-up-and-go they need to realize their full potential. Mining firms loaded with a geologic idea but little in the way of cash assets also come to the penny market. Respected securities analyst Steven Leuthold said of these companies, "There's been a lot of dream building going on."[4] And it's you, the small investor, who can help turn these dreams into a reality.

The primary aim of this book is to explain the mechanics and nuances of the lower-priced securities market for profitable investment. It's a book geared toward new investors. Because the stocks are priced so low, many who believed they could not afford to invest can avail themselves of this market. Nor should experienced investors shy away; the venture market is in many ways different from the stocks of the established exchanges.

In this book, I give many examples of actual companies in the venture market. These stories are employed to highlight important investment considerations. Of course, I simply could have said, look for companies that do "X" and avoid those that do "Y." However, specific examples of actual companies and their fortunes and misfortunes will give you a feel for the types of investment questions you'll be facing. These companies, much like their founders, are living, breathing entities with actual personalities.

Thus, I don't suggest strict investment formulas—for example, don't buy a stock with a price-to-earnings ratio of less than 10— because in many ways the penny market cannot be quantified. By presenting examples of actual companies, I believe I can give you a far better understanding of what to expect.

This book is divided into three main parts. The first section sets up the guidelines for venture stock investing: we'll look at the mechanics of the Over the Counter securities market, discuss what venture capital is and how it differs from other forms of capital, and then begin sketching a skeletal outline of how to evaluate potential investments. In the second section we'll jump into the main constituents of the venture stock market: high-tech, energy, mining, and new stock issues, and suggest questions that should be asked before any investment is ever made. The final section sums up all of this information by offering powerful investment strategies, guidelines on finding a venture stockbroker, and stories of some big winners in the market. When you're finished with this book you will have a more than adequate knowledge about the market, as well as the tools with which to find the next big winners.

PENNY ORIGINS

Before we embark on this journey to explore the lucrative lodes and gushers of the venture OTC stock market, a definition is in order.

Penny stocks have been around a long time. Denver Securities and Exchange Commission chief Robert Davenport once told me that penny stocks were issued in Denver in the 1880s when the city was the hub of a silver and gold mining explosion. A century ago, as today, risky companies needed capital in order to exploit the mineral resources of the earth. Selling stock in their companies to investors, these early pioneers discovered they could sell a lot more stock if they priced these issues for pennies. It didn't make any difference to them whether they raised $10,000 by selling 10 shares for $1,000 or by selling 100,000 shares for 10 cents.

Over the last decade, stock underwriters relearned the same thing: they could sell shares at $25 or 25 cents. Because these low-priced stocks are attractive to more investors, it's far easier for the 25-cent stock to move up to 50 cents than it is for the $25 stock to appreciate to $50. Nevertheless, an investment in either stock yields a 100% profit.

In the past, "penny stocks" referred to stocks that sold for under $1—literally for pennies. But nowadays, due to inflation, a penny stock has come to mean any security selling for under $5. However we choose to define them, the important part is that penny stocks have showed tremendous gains for investors—gains that have been far more than just pennies.

NOTES

1. Jerry Ruhl, "J. Daniel Bell Touts Penny Stock Mart," *Denver Rocky Mountain News,* February 16, 1981, p. 69.

2. C. Christian Hill, "Financing Concessions Conceal a Real Slump in the Price of Homes," *The Wall Street Journal,* August 7, 1981, p. 1.

3. "Twelve-Year Review of Oil and Gas Issues Reveals Big Returns," *The Denver Stock Exchange,* December 29, 1980, p. 5.

4. Michael Sivy, "Making Big Money on Little Stocks," *Money,* July 1981, p. 44.

2

OTC Outline

Plato Christopulos makes a decent wage in Salt Lake City although "his principal love," he says, "is the penny stock market. The secret," says the seasoned investor, "is flipping—buying a stock and then quickly getting out of it at a profit." You have to be lucky, he maintains. "Just two months ago I made $7,000 in five days from an investment in Justheim Petroleum. I bought 3,500 shares at $3 and flipped the stock when it hit $5."

Penny stocks catapult and collapse at incredible speeds, so speculators don't hold on to a profitable stock for too long. Profitable investment, as opposed to pure speculation, requires more foresight, investigation, and courage. "I remember Horn Silver," says Christopulos. "It traded at 2 cents in the early 1960s. Today, after a two for one stock split, it trades on the New York Stock Exchange as Freeport-McMoran for $32 a share." Christopulos laments selling out his 65,000 shares before it reached a dollar. "If I'd stuck with it, I'd be a multimillionaire today."[1]

Christopulos slights his profitable investment strategy when he says, "You have to be lucky." But he's traded actively for a long time and the rules of the game come almost as second nature. He knows, for example, what the spread is and what it indicates about a stock's growth potential. Moreover, he knows how trading in the Over the Counter market differs from that of the established exchanges. To realize clues, recognize nuances, and avoid pitfalls it's imperative to understand the basic trading mechanics of the OTC stock market. This chapter describes these market fundamentals and will allow new and seasoned investors alike to begin prospecting for the lucrative veins and gushers of the penny stock market.

Justheim Petroleum, Christopulos' pot of gold, originally raised $100,000 in the venture capital stock market. The company sold shares at 6 cents in order to generate the capital needed to explore for and to produce energy. By selling shares, the company sold a percentage of its assets to public investors. When Christopulos bought 3,500 shares of Justheim, in essence he bought a very small percentage of the company's five million outstanding shares. Because it sold shares to the public, Justheim is said to be "publicly owned" or "publicly held."

A company in need of money is presented with a wide range of financing alternatives. In theory, Justheim could have gone to a bank and obtained a loan. I say "in theory" because, in practice, no bank would have given the unproven company any money. The company could also have taken out a loan from the public by selling bonds; this is called debt financing. But instead, the company chose to sell shares of common stock to raise the money. This is called equity financing because the company sold some of its equity or worth to public investors.

From Justheim's point of view, selling shares offers the distinct advantage of never having to repay the money. The disadvantage is that the company is now owned by more people than when it was a private concern. Consequently, any earnings enjoyed by the company must now be shared by a larger group of people.*

A firm in search of its first funding from the public pool sells shares to investors, which are then traded in the OTC market. Nearly every publicly held concern from American Express to Xerox originally sold stock via this market. The explosive venture market has been called the Denver Over the Counter or Rocky Mountain Over the Counter market. These terms are a bit misleading. They give the impression that one central location houses all the furious trading activity where fortunes are made and lost in a matter of minutes. Nothing could be further from the truth. The OTC securities market operates in a completely different fashion than do the established exchanges.

* This assumes that earnings are not retained by the company and are distributed to the owners, the shareholders.

BIG BOARD EXCURSION

We're all familiar with the New York Stock Exchange. Occasionally, on a spectacularly up or dramatically down day, the evening news televises the frenzied activity on the trading floor of the Big Board. These people are gathered together for one specific reason: to make money for themselves, their firms, and their clients. Individually, they believe that they are just a little smarter than the next guy and therefore hope to wangle themselves a little better deal. These people or their firms own a "seat" on the exchange, giving them a right to trade on the floor. The majority of the seat holders act as either agents or specialists. Agents transact orders for clients while specialists oversee the orderly buying and selling of specific securities.

Let's say an agent working for Merrill Lynch receives an order from an investor in San Francisco. The order requests that the agent buy 100 shares of Exxon. It really doesn't matter where the order originates. It could be Oshkosh, Buenos Aires, or Paris—the order is still executed on the floor of the stock exchange located at the corner of Broad and Wall streets in New York City.

Our Merrill Lynch agent, order in hand, trots on over to the Exxon specialist's post. The Lynch buyer cajoles, dickers, argues, and smooth-talks the seller. The specialist feigns a lack of interest in the buyer's price. It's all part of the courting game known as trading securities. Finally the two tire of haggling when all that inhibits the trade is a fraction of a point. They decide on a price, shake hands, exchange paper, and the trade is complete. The agent speeds back to his desk where he reports, via wire to the San Francisco office, that the transaction has occurred. This simplified example illustrates how stocks are bought and sold on the exchange floor. The procedure, an auction, is pretty much the same for any of the stock exchanges: American, Vancouver, Spokane, Pacific, and so on.

Take this vision of the Big Board, already firmly embedded in our minds thanks to television, and turn it off. Trades in the Over the Counter market occur in an entirely different manner.

First of all, there is no single central location such as a trading floor. Instead, each brokerage house that buys and sells OTC stocks is, in effect, the trading floor. The brokerage house maintains an area where trades are effected, called the trading area or trading desk. In this specially designated section sits the firm's trader. He is in easy reach of a bank of telephones, video screens, and keyboard terminals. Traditionally, the trader is separated from the house's sales staff by a counter.

The OTC trader, upon receiving an order to buy or sell a security, simply gets on the phone and calls another brokerage house looking to buy or sell the same issue. Again, haggling over price occurs, this time over the phone. In this instance, however, the trade is negotiated, not auctioned. Finally the two traders agree upon a price and record pertinent information, and the trade is complete. Instead of zipping back to his post, the trader simply fills out a confirmation slip, slides it into an outbox, and awaits the next trade.

When the trader receives an order, he doesn't indiscriminately call brokerage houses around the country to find an interested party. If this were the case, the OTC market would come to a grinding halt. Instead, the trader relies upon the market-maker system to find a willing partner.

Market-making activity assures that an OTC stock doesn't just float in limbo, resting on the belief that someone always will want to buy and someone else, simultaneously, will want to sell. For an Over the Counter security to become just that, the company first must find a brokerage house willing and able to trade the security actively. The house makes a market for the stock. In becoming a market maker, the brokerage house agrees to trade the stock always—that is, to buy and sell a minimum number of the specified security. For low-priced OTC stocks, that minimum number is 1,000 shares. The market maker does not agree to price the stock too high; rather, the house simply agrees to purchase or sell the security at whatever price the market will bear.

This market-making function provides liquidity to the OTC market and ensures that the OTC market doesn't slip into periods of atrophy. Market makers are always willing (albeit sometimes reluctantly) to buy or sell a minimum number of shares at the stated or "indicated" price. The brokerage house does not do so out of some blind, benevolent allegiance to the security industry, of course. The market maker, the theory holds, buys the stock and keeps it in inventory, hoping the price will rise when the sale finally occurs. The market maker maintains a hedge known as the "spread," but we'll get to that shortly.

WHAT YOU PAY

Take a look in today's business section of your local newspaper. Unless it's Monday, it will include yesterday's closing quotes from the major stock exchanges and from the National Over the Counter list. If you look closely, you'll notice something dramatically different between the exchange-listed securities and the OTC stocks. The closing price for exchange securities amounts to one figure. This represents the price paid in the last auction of the day for that security. For OTC stocks, however, you'll see two closing prices—bid and asked. The bid price refers to what the market makers bid or offer to pay for your stock. The asked price, on the other hand, is the price charged to you by market makers for their stocks.

The asked price is always higher than the bid price. In other words, the amount you pay to buy a stock will always be more than the amount you would receive for selling it immediately after you bought it. The reason is simple. The market-making brokerage house agrees always to buy or sell a minimum number of shares. This can be expensive in three ways. The market maker must maintain a supply of stock in inventory to sell to you if you should so desire. Second, if he buys the stock and the market price drops, he's faced with a loss. Finally, if he's caught short when your order comes in, he agrees on the price and must then enter the marketplace to dredge up the stock. Even if he pays a higher price, he's already committed to you at the lower one.

An analogy to a supermarket probably serves to make the difference between bid and asked prices a bit clearer. A supermarket buys goods—say, canned peaches—at a wholesale price and then stocks the shelves with the goods. Thus, when an eager buyer enters the store, those canned peaches are sitting right there on the shelf just waiting to be bought. The supermarket sells the peaches at a retail price that covers the market's carrying costs as well as providing a little profit. Market making in the OTC world works in essentially the same fashion. Brokerage houses are often referred to as broker/dealers. The house acts as a dealer when buying and selling for its own account. As a market maker, the house hopes to generate a profit, dealing for itself. The house serves as a broker when it acts as an agent for clients and goes out to the street to buy securities. Just as a real estate broker aids others in buying and selling property, the stockbroker is a securities middleman. A third major function of brokerage houses is underwriting new stock issues. We'll explore this aspect in great detail in Chapter 8 on new stock offerings.

How much market makers bid and ask for stocks is contingent upon several factors, all related to supply and demand. The chief determinant in all markets is competition (well, maybe not all markets because government enters the fray, but that's a different story). If your brokerage house is the only one in the country to make a market for a particular stock, you could buy from or sell to only that house. Accordingly, the market maker can pay you as much as he likes to buy your stock. Conversely, he can charge others as much as he wants when he sells any shares in inventory. In this instance, the market maker monopolizes the market. Of course, as a sovereign investor you don't have to accept the price he's bidding or pay the price he's asking. You'll wait until the price becomes right to come into the marketplace.

If it's a hot stock with widespread interest, the exact opposite is true. A good many broker/dealers decide to become market makers of the security because of all the attention the stock is receiving. Becoming a market maker is a simple matter of filling out a form, filing with the National Association of Securities Dealers (NASD), and agreeing to buy and sell the security.* Trading volume—the number of shares bought and sold—runs very high for hot stocks. Competition for the stock is very keen. The price you pay or receive from any market maker will be very similar to what others are offering.

Now, you may wonder, "Why am I learning all of this seemingly superfluous information? Isn't this relatively unimportant vis-à-vis my own investment goals, which are to have a little fun and make a lot of money?" If this is your impression at this point, it's understandable. But I urge you to stick with it; as I've said from the outset, it takes work to invest profitably in the venture market. Learning the fundamentals of the marketplace is a neces-

---

* The National Association of Securities Dealers (NASD) is the self-regulating agency of the OTC security industry. It is composed of members of the various OTC brokerage houses.

sary prerequisite to recognizing clues and understanding the nuances of wise investing.

THE SPREAD

The difference between the bid and asked price provides a very broad assessment of a stock's market and its potential for appreciation. In broker circles, this difference is called the spread. The bid price for Empire Oil and Gas (a Denver energy stock that came out at $1 in 1979) amounted to $3.25 by mid-June of 1981. The asked price, what you would have had to pay, was $3.50. The spread was 25 cents. Disallowing broker commissions, house processing costs, and any other miscellaneous tacked-on charges, the stock's price must grow 25 cents before you recover your initial investment. In percentage form, Empire's security must appreciate approximately 8% as calculated below (see Table 1).

Table 1

Spread	=	Asked Price — Bid Price
Percentage Spread*	=	(Spread ÷ Bid) × 100
Empire's Spread, $0.25	=	$3.50 — $3.25
Percentage Spread,* 7.6%	=	($0.25 ÷ $3.25) × 100

* The spread divided by the bid price factor is multiplied times 100 to convert it to a percentage term.

This is one calculation that should be performed before any investment is made. Determining the necessary appreciation to recoup your investment places the price of the security in perspective. Lower-priced stocks generally tend to maintain a larger spread in percentage form than do their higher-priced counterparts.

For example, another venture stock issue, Float to Relax, recently sold for 6 cents at 9 cents.* The spread for Float's OTC

* Brokers often quote two figures in response to the question, "What's the price?" The first sum is the bid price and the second the asked. Not all new stock issues automatically appreciate dramatically. Float to Relax offers testimony to this tenet. Float originally sold for 10 cents. Once the stock started trading in the public's hands, it dropped to 6 cents. Anyone in on the ground floor immediately recognized a loss of 40% to his investment.

stock amounted to only 3 cents. On a percentage basis, though, Float's spread was 50%.

Float to Relax = ([9 cents − 6 cents]/6 cents) × 100 = 50% Percentage Spread

The investor in Float at this time must see an appreciation of 3 cents or 50% before regaining the original investment (exclusive of trading costs and fees).

If you were to entertain the idea of investing in either Empire Oil and Gas, bid at $3.25 with a spread of 8%, or Float to Relax, bid at 6 cents with a spread of 50%, which would be the wiser choice? Well, that's a tough question. At first glance, Empire would be the likely candidate because of the smaller percentage growth required to recoup the original investment. On the other hand, the potential for the 6-cent stock to double is much greater than for the other stock to do the same. These two investment possibilities highlight the risk-and-reward axiom of investing in securities. As a rule of thumb, the spread on stocks priced less than $1 will be greater than on their higher-priced counterparts. By the same token, the potential for appreciation is greater with the lower-priced stocks. Accordingly, the investor risks more on the 10-cent stock by virtue of the spread than on the $10 stock. But the possibility for reward is much greater when you trade in the pennies.

It's not a hard-and-fast rule that lower-priced stocks carry a larger percentage spread than do those stocks in the dollar-and-above range. If the investor narrows down the choices on the OTC investment menu to two stocks, both priced at about the same level, the spread can be a very telling sign. A hot stock maintains high trading volume and a large number of market makers. Competition for the stock remains very keen. Most likely, then, the stock with the greater appreciation potential also will maintain a smaller spread. This is easily explained. Market-making brokerage houses, like any retailer, know they don't have to charge a high mark-up to recover costs on a high-turnover item. However, for the stock that just languishes on the security shelves, the market maker incurs higher financing costs and, accordingly, charges a higher mark-up to recover carrying costs. This also fits in snugly with the supply-and-demand determinants of a stock's price. A fast-moving item in the securities biz generally means the stock is jetting upward. Conversely, any stock that's not moving generally drops in price as those who own the dullard try to unload it.

In 1971 the National Association of Securities Dealers (NASD) revolutionized OTC stock trading. The organization introduced a computer system called NASDAQ (pronounced NAZZ-DACK).* The NASDAQ computer keeps a running tab of what all market makers in the country are bidding and asking for every security in the system. Prior to its advent, trades in the system were slow. Very slow. Buying and selling OTC stocks takes place over the telephone. But before NASDAQ, the only way a trader learned the current prices was to call each and every market maker. For a stock boasting more than five market makers, this was a very tedious process to say the least. Accordingly, the market was relatively inefficient and trading volumes were relatively scant as compared with recent times.

Today, because of NASDAQ, instead of having to make extensive phone calls a house's trader simply punches in the stock's four-letter OTC calling card and the price appears on a video screen instantaneously.†

Not every OTC security is listed in the NASDAQ system. To become a member of the system, the NASD requires that certain standards be met, such as minimum asset size and a minimum amount of capital and surplus. In addition, the company must cough up a considerable sum to become a part of the system. In return, NASDAQ membership usually induces more broker/dealers to become market makers. As this leads to higher trading volumes, it also may add a few percentage points to a stock's price.

Often newspapers only quote NASDAQ securities. The National Over the Counter list is composed of those stocks that continually enjoy high trading volumes and meet certain financial requirements. Many penny stocks are included in the Additional National Over the Counter list. More than 30,000 companies' stocks are traded in the OTC market, but only a tenth of those are in the NASDAQ system. The reason that NASDAQ stocks

* NASDAQ is the acronym for National Association of Securities Dealers Automated Quotation system.
† For example, the two securities already discussed, Empire Oil and Gas and Float to Relax, employ EMPO and FLOT in the NASDAQ system.

are listed in the newspaper is simple: it's still a lot of work to call up market makers to find out the price of those securities not in the system.

OTC TRADING SIMPLIFIED

So let's put it all together. We have explained the rudiments of the Over the Counter market and how it differs from the established exchanges. We've even mentioned a primitive method of analyzing a security. But how does all this fit together and how do you, the new investor, make a trade?

The first step in the process is to call your broker. (Finding a broker and analyzing his suggestions are discussed in later chapters.) You suggest to your broker that you want to buy XYZ High Tech. You ask the price. He punches XYZH (XYZ's NAS-DAQ symbol) on his computer. It reports to him the highest bid price and the lowest asked price. You flip the numbers around in your head and determine the spread, and decide that all systems are go. You tell your broker that you want to buy. He writes down the information, says good-bye, and then runs at breakneck speed to his firm's trading area. Out of breath, he hands the slip over to the trader.

The trader has access to a more elaborate NASDAQ machine, and keys in the symbol. It tells him which brokerage houses make the market for XYZ High Tech. He searches for the lowest asked price—the one most favorable to you—and gets on the phone. Sometimes he will have a direct line to the other brokerage house. The trader asks if the price indicated is true, cajoles the other trader a bit, and finalizes the sale. The two traders exchange information on the particulars of the sale and *voilà*, the sale is complete. At that point your broker is informed of the successful transaction. That's it. Simple. And all this time you thought the securities business was so complicated. Well, it is. We've looked very superficially at the mechanics of the OTC market. But obviously there's more to making money in the OTC market than simply understanding how it works. We venture forward into the choosing of actual securities.

NOTE

1. Michael Sivy, "Making Big Money on Little Stocks," *Money,* July 1981, p. 48.

3

Venture Capital: The Risk and the Reward

J. Daniel Bell, whom we've already met, recently said that "the established brokerage houses of the East opt for slower, more predictable returns from securities issued by established corporations." The result, he continued, is that "many young companies —those with good ideas—are left begging for money."[1] Harkening back to Horace Greeley's adage about going West, Bell noted that these young companies are coming to Denver for funds.

Over the last five years, Denver and the Rocky Mountain region have earned the reputation of being the nation's number one fount of venture capital. This reputation recently was verified by Wall Street in Dun & Bradstreet's authoritative *Guide to Your Investments 1981*. "The hot spot for penny issues," reported the *Guide,* "is Denver."[2] Further authentication is offered by the 1980 yearbook of the National Association of Securities Dealers (NASD). The NASD's annual report pointed out that more publicly held Over the Counter companies called Colorado home than any other state but New York and California. The latter two areas have carved out safe niches for themselves by collecting capital for secure, essentially riskless investments. This leaves Colorado as the focal point for entrepreneurial capitalism.

What is venture or entrepreneurial capital, and how does it differ from other forms? Perhaps the easiest way to explain venture capital is to explain what it isn't.

When AT&T makes a public stock offering, the company hopes

to raise tens of millions of dollars. Most likely it will succeed. There are several possible reasons for wanting to raise such an awesome amount of money. Perhaps the company wants to reduce some of its debt. Or maybe it plans to expand operations, or, alternatively, to acquire another company. All of these moves would increase the worth of AT&T. The reason is simple: AT&T exchanges little slips of paper (stock certificates) for millions of dollars. It's a fairly wise financing move.

AT&T's secondary equity offering, for the most part, will be purchased by institutions. Bank trust departments and pension funds oversee the investment of enormous sums of capital. Money managers for these funds follow the legally required "prudent man" rule for investing—that is, investing as only a prudent man would. Further, managers of this type tend to be risk averters. Their livelihood depends not on spectacular growth, but rather on safe, solid, and regular upward movement. Accordingly, an investment in AT&T fits right into their scheme; a venturesome high-tech issue doesn't. Chances are fairly bright that AT&T isn't going to file bankruptcy proceedings. And even if the company did show signs of going belly-up, the institutions would have pulled out long before.

Another type of investor in AT&T's hypothetical offering might have been an individual, say a doctor, with large holdings on Wall Street. Our wise-but-conservative investor leans toward safe investments that provide steady growth with fairly healthy dividends. In short, our doctor friend is satisfied with, say, a 10% annual average return in exchange for its alleged safety. A penny stock doesn't match the doctor's investment objectives, either.

This brings us to another point. If AT&T raises all this money, what are the chances the value of the stock will double? Virtually nil. In fact, absolutely nil. Because of the larger equity value of the company (as with nearly all New York Stock Exchange-listed concerns), the potential for a 100% appreciation is almost nonexistent. It's simple mathematics. If a company's equity worth is $500 million, an increase of 100% works out to $500 million in growth—an impossibility.

By comparison, for smaller, venture stock companies, 100% growth is conceivable. If the total worth stacks up to only a million dollars, doubling of equity means growth of another million dollars. This is especially possible in the risky but lucrative world of resource exploitation (e.g., energy or precious metals). If a small company drills a wildcat well and it hits an enormous pool of oil, the worth of the company multiplies astronomically overnight. The stock price should follow suit. But "ifs" and "shoulds" aren't the kind of investment situations that risk averters and staid investors search out. Small investors, though, armed with some risk capital, are willing to accept the inherent risk in exchange for the chance to hit it big.

RISK CAPITAL

Up to this point, only fleeting references have been made to the risk-and-reward aspect of penny stock investing. Now it's time to explain what all this means vis-à-vis venture capital stocks and your money. If you have as little as $500 extra cash, a whole menu of possibilities emerges as to how you can dispose of it. You want to generate more money from the money—that is, you want to invest it. You can blow it by going on a Las Vegas gambling excursion (assuming you'll win, of course) or you can park the money in a risk-free passbook savings account. You plan to invest, speculate, or gamble intelligently. The two extremes—the Las Vegas foray and the passbook savings account—accentuate the risk-and-reward concept.

With a thousand dollars, you sidle up to the roulette wheel. The dealer nods his approval as you slink into one of the high-backed chairs. You're in a good mood and decide to risk all. On seeing your intentions with the ten $100 chips, the dealer gets you a free drink. Several of them, in fact. You haven't imbibed any of your whiskey sour yet so you're still a little cautious. The ten chips go onto the black spot. You start to perspire as the little silver ball spins ever so slowly around the wheel. It drops and starts bouncing from slot to slot. Finally, the ball comes to rest in a black number. You won and doubled your money. You had nearly a 50–50 chance and you won.

Now you've got 20 $100 chips as the alcohol starts to work its way into your system. Again, you decide to risk all. This time you shoot against higher odds. You place all $2,000 on number 25. If you win you'll have $72,000, while if you lose, nothing. The ball spins around. You sweat heavily as the ball drops down and crawls from slot to slot. Finally the ball stops. Number 26. It was close but you lose anyway.

Let's say that instead of going to Las Vegas, you salt away the money in a 5½% passbook savings account. After a year's time the compounded account will be worth slightly more than $1,055. Unless your bank and the U. S. Government were to fail, you could be sure that the extra $55+ would be there. Another option for your $1,000 would have been money market funds. These financial vehicles, managed by brokerage houses and others, buy commercial paper (short-term corporate loans) and government securities. You receive the average rate during the most recent time period, and therefore take a chance on the level of the going rate. Your risk of losing all is slim, of course, because the federal government and the major corporations probably aren't going out of business. Your only risk is what the interest rate will be when you pull out.

In short, there's a continuum of investment options open for your $1,000, ranging from high-risk, potentially big gains to low-risk, smaller gains. Venture capital stocks reside on the high side of the continuum, right up there with options and futures. The established stocks of the New York and American exchanges rank lower. Both established and venture stocks contain some risk, and both maintain the potential for gains. The difference is that venture stocks are riskier and potentially more lucrative by far. This is essentially a qualitative matter, as no foolproof system exists to quantify risk-and-reward relationships.

RISK-AND-REWARD CONTINUUM

Less Risky_____More Risky

| SAVINGS | MONEY | EXCHANGE | VENTURE | STOCK | COMMODITY | LAS |
| ACCOUNT | MARKET | STOCKS | STOCKS | OPTIONS | FUTURES | VEGAS |

The risk-and-reward dichotomy between venture stocks and New York Stock Exchange stocks can be seen in the graphic portrayal of Standard & Poor's stock price index of 500 New York securities and Howard Hebert's (president of Newhard Cook Advisory Services) price index of 160 low-priced stocks (see Chart 1).

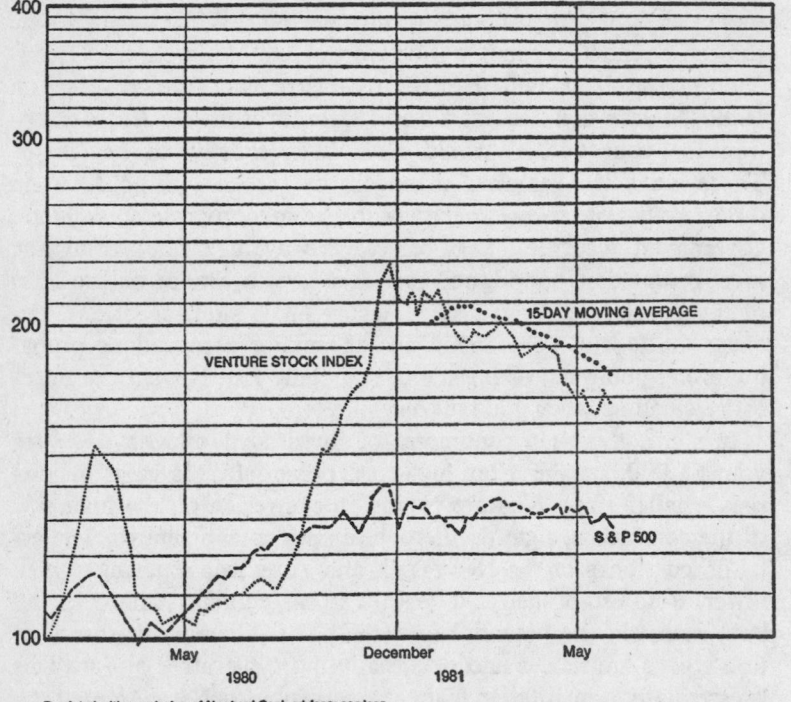

Chart 1
Venture Stock and Standard & Poor's Indexes

Reprinted with permission of Newhard Cook advisory services

From May 1980 through December 1980, low-priced stocks shot up 125 points as the S&P Index grew a relatively miserly 40 points. However, in the bear market that settled in after Reagan's election (January to June 1981), the penny stock index declined a full 55 points. The S&P Index fared better, dropping only 10 points.

If you had owned that famed crystal ball to forecast stock prices, you would have plunked down your $1,000 in penny stocks in May 1980. When you pulled out in January, the cyclic peak, your investment would have grown 119%. (This, of course, is all theoretical because an index tries to mimic stock price movement and is not an investment in itself.) By comparison, the S&P 500 investment would have yielded 40%—not bad, but only crumbs as compared with penny stock returns.

On the other hand, if you'd heard so much about the penny

market from friends with tremendous gains but hesitated and entered the market in January with your $1,000, you would have suffered a loss. The $1,000 investment in venture stocks would have caused you to lose $240 while a similar investment in the S&P stocks would have lost only $70.

Because of the volatile swings, which are par for the venture stock market course, the potential investor should consider devoting only resources he can afford to lose completely. In other words, your risk capital, the money you invest "at risk," should not be indispensable. An investor in the venture market must not only investigate the companies, but must also watch stock prices and trends on a daily basis. It'll be fun. If you'd invested $1,000 in the low-priced OTC stocks in January and then gone on a six-month vacation, your portfolio would have diminished by 25%. In the bear trend, however, some stocks didn't take a nose dive. Explaining why remains a difficult task. Special situations, such as encouraging revenue reports, new oil well discoveries, or scientific breakthroughs, help maintain some stocks' prices during doggy markets.

Another sign of fortitude among venture stocks is those issues that haven't gone wild. Most of the securities in the bull market of the latter half of 1980 traded to higher and higher prices. Not all, though. And when the vicious drop came, those that were swept up fell with equal vigor. In short, those securities not subject to dramatic swings tended to elude the bear trends. Charting stocks can help explain and illustrate this and make you more aware of the potential for reward as well as the risk of depreciation. We pick up this subject in Chapter 9, on the timing of trades.

THE WALL STREET OF THE WEST

Sparked by America's need to reindustrialize, Denver and the Rocky Mountain region grabbed the reins of this national drive. The revitalization of the American economy will not occur through corporations swallowing one another in the form of acquisitions. Rather, it takes entrepreneurs, armed with only a vision and venture capital, to make an attempt at achieving this goal. Most of them will fail. But some will thrive, and investing in those successful ventures is your aim.

Perhaps the reason for the West's growth in the last decade results from the paradigm of the Wild West. In this land, a man (or woman) could begin with virtually nothing but an ingenious scheme and transform it into a viable operation. This occurred a little before the turn of the century when early prospectors fled the East and came to the Rockies, lured by visions of gold. Most died paupers, but a few succeeded and became fabulously wealthy.

This same spirit survives today. Of course, the rules have changed. Instead of a pickax and mule, the modern-day gold prospector employs a stable of highly trained geophysical engineers to find the mother lode. Tomorrow's John D. Rockefeller doesn't aimlessly punch holes in the ground to tap gushers. Instead, today's oil finders meticulously scan seismic log charts of the earth's contours in order to detect unusual geologic formations.* High-technology inventors use computer chips to find solutions today to tomorrow's questions. The goal, though, persists as in the old days: to take an idea and transform it into a profitable reality.

The magazine *Inc.*, the *Fortune* of small companies, follows the progress of small entrepreneurial businesses. The 1980 wrap-up showed that Colorado was headquarters for nearly 10% of the fastest-growing firms in the country. The state, however, only houses slightly more than 1% of the nation's population. *Inc.* said, "The top firms share four characteristics. They are young, innovative, productive, and profitable." On average, these firms have been in business less than thirteen years. The magazine concluded its report by saying, "Start-ups not long ago, these firms are now the upstarts on the leading edge of high technology and creative marketing."³ The majority of Colorado's entries to the list were evenly divided between energy exploration and high technology.

One upstart, ranking as 1980's thirty-ninth fastest-growing firm, enjoyed revenue growth of 1,395% over the last five years alone. Polaris Resources, Inc., a Denver-based oil and gas firm, managed an annual growth rate of close to 100%. Stockholders' equity in the firm—the book value of shares outstanding—shot up more than double in a year's time, increasing from $650,000

* Seismic logs are reports of sound waves bouncing off the various geologic formations within the earth.

to $1.58 million in 1980. Yet, a chunk of Polaris could be had for 81 cents by midyear 1981.

Another firm typifying venture capitalism is Staodynamics, Inc., of northern Colorado. Staodynamics (pronounced Stay-o-dy-NAM-ics), another company included on *Inc.*'s listing of the fastest-growing firms, manufactures electronic instruments capable of arresting pain sensations. If properly connected to the correct nerve fibers, the device produces electronic shocks that effectively block pain. Thomas H. Thomson, president and founder, began working out of a garage in Boulder, Colorado, in the early 1970s. An engineer, he began by manufacturing four of the products per day.

Thomson, while having lots of fun in the garage, really couldn't get the undertaking off the ground. So in 1975 he came to the venture stock market for funding. Staodynamics sold stock to the public for $1 per share. Here was this character telling you that a little device the size of a cigarette lighter could eliminate back tension and other types of chronic pain. All he needed to start producing the invention was your money. Think what a leap of faith that investment would have been!

In 1981, Staodynamics racked up $4.8 million in sales of the electrical nerve stimulator and its other products. Your belief in the ability of Thomson and in the potential for the product would have paid off, handsomely. At last reckoning, a common share of Staodynamics was bid at $6.38, a gain of 538% in five years.

Why did Polaris Resources and Staodynamics approach public investors for their financing? The answer is simple: there's just no other way today to raise the needed money. A young company can't go to the bank because it doesn't have enough tangible assets with which to collateralize a loan. New companies usually boast only relatively intangible assets—an idea and management's ability. Most banks just aren't willing to stake a claim on such risky collateral, and bank financing isn't an option on the financing menu. Institutional funds aren't available either. We've already discussed institutions and their investing policies.

The unproven firm, then, has no place to turn except to well-heeled and not-so-well-heeled venture capitalists. The public investor hope to profit substantially from the risk. The two go hand in hand; the young firm, out to realize a vision and to make a lot of money, and the small investor, out to fund the vision and to make a lot of money.

VENTURE STOCK SUPPORTERS

The confluence of these two—small investor and entrepreneur —is made possible through the arrangement of the underwriter. An underwriter is an investment banker specializing in raising capital funds for start-ups and established companies alike. Broker/dealers who sell stock often underwrite stock issues as well. When Staodynamics decided to raise $550,000 and when Polaris Resources decided to raise $300,000, officers of these firms approached an underwriter. The underwriter agreed to sell the security for a cut of the proceeds. When the sale of the new issue took place, the needs of both the underwriters and the companies were met. Early investors in these two companies also were rewarded nicely for risking their money.

One effect of the explosive growth in new stock offerings is that firms specializing in underwriting also have enjoyed the same astronomical growth. The NASD's 1980 yearbook reported that Colorado also serves as headquarters for most of the Over the Counter brokerage houses in the country, again excepting California and New York—a fact that further validates this book's underlying premise that venture capital stocks are one of this nation's only hopes for reindustrialization.

Two Colorado firms in particular have expanded dramatically— one for the better and one for the worse. The first is Blinder, Robinson & Company. Meyer Blinder and Mac Robinson began the company jointly in New York in 1970. By the end of their first full year, the firm showed a slight profit at the same time as the Dow Jones Industrial Average sank to a cyclic low. Mac Robinson bowed out at that time, telling Blinder, "Meyer, I love you like a brother. Get out now or else you'll be broke in a year." Blinder didn't heed his partner's advice and continued plugging away. In 1977, Blinder decided that Denver was where the action was and moved his operation. Blinder chuckles when recounting the story of his partner's early departure because Blinder, Robinson & Company today stands as one of the nation's most prolific underwriters of new stock offerings. Among the more notable of Blinder's underwritings are Loch Exploration, Inc.'s $1.5 million offering and Biofuel, Inc.'s $2 million security sale.

Loch Exploration raised the money to prime the pump for its energy exploration efforts. The sale of the 10-cent stock went effective December 14, 1979, and by March 31, 1981, was selling at $1.94, a gain of 1,840%. Biofuel, powered by its plan to sell gasohol to the public, sold shares for 10 cents. This sale became effective on March 17, 1980. Less than a year later, on January 6, 1981, those shares sold for $1.19. Anyone fortunate enough to have puchased $500 worth of the stock, and then to have had the foresight to sell out on that 1981 date reaped a gain of $5,450. The reason for Blinder's success mirrors the reason behind the success of the venture market: the company has provided countless thousands of small investors with the opportunity to grab a share of America's future.

Another firm moving right along with the growth in the venture market was OTC Net. The name stands for Over the Counter Network. J. Carlos Schidlowski founded the firm in 1979. Two and one-half years later, Schidlowski claimed that his firm ranked as one of the nation's largest broker/dealers. OTC Net maintained twenty-five offices throughout the country, as well as a subsidiary operation in Geneva. Schidlowski had plans to open additional offices in such places as London, Paris, and Hong Kong to entice foreign money into the venture capital stock market.

Notable among OTC Net's offerings was Advanced Monitoring Systems, Inc. This company, which originally sold shares for 50 cents, manufactures and markets instruments capable of probing pipes to locate leaks. By late 1981, the stock traded in the $8–$10 range.

Unlike Meyer Blinder, though, Carlos Schidlowski could not handle success, and his firm has gone bankrupt. As with any young company, success must be planned for and nurtured. OTC Net couldn't maintain a dignified business posture; the back-office operations suffered serious difficulties and various excesses resulted.

Indeed, these two stories are indicative of the penny market itself—its risks and its rewards.

In these first chapters, we've laid out the basic framework of the venture OTC stock market. In the next chapter we begin looking at how you, the small investor, can analyze the myriad of stock issues. Special attention is paid to the high technology, energy, precious metals mining, and new stock offering fields, where most of the penny stock fever arises.

NOTES

1. Jerry Ruhl, "J. Daniel Bell Touts Denver Penny Stock Mart," *Denver Rocky Mountain News,* February 6, 1981, p. 69.

2. C. Colburn Hardy, *Dun & Bradstreet's Guide to Your Investments,* 26th ed. (New York: Lippincott & Crowell, 1981), p. 76.

3. Bradford Ketchum, Jr., "The *Inc.* 100 Fastest Growing Companies," *Inc.,* May 1981, p. 39.

4

Scrutiny, Scrutiny, Scrutiny

More than 30,000 stocks are traded in the Over the Counter market. A select few are going to be the big winners—and you'll pick these stocks. But what it calls for is scrutiny, more scrutiny, and, on top of this, yet more scrutiny.

Before buying a new suit or getting your car fixed, you shop around, compare the advantages and disadvantages of various options, and finally make a decision based upon your research. The same should hold true with venture stock investments. You shouldn't simply rely on your broker's advice and blindly plunk down your hard-earned money. Rather, you should plunge right into the investigation of various investment alternatives. After all, it's your money. In this chapter we outline some methods for evaluating the companies, based upon their potential and actual performance. We begin with two scenarios:*

Bob Arnold and Frank Benedict founded Benedict Arnold Exploration, Inc., in November 1978. They took the company public a year later, selling three million shares of stock at $1 each. Arnold contributed the financial brains and Benedict the petrochemical brawn. Together, the market said, they made a powerful team. During the first year, they took bold steps to develop energy resources. Then something went awry. Arnold left. Benedict changed the firm's name to Traitor Oil and the company was left without its major oil finder. To date (as of this writing), the company only produces 41 barrels of oil per day. Not very significant after three years in business. The stock, which had nudged $3, had dropped back down to 88 cents by mid-1981.†

*The names for these two stories have been changed to protect the innocent and, alas, the guilty. However, the details and numbers are factual.

†The author knows of this firsthand. I watched Traitor Oil's OTC security on a regular basis. When the price dropped from $2.93 down to $1.88, I believed this

Jeff Sharp brought his Summit Oil and Gas public in June 1980 through the sale of eight million shares of stock at $1 each. Sharp steered the direction of the company toward the contract drilling of oil and gas wells prior to its becoming publicly held. The market said, "Another powerful combination, Jeff Sharp and Jeff Sharp." Sharp understood that oil and gas exploration can take time before significant revenue flows commence. So, to bolster Summit's operations in the meantime, Sharp continued to emphasize contract drilling. A wise move. Revenues for the firm amounted to $2.7 million in 1980, up 43% from the previous year. The stock market was very appreciative of Summit's actions. In the first six months of 1981, Summit's OTC security reached a high of $4, a gain of 300% over its original price of $1.

What happened? Both companies set out with grand schemes, but one appears to be on the skids while the other one shoots for the stars. Basically it boils down to management or lack thereof. But how could you, as an investor, have predicted such divergent paths? The answer lies in fundamental analysis.

FUNDAMENTAL VALUES

"Fundamental analysis" is Wall Street's term for basing investment decisions on the underlying value of the company and its future prospects as well as on the promise of the industry and the economy. The other type of market sleuthing, technical analysis, is based on the premise that the company has little to do with the stock's price and that it's all just a matter of watching the price moves. The technical side of this market is discussed in the last section of this book.

Fundamental analysis suggests that profits can be made over the long haul by investing in solid, good, strong companies. Respected stock market analyst C. Colburn Hardy sums it up best: "Fundamental analysis, the value approach," he says, "is based on financial facts. It relies on economic forecasts and analysis of the corporation's present strength and past performance as indications of what can be anticipated in the future."[1]

---

to be a buy signal because the stock was at a new low. Boy, was I wrong. The stock dropped to $1.03 before I ditched it. My $500 investment was whittled away to $274, a loss of $226.

Buying stocks based on the company's underlying value can never go wrong. These worthwhile stocks may undergo short-term dips, valleys, and craters. But over the long haul the market corrects itself for past mistakes and continues upward. Let me amplify this point. Over the short term, bulls and bears rule the day. This is especially true in the venture market where volatile swings cut down past profits or bolster weak stock situations in a matter of minutes. However, if you purchase quality stocks, their long-run direction will most assuredly be upward.

Think for a minute about Xerox, which started its life as an OTC venture stock. Xerox was a glamour issue, suffering dramatic drops and enjoying lightning-like appreciation. But over the long haul, early investors in Xerox have not been disappointed. The same holds true for current venture stock investments. If you buy into a quality company (even though it's priced in the pennies), there's no reason for it not to reach stellar heights.

Of course, the venture stock investor must pay careful attention to ensure that the company remains in a forward-facing posture. Changes in management and in the industry's potential are enough to alter a very promising outlook into a bleak one. But how do you find quality?

AN EXCITING TALE

Accounting. Now before you skip to what may seem to be more exciting topics later in the chapter, let me digress for a bit on a personal discovery. I used to feel the same way the rest of the population does about accounting. Boring—except to CPAs and tax planners. But in the course of my work with *The National OTC Stock Journal* (then called *The Denver Stock Exchange* newspaper) and research for this book, I found it more and more imperative that I learn the rudiments of accounting to make sense of the pages and pages of financial tables that fill every document in the securities business. I discovered something else: it was fascinating. Company officials and stockbrokers can charm you no end with tales of their company's growth potential. But when you get right down to it, the bottom line tells all. These seemingly peripheral documents provide a black-and-white history of a company's accomplishments and disappointments. By understanding accounting statements, you'll be able to reconstruct the firm's journey through its corporate life as well as to spot a buying opportunity.

Before we get down to the nuts and bolts of accounting, let me interject another personal aside. For an article on one of the major energy firms making up the penny market, I spoke with the company's president. We talked about the newly discovered oil and gas wells and land acquisitions. No problem. Then the discussion turned to his company's recently released Form 10-Q (an SEC-mandated quarterly financial report). I questioned him about several line items on the company's balance sheet. He couldn't answer the questions and referred me to his accountant. I point this out not to belittle the man, but rather to suggest that many people out there—not only new investors and financial reporters, but public-company presidents as well—know very little about accounting practices.

Obviously, understanding accounting is very important to investing in penny stocks. If your broker should call you on the phone and tell you that he knows of a wonderful opportunity but you've got to buy now or else you'll miss it, your best response is to say, "Forget it." Chances are just as good that the opportunity to acquire a quality stock will be there a week from now, and you certainly don't have the time to gather all of the relevant information over the phone talking to your broker.

We start our magical accounting tour with the most basic of accounting documents, the balance sheet. The balance sheet picks one day in history to measure the worth of a company. It represents a snapshot photo of the company's financial position. The income statement, by comparison, shows the company's changing fortunes over a period of time: a quarter, say, or a year.

The balance sheet derives its name from the fundamental requirement that all of the company's assets must equal all of the company's debts, or liabilities, and net worth, or equity. Assets represent the cash, the properties, the equipment, and other similar items that give a company value. A corporation, however, is not a living entity in the accounting sense. Someone must own a claim to these assets. The two major groups owning a claim on the company's wealth are its creditors and owners. To facilitate the explanation of the balance sheet, let's look at Staodynamics' financial documents (see Table 2). Staodynamics, you'll recall, is the venture stock firm producing electronic anesthetizers.

Table 2

| | Fiscal year ending: | |
	2/28/81	2/29/80
Assets	$5,750,229	$4,846,380
Liabilities & Equities		
Liabilities	2,724,301	3,507,918
Stockholder's Equity	3,025,928	1,338,462
Total	5,750,229	4,846,380

GIVING WORTH

Assets are listed according to their degree of liquidity. Appearing first in this group are current assets (see Table 3). Generally, any asset that can be converted into cash or used in business operations within one year receives this designation. Cash comes first. Second come government securities because these can't be spent until they have been cashed in. Next in this subgrouping come accounts receivable. This represents sales the company has made, but for which it has not yet received payment. Accordingly, they are a less liquid asset to the company. Inventories are even less liquid. Before they can generate cash for the company, they must first be sold. Staodynamics' 1981 inventory figure amounted to nearly $1.3 million.

Table 3*

| | Fiscal year ending: | |
	2/28/81	2/29/80
Cash & cash items	$1,241	$1,449
Accounts & notes		
receivable	1,335	870
Inventories	1,246	1,138
Prepaid expenses	53	33
Deferred tax charges	51	8
Total	3,925	3,497

* Figures, in $1,000s, do not total exactly due to rounding.

Thus, if the company chose simply to close shop after manufacturing all of the products from materials on hand, the inventories, at cost, represent an asset of almost $1.3 million. Prepaid expenses and deferred income tax charges also are included in current assets because they will benefit the company within one year.

Next in line come those assets that are even less liquid: plant, property, and equipment (see Table 4). Buildings are included in this category, as are machines. These assets are recorded in the balance sheet at their purchase price. The acquisition costs of plant and equipment are allocated over the time the asset is in use. This cost is charged against the asset, decreasing its book value each year. For example, Staodynamics had acquired fixed assets, not including land, for almost $1.71 million as of February 28, 1981.

Thus, the book value of plant and equipment is the acquisition price less the accumulated depreciation. When the acquisition price of the land (which is never depreciated) is added to this figure, the total represents the current book value of plant, property, and equipment.

The final category on the assets side of the balance sheet is called "other assets." Typically these represent "book" assets, which cannot be sold to generate cash in the usual way. For example, Staodynamics acquired another firm in fiscal 1981, Wyoming Biotelemetry (see Table 5). Staodynamics, however, paid more for the firm then would have been dictated by the net asset value of the acquired company. Because all items on the balance sheet are recognized at their cost of acquisition, the cost in excess of the actual book worth of Wyoming Biotelemetry is included in this "other assets" category. Other possible entries in this category include long-term investments and intangible sources of wealth, such as goodwill and trademarks.

Table 4*

| | Fiscal year ending: | |
	2/28/81	2/29/80
Building & improvements	$379	$369
Production & lab equipment	950	689
Office furniture & fixtures	226	96
Data processing & automotive equipment	155	85
Subtotal	1,710	1,239
Less accumulated depreciation	466	305
Land	38	38
Total	1,282	972

* Figures in $1,000s.

Table 5*

	Fiscal year ending:	
	2/28/81	2/29/80
Cost in excess of net assets of acquired company	$269	——
Unamortized debt expenses	187	$325
Other	87	52
Total	544	377

* Figures, in $1,000s, do not total exactly due to rounding.

Taken together, current assets; plant, property, and equipment; and other assets represent the total value of the firm. For Staodynamics, the complete asset worth of the firm in fiscal years 1980 and 1981 was $4.9 million and 5.75 million respectively (see Table 6).

Table 6*

	Fiscal year ending:	
	2/28/81	2/29/80
Current assets	$3,925	$3,497
Property, plant & equipment	1,282	972
Other assets	544	377
Total Assets	5,750	4,846

* Figures, in $1,000s, do not total exactly due to rounding.

TAKING WORTH

Liabilities and stockholders' equity make up the other portion of the balance sheet. This section represents the claims held against the company's assets. Liabilities represent the company's debts, while the remainder of the assets—the equity or net worth —represents the portion owned by the shareholders.

The liabilities section is constructed in similar fashion to the assets. Current liabilities come first. These are debts that must be paid within one year's time (see Table 7). Included in this section for Staodynamics are notes payable for goods and services, taxes, payroll, and the current portion of the long-term debt. The next

Table 7*

CURRENT LIABILITIES	Fiscal year ending:	
	2/28/81	2/29/80
Accounts payable	$159	$198
Current portion of long-term debt	47	36
Accrued expenses (payroll, etc.)	321	231
Other current liabilities	57	50
Total Current	584	515

* Figures in $1,000s.

step down the balance sheet brings us to long-term liabilities, those due in more than a year's time. Staodynamics issued $2.979 million worth of debentures in 1979. By 1981 the company still owed $2.1 million to the note holders (see Table 8). Deferred income taxes, a potential future tax liability, also appear.

The final portion of this section of the balance sheet is stockholders' equity. This refers to the ownership of the company's assets attributed to the shareholders. If the company liquidated its assets, the firm's creditors would be paid first and the remainder would then be distributed to the shareholders.

Table 8*

	Fiscal year ending:	
	2/28/81	2/29/80
Long-term debt	$2,100	$2,979
Deferred income tax credits	40	15

* Figures in $1,000s.

This section consists of three major subcategories: common stock, paid-in capital, and retained earnings. A portion of the common stock entry plus a portion of the paid-in capital represents the shareholders' original investment in the company. Each share of stock issued by the company is assigned a par value. "Par value" is essentially a meaningless expression with origins in the 1930s. The common stock (sometimes called capital stock) is simply the number of shares outstanding multiplied by the par value.

In the venture stock market, par values are typically 10 cents, 1 cent, or a tenth of a cent. Paid-in capital shows the excess over par for stock originally issued, bought back, or retired. If the par value has changed or if the company has received a donation, both of these events are reflected in the paid-in capital section as well. Thus these two subcategories represent the investment in the company plus any stock-related changes.

A company, though, is a living, dynamic organism. If the firm managed to generate a profit during its existence, management has several options. We'll discuss those options shortly. If the managers decide to hold on to the net income, then, this money will be attributed to the shareholders in the stockholders' equity section. Because these earnings do not represent investment, they cannot be included in either of the two sections already discussed. Net income is added to the retained earnings section.

Taken together, these three line items constitute the balance-sheet heading of stockholders' equity (see Table 9).

Table 9*

STOCKHOLDERS' EQUITY	*Fiscal year ending:*	
	2/28/81	2/29/80
Common stock†	$ 19	$ 13
Paid-in capital	2,311	872
Retained earnings	696	453
Total	3,026	1,339

* Figures, in $1,000s, do not total exactly due to rounding.
† $0.01 par value; 5 million shares authorized; 1,935,247 shares issued and outstanding in 1981 and 1,342,998 in 1980.

And remarkably—or perhaps not so remarkably—this figure, when added to the current and long-term liabilities, equals the total assets of the company. Of course, it must balance out because the creditors and the shareholders are the only groups owning a claim to the company's assets.

In admittedly oversimplified form, we have, by looking at its components, looked at the balance sheet. It's really not that formidable—just a matter of knowing what the terms mean.

IN COMES AND OUT GOES

Let's continue our journey into the dark valley of accounting in order to shed a little more light on how changes occur in the retained earnings section (i.e., whether the company makes or loses money).

The income statement depicts the changing fortunes of the firm over a specified period of time, usually a quarter or a year. This is distinctly different from the balance sheet, which represents the position of a firm at only one point in time. In essence, the balance sheet takes a snapshot photo of the firm whereas an income statement takes movies. But enough analogies; on with the components of the income statement.

The title of this document is a little misleading, as it suggests only one third of its constituents. Every income statement encompasses three basic areas: income to the company's coffers, outgo from same, and what's left, or net income.

Revenues are fairly straightforward. This designation includes any funds generated through the sale of the company's product or service. Other typical sources of income for venture stock companies include interest income from certificates of deposit and rental income. It's very important to examine closely the source of the company's revenues.

For a venture stock company, still in its start-up stage, a large portion of the firm's income will be derived from interest-bearing certificates. When a company first goes public, it's usually awash in cash for a short time thereafter. And instead of spending money like a drunken sailor, the wise controller invests in short-term certificates of deposit. After several years of operation, though, it's possible for the firm to be still receiving most of its income from interest-paying securities. If this is the case, you should ask yourself, "Why aren't they spending money on operations," and you should not invest.

The next step down the income statement shows the direct expense to the company of producing the aforementioned revenues. This includes wages directly attributable to production, cost of materials, and maintenance of plant and equipment. These are usually under the heading of "cost of sales." The difference between the two sums, revenues and cost of sales, represents the gross profit.

The above expenses are those directly attributable to the production of the goods for sale. Other expenses go into producing and selling the product as well. These are operating expenses, which include maintaining the office.

The next expense is a little more abstract, or at least less clearly observable. This is depreciation, which can only be applied to fixed assets. As mentioned, the concept of depreciation is that the cost of, say, a piece of machinery must be allocated over its expected useful life. Since accounting follows the principle of matching expenses with revenues in the period incurred, the cost of the machine must be spread over those years in which the machine is contributing to revenues. It would be difficult, if not impossible, to match the entire cost of the machine with the revenue it was responsible for in a single year of operation. So even though no cash outlay is required after the machine has been purchased, the company is allowed to show a portion of its cost on its balance sheet as depreciation, an expense that can be deducted from each period's revenues.

After all of these items are subtracted out of gross profit, the income from operations, the operating margin, remains. Now things begin to get interesting. The operating margin describes how well the firm is doing.

Deducted from the operating margin is the interest paid during the current period. The company, to undertake its appointed business, may have borrowed money at one time or another. Even established companies borrow substantially to cover short-term cash needs. Many venture stock companies, though, cannot qualify for or cannot afford a loan. As has been explained, this is one of the prime causes behind the emergence of the venture stock market.

Once all of these costs are deducted, earnings remain. The company reports interest earnings, as well as interest paid out, in the section on operating margin. Of course, good old Uncle Sam wants his piece. Federal and other taxes must be paid before you arrive at the final entry—what the company actually earned.

The net earnings figure (that is, the profit) is the most interesting comment on the income statement. It depicts what the company has accomplished.

Management has several options regarding the dispersal of its profits. The money can be distributed to shareholders through a dividend; another alternative is to credit the profits to the retained earnings section of stockholders' equity.

Your job as a venture stock investor is to sift carefully through the income statement and compare the current situation with that of earlier years. Accounting legerdemain can reduce profits in one year and then skyrocket them in the following year. It is not so easy to do this year after year.

Another factor behind up-and-down profits is nonrecurring items. Sometimes a company will enjoy a one-year gain that cannot be expected to recur. For example, oil and gas companies sometimes sell off pieces of acreage. As they can never resell the same piece, the event would be recorded as a nonrecurring gain. Some energy companies, though, make it a business to buy and sell acreage, in which case this type of "nonrecurring" item could be expected to reappear despite its name.

If you discover that profits have increased but expenses have soared even more, then you should try to determine why this is so. On the other hand, if profits have risen and costs have not gone up as much, this may alert you to wise financial management.

IN THE REAL WORLD

Rather than continuing to pose hypothetical income statement queries, let's analyze Staodynamics' 1981 income statement, as shown in Table 10. In financial tables, parentheses surrounding a figure indicate a negative sum—e.g., (1850) = −1850. In 1981, net sales for the company rose to $4.78 million, an increase of 88% over 1979. Direct costs of these sales grew by less, up 83%. Because the cost of sales did not rise as rapidly as net sales, the gross profit flew even higher, up 91%. This suggests that the firm may have become more efficient.

Running down the income statement, we come next to operating expenses. You'll remember that these are the fixed and variable costs of operating the business. The increase of only 75% suggests that the firm enjoyed even greater economies of scale. All told, management was able to retard the growth in expenses relative to the growth in sales. Income from operations, the sum-

Table 10*

Fiscal year ending:

	2/28/81	2/29/80	2/28/79	1979–81 % change
Net sales	$4,780	$3,269	$2,550	+ 88%
Cost of Sales	(1,850)	(1,230)	(1,014)	+ 83%
Gross Profit	2,930	2,038	1,536	+ 91%
Operating expenses	(2,537)	(1,866)	(1,451)	+ 75%
Income from operations	393	172	85	+ 362%
Other expenses	(154)	(136)	(69)	+ 123%
Income before taxes	239	36	16	+1,394%
Income taxes, benefits (expenses) & other	4	(9)	44	NA
Net Income	$ 243	$ 27	$ 60	+ 305%

* Figures, in $1,000s, are rounded and may not total exactly. Indented lines represent summation of income statement at that point.
NA = Not applicable

mation of the income statement figures mentioned thus far, grew 362%.

Interest payments for money borrowed and received from loaned funds usually is separated from the operations expenses. This is an old accounting practice that stems from the days when interest was considered usury and carried with it a negative connotation. The interest charges in Staodynamics' statement is included in the "other expenses" section. You'll notice that these costs grew 123%, up considerably over the costs in each of the last three years. The financial documents accompanying the annual report explain why. In this instance, it is because Staodynamics sold bonds totaling nearly $3 million in 1980 and was saddled with high interest payments as a result.

Now we've arrived at the company's income before taxes. The growth is more than healthy: it's spectacular. The company's income before taxes in 1981 was up from a mere $16,000 in 1979 to $239,000 in 1981, an increase of 1,394%. This certainly gives the company a positive aura. Now it's just a matter of deducting income taxes and an extraordinary loss the company suffered to arrive at the firm's after-tax profit. Because a tax credit ballooned

Staodynamics' after-tax income in 1979, 1981's profit growth is not as spectacular as the growth of before-tax earnings. Nevertheless, net income shot up 305% in just three years. In other words, Staodynamics increased profits 305% while sales grew only 88%. As mentioned, this growth earned the company recognition as one of the country's fastest-growing small businesses. Next, we'll look at how Staodynamics utilized those profits.

The preceding section on the two most important financial documents shouldn't cause you to put this book down and turn to greener pastures. The reason for such a careful examination is simple: accounting is important. Penny stockbrokers will go to great lengths to impress you with the durability and profitability of their favorite companies. But until you actually scrutinize the financial fingerprints of the firm, you can't be sure.

WHAT TO DO WITH PROFITS

Most venture stock companies don't pay dividends, while many New York Stock Exchange (NYSE) companies do offer dividends, ranging from stingy to generous. Dividends are nothing more than a portion of a company's earnings distributed to its shareholders. Because most NYSE companies are old-line, established firms that have been paying dividends year after year, the income to be derived from holding a NYSE-listed stock can be estimated fairly accurately. Accordingly, the yield on investment—the amount returned through dividends relative to the price of the stock—also can be estimated. Nevertheless, it should be remembered that dividends are funds not plowed back into the company.

Venture stock companies don't issue dividends for two very good reasons. First, many of these companies don't enjoy profits that can be distributed. Some companies, though, do turn a profit —and well they should, after several years in business. But this money isn't returned to the owners directly. Instead, the money goes back into the firm to increase its asset value. This is a wise move because these companies, in general, are idea-rich but asset-poor. Holding on to earnings increases the worth of the company and should increase the stock price, at least in theory.

Let's look again at Staodynamics to see how retaining the profits, as opposed to paying dividends, improves the asset worth of the share. In 1981 Staodynamics turned an after-tax profit of $242,598. The company retained all of these earnings and credited them to the shareholders in the retained earnings account (see Table 11).

Table 11

STOCKHOLDERS' EQUITY	2/28/81	2/29/80	Percent change
Common stock*	$ 19,352	$ 13,430	+ 44%
Paid-in capital	2,310,572	871,626	+165%
Retained earnings	696,004	453,406	+ 54%
Total	3,025,928	1,338,462	+126%

* $0.01 par value; 5,000,000 shares authorized; 1,935,247 shares issued and outstanding in 1981 and 1,342,998 in 1980.

The firm's retained earnings grew from $453,406 to $696,004. However, shareholders' equity grew by considerably more than this amount as a result of the issuance of an additional 600,000 shares of stock. Conversion of debentures, exercise of stock options, and other methods were responsible for more shares issued and outstanding, the major cause of the increase in stockholders' equity and corresponding increase in assets. Thus the book value for stockholders exploded from just under $1.34 million to more than $3 million.

The book value per share provides an interesting comment on the share's market worth (see Table 12). To calculate it, divide the Stockholders' Equity by Shares Outstanding ($\frac{SE}{SO}$) as shown in the following table for Staodynamics.

Table 12

	Stockholders' Equity	÷	Shares Outstanding	=	Book Value Per Share
1981	$3,025,928		1,935,247		$1.564
1980	$1,338,462		1,342,998		$0.997

On February 29, 1980, the net actual book value of owning a piece of Staodynamics was about a dollar. A year later it shot up 56% to $1.56. This certainly looks good. After an examination of the fundamentals, you decide to buy into Staodynamics and call your broker periodically during the following quarter. You are aghast to find the stock selling for between $3.25 and $5. You learn that a year earlier, the stock sold for between $2 and $3.13. First, you knock your head against the wall for not buying at $2 and then selling at $5. Second, you rub your head and ask yourself, "What's going on?" At the end of fiscal 1980 the worth of the stock in tangible assets amounted to about $1, yet the stock sold for between two and three times that amount. A year later, after the value had increased, the stock again was selling for between two and three times the new book value. What gives?

A STOCK'S PRICE = (? + ? + ?) / ? × ?

The price a stock commands on the market, and in particular on the venture OTC market, is a curious concoction composed of book net worth, earnings anticipations, industry potential, market estimations, management potential, and, above almost all else, hope. As can be seen by the following list of venture issues, the book value of the company's stock seems to have little direct correlation with the market selling price (see Table 13).

Table 13

Company	Book Value	Market Price*
Electromedics	$0.062	$2.595
Oiltech	0.109	2.44
Parallel Petro.	0.095	0.719
Premier Energy	0.103	0.60

* The market price is the average bid price during each company's fourth quarter of fiscal 1980, at which time the book value was calculated.

So, again, what gives?

Theoretically, we could assume that the price of a stock should represent its worth today plus an estimate of future growth. The only way a company can increase its per share value is by profiting and then retaining the earnings. Thus, the worth today should be the book value plus an estimate of earnings growth per share. As always, an example serves to make this a bit clearer. Let's say High Orbit Tech (HOT) has a book value equaling $1 per share today. Earnings per share over the next ten years will be 10 cents each year. (In the make-believe world of examples, one automatically knows this information.) The worth of the share today should be $2 (see Table 14).

Table 14

Present Book Value	+	Future Earnings	=	Est. Market Worth
$1.00	+	($0.10 × 10 years)	=	$2.00

This estimate doesn't take into account that the growth occurs over ten years, not immediately. And investors, no-nonsense lot that they are, would prefer to have the extra dollar in earnings right away instead of waiting for ten years. A simple illustration of this concept is provided by a passbook savings account. Anyone with an extra dollar invested in a passbook account paying 5½% says, in effect, "I'm willing to forgo spending that dollar right now in exchange for owning $1.055 a year from now." This also works the same way in reverse. The non-saver says, "Instead of having $1.055 a year from now, I want to spend the dollar right away."

To arrive at the correct market price of HOT's stock, we must calculate the present value of the ten years' earnings and add it to the current book worth. For HOT the question becomes: What is the $1 of current book worth plus ten cents per year earned over the next ten years worth today? If we assume that the investment money would otherwise have been placed in a passbook savings account paying 5½%, the calculation is relatively easy. In a bank account, 9.5 cents would grow to 10 cents in a year. Conversely, 10 cents a year from now is worth only 9.5 cents today. Similarly, the present value of having 10 cents two years from now is only 9 cents, five years from now, 7.7 cents and, finally, ten years from the present, only 5.9 cents. Totaling up the figures for each year (9.5 cents plus 9 cents and so on to 5.9 cents) shows that the earnings of HOT have a present value of only 75 cents for investors who keep their money parked in savings accounts. So the actual market value of the stock today should be $1.75 (today's book assets per share plus discounted future earnings), not $2 as previously estimated.

Ascertaining the present worth of any stock revolves around

finding answers to two major questions: what is the appropriate interest rate at which to discount earnings, and what earnings are predicted for the future. If the investor in HOT takes advantage of higher-yielding investment vehicles, then the 5½% discount rate is unrealistic. Let's say the investor can invest for ten years in a security that pays an annual dividend of 10%. He is prepared not to spend the dollar today in exchange for owning $1.10 a year from now. Conversely, a dollar a year from now is worth 91 cents today and the appropriate discount rate is 10%, not 5½%. If this is the case, ten years' worth of dimes is 61.45 cents, not 75 cents or $1, and, to this investor, the price of HOT shares (present price plus future earnings) should be $1.6145.

The price of a stock, however, is anything but certain. Investors come into the marketplace with different time values associated with their money. Another major force acting upon a stock's price is the earnings estimate. Once a company gets off the starting blocks and begins showing a profit, the stockholders' equity can be expected to grow. Obviously, investors' views as to future earnings growth have a very substantive impact on the selling price of that security.

For many venture stock companies, though, the prime question isn't what earnings will look like over the next several years; rather, the major question is whether or not the company will survive. Investors come to the venture market with widely varying views as to how well the company will perform. For this reason, the price of the stock for some companies cannot be strictly evaluated by the method suggested above. Nevertheless, for those companies showing a profit, this is a good starting point from which to evaluate venture stock investments. It leads us to the question of ratios.

RATIO, RATIO, WHO'S GOT THE RATIOS?

Let's put it all together. We discussed how the equity in a company, or the book value of a company's stock, can grow. Next, we suggested a method for evaluating the market value of a security. The relatonship between these two—the earnings of a company and the price of its stock—is termed, in the securities business, the price-to-earnings ratio.

The price-to-earnings ratio, or the PE as Wall Street analysts refer to it, measures the current price of the stock and compares it to the most recent earnings report. If you know nothing about stock market analysis, knowing the price-to-earnings ratio is like having a road map of Uruguay for driving in Greenland. PEs are only good if you work with them on a daily basis and can derive meaning from them. For example, when Staodynamics sold for $3.25, its yearly per share earnings amounted to 14 cents. Hence, its PE ratio was approximately 23. Stock analysts will compare the PE of a certain company to those of other companies in the same industry to make investment judgments.

Ray Dirks, former king of New York venture stocks, said, "What most investors—and many brokers—don't understand is that the true significance of the ratio is understood only when you take its reciprocal."[2] The reciprocal of the PE, the earnings yield, reduces the relationship between price and earnings to a readily comprehensible form.

Very simply, the earnings yield depicts the theoretical return on your stock investment. As an example, let's look at the earnings yield of Burton-Hawks, Inc., a Wyoming energy exploration firm. On April 14, 1981, Burton-Hawks sold for $5.75. For the preceding year, earnings per share amounted to $1.30. Hence the price-to-earnings ratio, the PE, was 4.4. Big deal. What does this tell you? Unless you're an experienced investor and can compare this with other small energy firms, it tells you nothing. But if you flip the ratio on its head, something more interesting emerges. To arrive at the PE, $5.75 is divided by $1.30. The earnings yield, $1.30 divided by $5.75, amounts to .23 or 23%.

In words, this tells you that a $5.75 investment in Burton-Hawks results in earnings growth of $1.30. Remember, you own a little piece of the company and any profits can be considered yours. The earnings yield suggests you receive a 23% return on investment. This, of course, is all theoretical because Burton-Hawks, like other venture stock companies, retains earnings in order to spark more growth.

The earnings yield should not be confused with the stock yield figures that appear in the quote section of newspapers and investment guides. The stock yield figure reflects the dividends paid out relative to the price of the stock. Because dividends are only a portion of the total earnings, the stock yield figure is only a portion of the earnings yield. (See Table 15.)

Table 15

Stock Yield*   = $$\frac{\text{Dividends Paid}}{\text{Stock Purchase Price}}$$

Earnings Yield   = $$\frac{\text{Year's Retained Earnings} + \text{Dividends Paid}}{\text{Stock Purchase Price}}$$

* The yield figure newspapers print in stock tables is the stock yield.

In the selection of penny stocks, yields—PEs or their more useful stepbrothers, earnings yields—are of limited value. If you're a
seasoned investor you might be taken aback by the last comment,
but hold your horses and I'll explain why. The companies
discussed thus far are, by and large, young companies that have
not achieved substantial earnings. That's why many of them are
still referred to as development-stage companies. Yields are virtually nonexistent because very few of the companies pay out dividends. Earnings, if any, are erratic at best, and the earnings yield
does not provide a stable yardstick. In fact, the return on investment shown by the earnings yields for many of these companies is
minuscule and would cause even the most neophyte investor to
stand back, scratch his or her head, and ask "What kind of investment is that?" I have selected several stocks at random from
the *Northwest Investment Review*'s list and reproduced their
market price as of April 1981 and associated ratios (see Table
16).

Table 16*

Company	Mkt. Price	PE	Earnings Yield
Amer. Nuclear	$5.50	18	6%
Antares Oil	3.88	39	3%
Bear Body	0.31	10	10%
Clayton Silver	2.25	15	7%
Northair Mines	4.40	9	11%
Search Nat. Res.	1.00	20	5%
20-10 Products	2.63	11	10%

* "Earnings Estimates," *Northwest Investment Review*, June 8, 1981,
11:6–8.

As you can see from these selected securities, venture stock evaluation does not call for the same set of rules as do New York stocks. Stephen F. Marsters, Denver's chief deputy district attorney, in a candid moment commented, "It's difficult to see the value of a penny stock when Texaco is selling for four times earnings [Texaco's PE] and these guys [penny stocks] sell for 100 times their last year's deficit. Something's going on that is not relative to intrinsic value."[3]

Mr. Marsters' final comment about intrinsic value completely misses the mark with regard to venture stocks and venture stock analysis. Very simply, intrinsic value is largely measured in qualitative terms.

Let's look at one of the companies on the above list which, if evaluated by standard methods, would be thrown to the bottom of the list of potential investments. Search Natural Resources is a good example. When the chart above was constructed, Search's OTC stock sold for $1, a price twenty times the previous year's earnings—a laggard if there ever was one. Why invest in a non-interest-bearing security that only returns 5% in asset growth with loads of risk, when you could go down to your bank and invest at 5½% and be assured of a return? The answer is Cory Campbell.

Campbell, a wunderkind of the oil industry, founded Search in 1980. Prior to Search's emergence, Campbell worked for other firms and could claim an almost unheard of wildcat well discovery rate, 80%. This is head and shoulders above the national average, 30%. In January, *The National OTC Stock Journal* reported that Campbell's company produced oil at the rate of 15 barrels per day.[4] Only five months later, Search claimed to produce 150 barrels of oil per day, a tenfold increase. Campbell's efforts have not gone unnoticed: Marvin Davis, owner of the largest privately held oil exploration outfit in the country, hired Campbell to perform exploratory work for Davis Oil.

Cory Campbell is an oil-field hero, but he lacked the solid financial background with which to construct a public company. So, before selling stock to the public, he put together a staff of financial experts and managers to help run the company. At first the OTC stock market was appreciative of Campbell's efforts. Search went public in October 1980 by selling two shares of stock and one warrant for $1.20.* Before the dust settled, Search's units sold for more than $6. Any investors who had bought in on the ground floor recognized a gain of more than 400%. By late 1981, though, Search's price had slithered down to slightly more than $2 which, company officials claim, actually undervalues the price of the share relative to the company's assets.

At this early juncture, the balance sheet for Search doesn't read very well. None of this management potential shows up on the balance sheet. After several years, no doubt it should. But today an investor looking solely at the balance sheet, income statement, and PE ratio would wonder, "What kind of investment is that?"

It's a typical venture stock investment. While the outlook for Search appears good—strong management, wise conservation of financial resources, and early positive results—there's no assurance that Search's future quest for energy won't be in vain. Remember, you're buying hopes and dreams first, and solid tangible assets second.

VENTURE FUNDAMENTALS

Through the preceding scenario, as well as in the other venture stock stories, I've alluded to two basic tenets necessary in the evaluation of these issues. First, look at the market the company is entering. Second, look at management's background and judge whether or not they are capable of succeeding at the endeavor. In other words, you must rely on an analysis of the company's potential rather than its past achievements alone. As securities lawyer Bruce G. Cohne suggests, "The 'Penny Market' is unlike any other stock market in that companies do not necessarily trade upon the market value of the assets or the company's earnings. Many times, companies trade upon the enthusiasm and persuasion of the market."[5]

In buying venture stocks, you're investing in the industry's outlook and in the management's potential. Accordingly, you must investigate the industry's potential in addition to that of the com-

---

* A warrant is a long-term option enabling the holder to buy a share of stock for a specified price, regardless of the current market price of the share. Warrants are discussed at considerable length in the eighth chapter.

pany. The market for energy is fairly straightforward. As long as OPEC exists and as long as the nation remains a net importer of energy, the market for domestic energy will be strong. Precious metals have been in demand from time immemorial. Prices fluctuate, but there will always be a market for precious metals. Indeed, this market could grow stronger if the whispers concerning a return to the gold standard prove correct. Interest in domestically produced strategic metals is also growing and several venture stock companies are begining to take advantage of this industry's potential. Solar, on the other hand, has been placed on the back shelf. At one time solar energy, believed the cure-all to OPEC-induced ills, spawned a mini-explosion in the penny market. Once it became known, however, that solar energy was still in the embryonic stage, the market's fervor cooled considerably. The outlook for high-tech companies is a little trickier to evaluate. Of course, there will always be interest in time-saving and advanced products. And the 1980s have been dubbed the decade of the computer chip. But whether or not what the venture stock company produces is state-of-the-art or obsolete is another question. We'll present some suggestions about how to analyze a company in the high-technology field in the following chapter.

The second consideration in venture fundamentals concerns management. By and large, the firm's management should have the capabilities, the background, and the hands-on experience to make the venture succeed. The fortunes of the penny stock market have encouraged an inordinate number of lawyers and stockbrokers to jump into fields that they would never have considered otherwise—e.g., drilling for oil or mining for gold. This isn't to say that a venture headed by a lawyer or a broker can't succeed; some have. According to textbook theory, the stereotypical chief executive office should have managerial experience and hire others to do the dirty work. But most of the firms in this market are small businesses. And if you've ever been involved in a small company, then you know that the chief executive officer does everything from signing checks to making coffee. On your mental checklist, you should consider whether or not management has direct experience in (1) the industry, and (2) running a small business. Another warning: Make sure the persons with experience are going to run the company on a daily basis. Many times a company will assemble a galaxy of industry stars to sit on the board or serve as officers, but in practice, an ex-gas-station jockey is going to run the whole show.

The company prospectus or offering circular (the offering document for the original public sale of securities) is a good source from which to learn of the management's background. There, in terse language, the board of directors' working lives are summed up in ten or eleven lines. Every prospectus includes this information. Often the annual report will also contain such information. But if the company has been in business for a number of years, the balance sheet and the income statements are better testimony to management's ability than where they went to high school and college.

For a company still in its corporate infancy, the managers' background is really the only way you can gauge a particular company's potential. Evaluating many venture stocks in terms of sheer financial data is secondary to the qualitative aspects. Frequently, though, the line separating potential and actual management achievement blurs imperceptibly with the dreams. For this reason, try to make certain that your information about the company is correct, up-to-date, and not exaggerated. Some companies will mount a public relations effort to circulate accurate information about the firm. Some, though, resort to hype to move their stock. All other things being equal, you should invest in the firm that employs a vigorous PR program over the one that doesn't. However, you should be wary of those that tout their stock seemingly without paying attention to the business itself.

As a venture stock investor, you should be very wary of hype portrayed as fact. I have explained in this chapter that there's more to wise investing than simply listening to whispers. Fundamental analysis provides the backbone to long-term profitable investment. If you follow some of the guidelines established in this chapter, such as looking at management, obtaining the annual reports, and examining the key financial statements, you'll begin to get a feel for what looks like a potentially profitable investment and what does not.

The mainstays of the venture market are high technology, energy, and mining securities, as well as new stock issues. In the next section you'll be learning a lot about these different areas—

probably more than you anticipated, but no more than is absolutely necessary.

The most important aspect of investing in the venture market is learning to select strong, growing companies. And the only way you'll be able to accomplish this is by acquiring a knowledge of the industries and the terms peculiar to each. Many examples of actual venture stock companies are presented in the following chapters. They will provide a familiarity with the types of investments you'll be considering. You'll learn a methodology for investigating any company, regardless of its industry. With this knowledge you'll be able to ask the right questions and understand the answers. Let's jump in.

NOTES

1. C. Colburn Hardy, *Dun & Bradstreet's Guide to Your Investments,* 26th ed. (New York: Lippincott & Crowell, 1981), p. 40.

2. Ray Dirks, *Heads You Win, Tails You Win* (New York: Bantam Books, 1980), p. 35.

3. "A Tarnished Penny Stock Market," *Business Week,* June 29, 1981, p. 104.

4. "Despite Davis Deal Hoopla, Search's Plans Stay Unfazed,' *The Denver Stock Exchange,* January 26, 1981, p. 1.

5. Chris S. Metos, *The OTC Penny Stock Digest,* ed. Mark A. Scharmann (Salt Lake City: Chris S. Metos, 1981), p. 12.

PART TWO

THE MOVERS: FASTEN YOUR SEATBELT

5

High Technology:
Much Ado About the Future

Money magazine had this to say about high-technology stocks and investors in these clearly chancy ventures:

> Young or old, new to investing or veteran of many booms and busts, nearly every stock buyer dreams of discovering a nascent Xerox or IBM and settling back to watch a few thousand dollars grow into a fortune. Alas, the companies that achieve such fabulous success are rare. But there are many obscure stocks that over the past few years have rewarded astute investors with superlative profits.[1]

And it's in today's venture OTC market that astute investors will find tomorrow's Xerox or IBM. Usually, banks politely but firmly shut the door on these young firms that have an idea or an invention, but few tangible assets. However, many small investors willing to take a risk have invested, and continue to invest, millions of dollars in such fledgling companies.

An investment in a high-tech venture stock requires special research and extra scrutiny because the intricacies are often difficult to comprehend. Such investments can be relatively unknown quantities; nevertheless there are precautionary measures you can take to make sure that you don't end up with 1980s computer-chip Edsel.

With regard to new companies, called start-ups, the way to begin analyzing the investment is to understand what the company is trying to accomplish. A new high-tech concern, (IRIS) (whose acronym stands for International Remote Imaging Systems), provides a good example. The company plans to break into the urine analysis market, and, after that, hopes to begin producing machines capable of analyzing blood specimens. In the prospectus for the company's December 1980 public sale of stock, the uses of their device are explained as is the potential size of the market. IRIS sold several million shares of stock, priced at $1, by convincing investors that there was indeed a market for their product. The second major question for investors—and perhaps the overriding concern—was whether or not management had the engineering know-how to build the device and the business acumen to market it successfully. For any high-tech investment, it all boils down to these two concerns: management ability and market receptiveness.

After the initial sale to the investing public, IRIS's stock rose as high as $4 before crashing down to $1.12 several months later. The market's euphoric first judgment doesn't necessarily reflect the fortunes of the company. On the contrary, during the wild price gyrations of its stock, IRIS hadn't produced a single commercial urine analyzer.

Another high-flyer in the high-tech venture market has been Denelcor, Inc. This computer company originally sold one million shares for $1 each in August 1978. During the final quarter of the company's fiscal 1980, shares of Denelcor, on average, were bid at $16.44. Despite the fact that the company has never turned a profit (except for a meager one in 1976), sales have generally taken an upward course.

Let's look at Denelcor's business. The firm's 1980 annual report explains that "Denelcor designs, manufactures, markets, and services large-scale, high-speed, general-purpose parallel computer systems for scientific and commercial applications. The company's Heterogeneous Element Processor (HEP) incorporates the Multiple Instruction Stream, Multiple Data Stream architectural concept for the first time in a commercially available form."

Now, unless you were an expert, would you have laid down your hard-earned money in a company that purports to produce "parallel computer systems"? If you had done a minimal amount of research on the firm, you would have learned about Denelcor's computers as well as the expanding market for this product. And you would have been greatly rewarded for your work and foresight by the stock's price appreciation.

Both of these examples point out something else as well. Denelcor's stock didn't climb along a straight upward path. Instead, after the first year of public trading the stock, on average, slipped back down to $3^{11}\!/_{16}$ bid. Only in 1980 did the market seem receptive to parallel computers (see Chart 2). IRIS's stock is still young and low on the growth curve; the verdict is not yet in. In other words, investing in a high-tech stock generally requires patience while you wait for the firm's product to come to fruition.

WHAT IS HIGH TECH?

Much science fiction baggage has become attached to the words "high technology"—everything from genetic engineering to robotics. High-tech has come to be a catch-all term that includes the latest advances in medical technology, TV and cable hardware, energy conservation, ultrasonic security devices, computer software, and a great deal more. New York *Times* science editor William Stockton wrote that "more than a century of unprecedented scientific achievement has laid the groundwork for a coming century of astonishing technological accomplishment."[2] Indeed, well-designed and well-engineered products are a major source of tomorrow's profits.

The resurgence in the high-technology field stems from two root causes. First, Americans realized that if they wanted to regain their role as the world's leading innovators, they would have to push forward—rapidly. And as the laws of economics predict, when there's money to be made by filling a void, private entrepreneurs will move in and attempt to fill it.

The second cause underlying the resurgence in the high-tech field has been the development of the computer chip. This little silicon device, which could—and did—replace whole roomfuls of old main frame computers, spawned an incredible assortment of applications. In the late 1950s and early 1960s, the space program was the cutting edge of high-tech; today, it's computer technology. And just as in the space program, there are numerous spin-off products creating mini-industries. The only limits to the

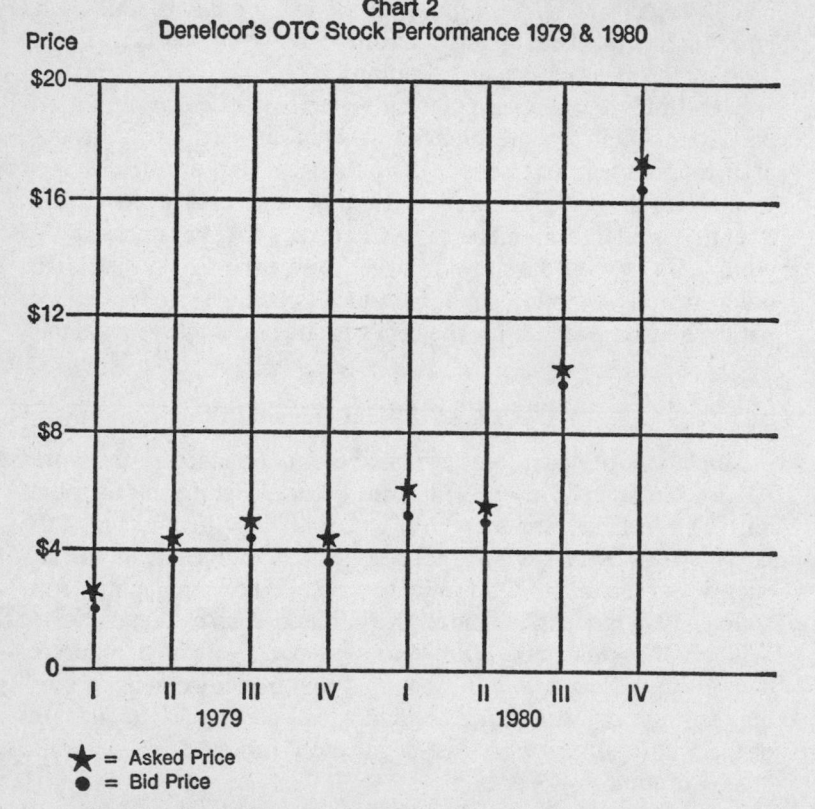

Chart 2
Denelcor's OTC Stock Performance 1979 & 1980

★ = Asked Price
● = Bid Price

NOTE: Bid and asked prices are average of quarterly highs and lows
Source: Denelcor, Inc., 1980 annual report

uses of the chip—aside from the availability of money, of course
—appear to lie in the creativity of engineers who design the pro-
grams.

The venture stock market has provided the needed capitalization for many of these companies. As the stock market for
high-tech grows, there will be many new companies coming to the
public, of which some will prove worthwhile and others worthless. Clearly, you need to be able to pick the valuable ones. Let's
look at four high-tech companies that have come to the Over the
Counter market. These will provide the basis for the investment
strategies suggested at the close of the chapter.

TALKING BIOFEEDBACKS

In 1980, Electromedics, Inc., was the forty-seventh fastest-growing small business in the country. Sales in 1980 were more than $3 million, 1,139% higher than sales in 1976. Optimistic signs were not always in evidence, though: the company endured the traditional trials and tribulations that are the lot of any small business.

Electromedics went public in 1972, selling shares at $1.25. By 1976 the bid price had grown to $4.50. At that point, apparently, considerable question arose in the investing public's mind as to whether Electromedics and its electronic thermometers would ever make the big breakthrough. By the end of 1979 the stock's price had slithered down to 38 cents. But as the firm's health improved, the price recuperated, to trade in the range of $4 in early 1981.

Electromedics manufactures a broad line of electronic temperature-gauging units with medical, veterinary, and industrial applications. The company claims that 100 hospitals use its disposable electronic thermometers. In 1980 the company unveiled a temperature-measuring device that reports a patient's temperature verbally. That's right, it talks.

The new talking thermometer helps a person to relax his or her body. Electromedics asserts that the thermometer, a tool for clinical biofeedback training, can "alleviate the occurence of migraine headaches, overcome speech impediments, improve cardiovascular health, and a host of other bodily conditions through control by state of mind." The company hopes that biofeedback training will become more prevalent and that the talking thermometer will gain widespread acceptance. This certainly requires a leap of faith on the investor's part. But then, many others have asked investors to make a similar leap: Edwin Land, you'll recall, claimed that a hand-held contraption was capable of capturing images and then reproducing them in a matter of seconds via his Polaroid invention.

Electromedics, though, isn't placing all of its eggs in this talking "basket." The company continues to push its disposable elec-

tronic thermometer, hoping to carve itself a major niche in the
tough medical market. The firm also emphasizes research and development, where work is currently underway to develop a den-
sity altimeter for small aircraft and a computer chip capable of
measuring temperatures between —70 and +2,000 degrees Fahr-
enheit.

Now, before you run out and invest let me add several caveats.
First of all, the company lost money from 1973 through 1979.
The firm's first profitable year was 1980, and even then profits
were slim, amounting to only 4 cents per share. There's no assurance that Electromedics will ever capitalize on what seem to be
some promising developments. Furthermore, there's no assurance
that the market for Electromedics' OTC security will ever regain
its momentum and surge forward. After all, there's no certainty
that another company won't come along and introduce a thermometer that not only talks but listens, too, possibly rendering
Electromedics' product obsolete.

The serious question one must face before investing in a high-
tech stock is whether the product has long-term sales durability or
is just a flash in the pan. And unless you're an expert in the field
(of thermistory in this case) there's really no way for you to
assess the company's potential on your own. Chances are, your
broker is no expert in the field either. For this reason it's a good
idea to read brokerage house research reports and, if possible, articles in trade magazines concerning the company's product.

Tom Ullman, syndication manager of a large brokerage house,
summed it up best: "Sure, everyone's got a neat idea. But it's
important to go further than that."[3] Ullman suggests that investors
look at how many applications a device has, as well as at the
management's experience in the particular field.

NOTHING BUT INITIALS

NBI, Inc., was founded in 1972 by disgruntled employees of
one of the nation's largest computer firms. The company survived
on private sources of capital until 1979, at which time the firm
approached venture-minded public investors. And while NBI
originally sold public stock for $20 (which does not meet our
definition of a penny stock), the company offers a stirring example of a recently-gone-public high-tech firm. After two years of

public trading, the adjusted stock price had more than quadrupled. Early investors in NBI may have found the next "nascent Xerox or IBM."

The founders of NBI believed that the whole field of information processing was on the brink of a revolution, and they wanted to take part. These fellows had the engineering know-how to produce the office machine of tomorrow, the word processor. So, on two counts, NBI met our requirements for a potentially successful company: management understood the technical requirements of the industry and the market thirsted for its products. The only question yet unanswered was whether or not the managers had the business wherewithal to make the venture succeed.

The venture stock market and the established exchanges too are littered with the wreckage of companies managed by engineers and oil-field hands. The success of these people in their own industry was sufficient to convince investors that they knew industry requirements well enough to manage a public enterprise and make it thrive. These experts discovered that in order to succeed they had to know more than simply how to find oil or how to design a computer. Instead, success demands a magic elixir of industry experience and financial and business acumen. These combined qualities, then, are another crucial indicator for high-tech investors to look for. Close perusal of the financial documents, particularly several of the recent income statements and the most recent balance sheet, present very telling signs as to whether or not the managers can handle the business.

NBI appears to have succeeded on the final count. The company's revenues jumped from a relatively modest $459,000 in 1976 to a tremendous $32.9 million in 1980. What's more, there doesn't seem to be any slowing of this phenomenal growth. For the company's third fiscal quarter in 1981, NBI President Thomas S. Kavanagh stated that "NBI again reported its highest level of operating results." As compared with the third quarter of the preceding year, revenues soared from $8.7 million to $14.3 million, a gain of 65%. Net income—profits—appreciated even more grandly, up 125% to $2 million.[4]

NBI's dramatic growth derives primarily from the invention, production, and market acceptance of its word-processing equipment. Kavanagh asserted in the 1980 annual report that "NBI is rapidly emerging throughout the world as the supplier of the most technologically advanced yet highly useful word-processing and information-processing systems in the office automation industry today." He backed up this claim by stating that NBI has been "growing at an average compound annual rate in excess of 150% in a market estimated to be growing at only a 50% rate." The skyrocketing growth is the result of an extensive and aggressive distribution system composed of direct sales offices and manufacturer's representatives. Plans in 1981 called for a nearly one-third increase in the number of direct sales offices.

The stock market has been quite receptive to NBI's abilities and potential. Fundamentally, NBI appears to be a quality investment. Company officials had the business smarts to recognize an expanding market, along with the computer-chip talents to build a product the market desired.

THERMATRON AMBIGUITY

Now we turn to a company that hasn't been nearly as successful; "an enigma" is how Thermatron's president, Bruce Murphy, described his firm. So far, Murphy's Thermatron, Inc., has piloted a strange course through the energy and high-tech fields. The company was born in 1977 as Emerald Resources, a privately held concern. In 1978 the company sold shares to the public for $1 each and changed its name to Thermatron. Dumping its energy holdings, it acquired the patent for a microwave heating device and thus qualified for a high-tech name.

The company branched out into several related areas, producing an energy-conservation device for the home and hand-held thermometers with industrial and consumer applications. Although sales were building, revenues never did overtake the growth in costs; after three and one-half years in business, Thermatron still hadn't shown a profit.

This corporate schizophrenia continued through mid-1981. Reversing itself, the company divested itself of its high-tech workings and reentered the oil and gas field in full force. The microwave heater, which had given the company its name in a time of high hopes, was never completed.

Thermatron's problems may have been with management or with the product itself. Murphy is an intelligent man, a former lawyer for a Cheyenne, Wyoming, energy firm. Noticeably absent from his background was any work in the high-tech field. Murphy himself said he had no experience in the operating end of an oil and gas company, nor any knowledge of microwave electronics. He didn't allow these deficiencies to get in the way, though. As he said, "I saw the opportunity and the product [the microwave heater] intrigued me." He and his brother convinced the investment community of the opportunity and Thermatron was on its way.[5]

The stock, underwritten by American Western Securities, originally sold for $1. Then the company and the underwriter decided the stock's appreciation potential would be greater if the stock were priced lower, and the stock was split 10 for 1. This effectively altered the original offering price to 10 cents. In October 1980 the stock dipped to 3 cents. Then in December it vaulted back up to 25 cents. But by mid-1981 the price had dripped back down to 7 cents.

The concept itself may have been impossible for management to transform into a viable business opportunity, or perhaps the fault lay in the product. On the face of it, a microwave heater sounds considerably more feasible than a talking thermometer. Appearances can be deceptive, though, and this is the reason to talk with experts and learn whether there's a market for the product before taking a particular high-tech plunge. Indeed, one day Thermatron (or whatever it is called by then) may succeed.

But the lesson to be drawn is that venture stock investors should not hold a stock that:

1) may take several years before it begins to move, or that
2) may never get out of the starting blocks.

Indeed if, after several years of corporate life, a company still vacillates in its direction, the wise investor will beware.

THE MENU EXPLOSION

In late 1980, a company with a futuristic name appeared among the nation's top ten most actively traded securities on an almost daily basis. The company's OTC stock hung in there at between 3 cents and 12 cents for most of the year until the year-end trading frenzy jolted the stock up to $1.31. And then, with an equally heavy-handed swipe, the penny market demolished many investors' gains as the bid price plummeted to 31 cents. In short, there was quite a bit of commotion over Sci-Pro, Inc.!

Sci-Pro is another firm that entered the public realm with one intention and then altered its course down what appeared to be a more lucrative avenue. The company began operations in 1976, developing biomedical computer products. After researching the market and failing to enter it successfully, Sci-Pro abandoned this area to enter the restaurant computer field. Currently, the company's only product is the "Hospitality Manager."

Alan Boxer, Sci-Pro president, explained that the machine, fabricated from specially programmed computer chips, is a desktop computer. It is designed to deal with a restaurant's accounting needs. Expectations ride high for the computer and its marketability. In November 1980 Boxer believed that no comparable model existed in the market.* He hoped that the product would become the "dominant force in the hospitality accounting area" because, he claimed, the machine can take care of about 75% to 80% of the "total data and information management requirements necessary for modern food service."

Along with the standard restaurant accounting procedures such as payroll and periodic sales reports, the computer is also capable of what Sci-Pro calls "the menu explosion," using a detailed program that analyzes current costs and profit margins for each menu item. The restaurant's managers can then react immediately to any adverse cost situations. Boxer gave an example: if the price of hamburger shoots up 15% per pound, the restaurateur won't know the effect on profits until several months later when the accountant does the books. With the Hospitality Manager, Boxer asserted, it's possible to stay abreast of profit margin fluctuations and adjust menu prices accordingly. Boxer finished his pitch by claiming that the Hospitality Manager can save $12,000 to $15,000 yearly in inventory costs alone for a restaurant grossing $500,000 per year.[6]

Here are a few additional facts. Sci-Pro has never turned a profit. Its net loss of $689,120 in 1981 was more than triple the previous year's loss. The heightened activity of Sci-Pro's OTC security at year's end stemmed from hints of a tremendous sales contract and the fact that the company's first computers were beginning to roll off the production line.

---

* The wise investor would look at both sides of this contention: Either Sci-Pro was in for a bonanza or else no other firm deemed it worthwhile to manufacture such a product.

At first glance—and maybe at second glance as well—Sci-Pro appears to be moving forward once again. Nevertheless, one should not base an investment in Sci-Pro merely upon enthusiastic remarks concerning the Hospitality Manager. Furthermore, Alan Boxer, who just recently took over the company, may or may not be competent enough to turn the business around.

The more you can find out, the better: research, research, research, and scrutiny, scrutiny, scrutiny, are paramount for successfully investing on the basis of a high-tech company's fundamentals. Northwestern University Professor Rolf Banz suggests that investors in venture stocks are well advised to adopt a "buy and hope strategy."[7] I would add that investors should first research, and only then "buy and hope."

A HIGH-TECHNOLOGY PROGRAM

I hope I haven't fatigued you with these short surveys of four high-tech firms. These examples were provided to give you an idea of the different situations you might face as a high-tech investor. A high-tech firm is nothing if it just has a good idea. As we have seen, it takes a particular combination of idea, capital, management, and market before the company can get moving. The OTC market generally appreciates the phenomenon when the various elements come together in a successful formula.

Before jumping into a high-tech venture, first look at the company's age. When it comes to brand-new companies, those seeking venture capital from the market for the first time, you won't have much to go on. We'll take an in-depth look at analyzing new issues later in this section. In any case, you should get a copy of the prospectus or offering circular for the high-tech issue. Decide whether the invention and the plan of action seem credible. Typically, this information should be obtained from someone other than your broker. He is not a disinterested party in any matters relating to the sale to you of a security. It is likely that his house is a member of the selling syndicate or underwriting group for the new issue, so there will be a great sales push. Furthermore, look at the disbursement of proceeds from the offering. Does it seem that an inordinate amount of money is allocated to salaries or to old debts, with a relatively small sum devoted to actual development of the product? If this is the case, look elsewhere to invest.

The mid-life high-technology firm presents a much more interesting and challenging proposition. The term "mid-life" refers to a company that is already manufacturing a product, that has a marketing force, and that has achieved considerable sales. This doesn't necessarily mean that the company is turning a profit.

For such companies, find out whether or not sales are growing at a fairly healthy clip. In addition, it's important to look at total revenues. Often one year's revenues will jump solely because the company sold something of considerable value, such as land or patent rights. A nonrecurring item such as this cannot be used to assess the future revenue growth of the firm.

Besides sales growth, another important sign of a strong mid-life firm is the percentage of resources devoted to marketing. As we stressed earlier, a chief consideration is whether or not anyone will buy the machine, once it is built. High-tech firms must use aggressive marketing techniques if their innovative products are to gain market acceptance. This is especially true of firms in the medical field. For good reason, medical authorities are often reluctant to utilize a snazzy new device until it has been proven to work. Medically oriented high-tech firms must work extra hard to convince the medical establishment that their product is worthwhile, consistent, and, above all else, safe.

If the firm you're considering is not yet turning a profit, find out when management believes the red ink will turn to black. Sometimes this information can be found in the president's message, which is included in the annual report. Other times, you'll have to talk with your broker or call the firm itself. Furthermore, you should make certain that the profit is based on increased sales alone. Remember, while the firm may be operating in the red now, at some point it must begin making money if the value of your shares is to appreciate over the long haul.

OTC APPLAUSE

As an example of the above method of analysis, let's look at Denelcor's 1980 annual report. Denelcor is the "parallel computer" company mentioned earlier in the chapter. From the statement of operations, we find that sales in 1980 amounted to $2,604,814 (see Table 17).

This is a fairly substantial amount for a young company. As compared with 1978, sales increased 56% from $1.7 million. Sales in 1980, though, actually fell by $93,887 (or 3.5%) from the preceding year. This should raise a question in the investor's mind. "Why did sales decrease?" Turning to the president's message, we find that this drop resulted from "the lack of commercial orders for the HEP [the firm's primary computer]." This certainly doesn't answer the question and no further explanation is given here. In this instance, potential investors should investigate further to learn why the decline occurred. Another figure the alert investor would notice shows that to achieve this lower level of sales, costs rose. The gross profit declined $195,736 as the cost of goods sold and contract costs edged up from $2.3 million to $2.4 million.

Running down the income statement to expenses, we find them up by 59%, a considerable increase. This represents a 52% growth in general and administrative expenses, a 70% jump in marketing efforts, and a 61% heightening of research and development costs. On the surface, this looks like positive evidence that the firm is doing what it should be doing: both marketing and research and development are chief concerns. Again, you should scrutinize the annual report to determine more specifically how the firm is expanding its efforts in these areas. In the president's message to shareholders, David R. Miller, Denelcor's president and chairman, explains that the firm engaged Field Marketing to sell its product. Further perusal of the annual report reveals Denelcor's thrust in research and development. However the expanded administrative expense, smaller in percentage terms than the gains in the other two areas, is not explained.

The total loss for the year, $662,311, results, then, from higher direct and indirect expenses while sales declined. The cautious investor would persevere and find out why sales slumped.

Despite the overall loss, the OTC stock market seemed receptive to Denelcor's efforts and potential. As has already been shown, the stock, on average, jumped from a low of $2.50, bid in the first quarter of fiscal 1979, to $16.44 at the end of fiscal 1980 (see Chart 2).

The other variety of mid-life company is the one whose identity

Table 17

Denelcor, Inc.
Statement of Operations

	Year ending December 31:		
	1980	1979	1978
Net sales and contract revenues	$2,604,814	$2,698,701	$1,673,636
Cost of goods sold and contract costs	2,383,910	2,282,061	1,340,560
Gross Profit	220,904	416,640	333,076
Expenses:			
General & Administrative	590,274	387,612	191,978
Marketing	348,980	204,979	168,133
Research & Development	249,541	155,378	50,317
Total	1,188,795	747,969	410,428
(Loss) from operations	(967,891)	(331,329)	(77,352)
Other income (expense):			
Interest expense	(52,340)	(69,690)	(22,606)
Interest income & other	357,920	6,242	73,253
Total	305,580	(63,448)	50,647
(Loss) before income taxes	(662,311)	(394,777)	(26,705)
Credit for deferred income taxes	–	24,700	7,100
Net (loss)	$(662,311)	$(370,007)	$ (19,605)

is ambiguous. A look at the income statement for such a firm will be a bit disheartening. Nevertheless, you should not be scared away—at least not yet. Find out whether the company changed course in midstream. Perhaps management finally decided that the product wasn't going to sell well. If this proves to be the case, determine whether or not they're seeking other products or just crying in their beer.

Also, look at the managers. Have they changed recently and does this event suggest that better days are in the offing? In short, venturing into a mid-life high-tech company that doesn't yet look worthwhile requires considerable qualitative evaluation of its potential. Of course, you could always "buy and hope," but analyzing the company is a better strategy.

For the more seasoned high-technology firm, you should review the balance sheet, income statement, and the qualitative features of the annual report. You should look as well at the firm's profit record during the preceding several years and at management's forecast of future profit growth. For the older firms—those that were once penny stocks—the more traditional yardsticks are fully applicable: earnings yields, PEs, and so forth. Nevertheless you should still talk with the experts and carefully read research reports on the company.

This completes our section on how to evaluate high-tech situations. While many of these companies' products are very difficult to evaluate, you can still look into the company itself. After all, it's your money, and a research-then-invest strategy is always better than the "buy-and-hold-your-breath" method.

NOTES

1. Michael Sivy, "Making Big Money on Little Stocks," *Money,* July 1981, p. 42.

2. William Stockton, "U.S. Needs Shot of Pride to Rev Up Lagging Technology," Denver *Post,* July 5, 1981, Sec. 2, p. 1.

3. "Technology Wave Rides High Above Flagging Oil and Gas Market Leaders," *The Denver Stock Exchange,* June 29, 1981, p. 1.

4. "NBI: The High Tech 'Cadillac,'" *The Denver Stock Exchange,* June 29, 1981, p. 5.

5. Bruce McWilliams, "Thermatron Will Place Major Emphasis on Oil and Gas," *The Denver Stock Exchange,* December 22, 1980, p. 6.

6. "Sci-Pro's Computer Brings Price High," *The Denver Stock Exchange,* November 22, 1980, p. 6.

7. Sivy, p. 43.

6

Energy: Gusher Bonanzas

The energy cauldron was at full boil for most of the 1970s. Only in 1981 did energy prices drop to a simmer as the fire cooled. What had happened is no secret: the industrial world's consumption of oil had slackened while greedy OPEC nations continued to produce millions of barrels of oil and sell them for too high a price. The result, the alleged oil glut.

Daniel Yergin, Harvard energy economist, laid the myth of an oil glut to rest. "Right now [in 1981], it's easy to believe that the problem has solved itself. It may not be so easy in" several years.[1] Yergin explained that any number of international variables, such as the loss of Saudi Arabian "friendship," could easily put the United States in another precarious situation.

When the price of oil began to stabilize, the price of Big Board oil equities began to fall. Future profit projections were based on the continued unrestricted upward trajectory of oil prices. Thus, when future profit projections were scaled down, the current selling price of these stocks also underwent a correction. At the same time as the Big Board oil stocks fell, the penny oil stocks collapsed. *The National OTC Stock Journal*'s index of penny oil stocks plummeted one third during 1981.

The underlying basis for their decline, though, is not so easily explained. Many of these companies are still in the start-up stage. The chief consideration is not what price they'll be able to command for their oil; rather, it's whether or not they'll be able to find any oil.

After such a rapid devaluation, penny stock market investors should have shied away from these declining investments, right? Well, not exactly. In fact, many of these companies' stocks were undervalued. But before running out and buying any oil and gas issues, you should consider your own view of the future of this industry. If you believe that solar power or some other alternative energy form will challenge, overwhelm, and replace fossil fuels' importance in the next five years, then it would be contradictory for you to invest in a going oil and gas concern. On the other hand, if you believe that OPEC will continue to overshadow world energy production and prices, and that American energy entrepreneurs will play an increasingly important role in America's future energy scenario, then an oil and gas investment might be right for you.

ENERGETIC TRANSITION

The economics of energy exploration has changed dramatically over the last decade. By 1981 the price of a barrel of crude oil had been jacked up 308% from its pre-embargo price; natural gas skyrocketed even more—up 575%. Oil and gas wells that were at one time capped as uneconomic are now more than profitable.

As the economics shifted radically, numerous oil-field hacks went into business for themselves. Again, the reason is simple: oil and gas became more profitable and more people entered the industry. Between 1973 and 1974, the time of the embargo, employment in the energy business rose 91%, "almost six times the growth rate of jobs in the private non-farm economy."[2] The gradual decontrol of oil prices, which began on April 4, 1979, spurred an even greater rush to the land. Since then, employment in the oil and gas industry has grown at the rate of about 6,600 jobs per month. The total number of drillings in the United States was up by more than a fifth in 1980 over 1979.[8]

Paralleling this growth in activity, there has also been an explosion in the number of small energy exploration and production outfits. Many of these firms originally became capitalized through friends and other sources of private capital. At a certain point, many realized that they wouldn't be successful without a huge inflow of capital. And that's the point where the venture stock market enters the scene. In fact, the emergence of this market is linked chiefly to the demand for funding by these energy firms.

Whenever a massive economic transformation takes place, it's inevitable that a washout will follow the boom. Many individuals go into businesses that they probably should avoid. They fail because of insufficient funding and because of poor management. The point that should be emphasized is that it takes more than a successful, competent geologist for a company to be able to turn a profit. The seeds of any successful company are quality management, a good product, and a receptive market. In the oil and gas industry, the product is fairly standardized and the market, at least in the near term, is very receptive. Accordingly, all you need to look for is quality management.

But an oil and gas situation is, in some respects, even more difficult to analyze than other venture stock industries. All oil and gas companies, at similar stages of their corporate lives, tend to have the same appearance—that is, most firms are run by seasoned management, many own an inventory of producing and nonproducing land, and, finally, all enjoy an eager world market. Nonetheless, subtle distinctions emerge under an astute investor's magnifying glass.

The aim of this chapter is to give you a brief familiarity with the workings and the jargon of the oil and gas exploration business. As an investor in an exploratory oil company, you'll be receiving notices from your company of their achievements. The following section will help you to interpret these as well as to evaluate potential investments. We'll look at the basics of energy exploration as well as at the method used by the companies to put together the massive sums of money needed to drill a well. Then we'll turn to the investment side of the picture. The final section explains the nuances of venture oil stock investing.

FINDING OIL

In the most basic sense, oil and gas exploration requires three steps: buying land, punching a hole in the ground, and then either finding or not finding oil and gas. It's that simple. What makes it risky is that no one knows a surefire way to find these hydrocarbons. There are all sorts of hints, such as geologic anomalies, oil-tar sand outcroppings on the earth's surface and the like, that guide geologists. But as yet no one has determined an exact method of finding these energy resources.

Before the penny stock oil company can drill a well, the firm must first acquire the land upon which to drill. In the oil industry there are basically two kinds of land: producing and nonproducing. Producing land contains at least one well that is producing from the oil field below. Conversely, nonproducing land is acreage that has not been drilled or on which no oil and gas is currently being produced. This is not to say that the land doesn't contain any oil. Rather, there is a chance, a prospect, that the land can produce; hence it is called a nonproducing prospect. In the hell-for-leather rush to produce energy, the price of both producing and nonproducing land has been bid up considerably. Producing land is much more expensive. In the mining industry, the firms buy up claims—legal rights—to mine the earth. In the oil industry, however, firms buy up leases or leaseholds. This land is rented from federal or state governments, or from private persons who own potentially productive lands and will sell the right to drill for oil or gas for a specified period of time.

The Geology of Petroleum, a leading textbook for soon-to-be oil finders, said this about oil and its exploration:

> We have yet no direct method of locating a pool of petroleum. We know of no physical property of underground petroleum that we can measure at the surface of the ground. The petroleum geologist's approach to the discovery problem must therefore be indirect. Each pool of hydrocarbons is unique. We may think of a pool as the end result of twenty or twenty-five variables of which only a few can be ascertained in advance.*[4]

Finding these twenty or twenty-five variables is the reason for the existence of a mini-industry. Many esoteric methods are employed to locate the critical indications of oil and gas. One method requires sending sound waves through the surface of the earth, waiting for them to bounce back, and then charting the time required for the echo. The resulting data, called seismics, are recorded on a graph. Back in the lab, trained geophysicists scan the charts in hope of detecting anomalies, the breaks in the subsurface geology that indicate the possibility of an oil and gas trap.

Another method, similar in purpose, is to photograph the to-

* The reader-investor is well advised to keep this in mind when a broker or company president asserts that oil is in the ground on the company's new but yet-undrilled prospect.

pography from airplanes. Such pictures may show unusual contours in the earth's surface, possibly indicating an anomaly underneath. And that by no means exhausts exploration techniques; there are countless other methods of detecting these variables.

Young oil companies will sometimes retain a geologist to interpret this data. In other instances, the firm simply contracts out for the work. Once it has been determined from the surface that all systems are go, it's time to punch a hole and ascertain the accuracy of the geologic prediction.

DRILLING A WELL

To drill a prospect, the company must first arrange to get a drilling rig to the site. In recent years obtaining a rig has become somewhat difficult. Because of the stepped-up drilling activity of U.S. oil companies, the nation's rig inventory has not been able to satisfy the growing demand. In fact, "new rigs [were] being put up in the United States at the rate of nearly four a day in 1981—a 50% increase" over 1979.[5]

When the drilling rig pulls up to the site, all preparatory work has been completed. The prior geological work targets a specified depth where it is believed that oil will be found. Some wells need to be drilled only a few thousand feet into the earth, while others may require drilling of up to 10,000 feet and more. Rig capabilities vary, and for the deeper wells more expensive, heavy-duty rigs are required. Keep in mind that the total cost rises considerably for each foot drilled. Investors should determine the depth of the wells the company is betting on. If the company only drills to 2,000 feet and the well comes up dry, then the expense won't be nearly as great as if a 20,000-foot well proves to be dry. When the rig starts turning, this is called "spudding the well." After the well has been drilled to the total targeted depth, it is said to have reached the casing point. The drilling rig is wheeled away and the operators begin testing whether or not there's any oil in the ground. Even if oil or gas is found, this doesn't necessarily mean the well is successful, however. Further testing is required to make certain that pumping the liquid out of the ground and then shipping it to a refinery are economically feasible. And unless the well looks like a worthwhile undertaking, the company just throws in the towel and moves on to the next prospect.

On the other hand, if tentative tests prove that the site does contain commercially recoverable reserves of petrochemicals, then casing the well begins. Casing, another of those picturesque oil and gas terms, means constructing a wall within the well. The wall, which is built from the surface all the way down to the pool, assures that the oil won't get drained away on its trip to the surface. After casing is finished, the completion unit moves in and a pumping unit is built on top of the well.

Once the oil begins flowing, the major worry is out of the way and the company must simply make sure that the oil keeps flowing. For the first few days or weeks of operation, the well will produce at a greater rate than is to be expected over the rest of its productive life. During the first few days, it rids itself of much of the pressure that has been building for thousands of years. After the tap is broken, the rate of recovery slows down and a constant but decreasing flow is assured.

Thanks to advances in the petroleum field, geophysical engineers can look at several of the variables disclosed by the producing well and estimate the size of the oil pool. Their estimation, while rough, is better than none at all. It gives the company and investors alike a yardstick by which to evaluate the size of the resource and its impact on the fortunes of the company. Later in this chapter we'll explain how oil stock investors can use this knowledge to evaluate a company's stock price.

The first well drilled in an area is dubbed the exploratory well. It is drilled outside an area of proven oil and gas reserves or within a proven area but to a previously untested depth. In the idiom of the oil field, the exploratory well has come to be called a "wildcat" and one who drills exploratory wells is called a "wildcatter." This is a revered title similar to the prospector in the mining industry or the inventor in science. According to *The Geology of Petroleum*, it carries none of the connotations of its use in the term a "wildcat strike" (a labor walkout unsanctioned by the union).[6] In 1980, more than 11,000 wildcat wells were drilled all over the country; approximately 70% were dry holes. The dry hole rate fluctuates from region to region and is about 85%–90% in the Rocky Mountain area.

If the venture oil company acquires land just adjacent to another producing well and proceeds to drill, this new well is called a development well. It must be drilled to approximately the same depth as that of the producing well to receive this designation. Industry hands sometimes call development wells "confirmation" wells because the second and subsequent wells confirm the presence of hydrocarbons and the size of the pool. Subcategories in the realm of development wells are step-outs and offsets. Offset wells are drilled close to the already producing well, while step-outs are drilled slightly farther away in an attempt to define the parameters of the field. The spacing of development wells is geologically determined. Company managers try to recover the maximum amount of oil possible within a given time while expending the minimum amount of money.

The modus operandi of the oil and gas industry is very complex and is littered with claims of surefire methods to discover oil, alleviate costs, reduce risk, and lessen the problems associated with drilling. But when all is said and done, drilling a well is risky and expensive. How do venture stock companies, armed with only several million dollars, complete an exhaustive drilling program?

OIL FINANCES

In any business venture, the ability to produce the product is only one aspect of the endeavor. Another major consideration is raising the money with which to finance the undertaking. The oil industry is no different; recent venture stock offerings will raise several million dollars. Managers for these companies could buy a few land leases and proceed to drill the wells themselves. For young companies, though, this is entirely inadvisable. As stated, drilling an oil well is very risky. The landscape is composed of more dry holes—"dusters"—than active producers. So if the well turns out to be unproductive, the company has sunk a good portion of its own funds into an unrecoverable resource. All they'll have to show for their efforts is a deep, long hole, and perhaps some geological data confirming that there's no oil in the ground. The company is out a considerable sum of money, and will have that much less with which to drill the next well.

In the oil industry, and especially among young companies, it is common to share the risk with others in exchange for some of the revenues if the well is a producer. This is accomplished in numerous ways, sometimes with other members of the industry and sometimes with outside sources of funds.

Let's add some more texture to this concept of risk sharing through a hypothetical example. We begin our foray with a trek up to a piece of land in Montana. The land sits squarely above the Overthrust Belt (see footnote page 5). A poor old farmer owns the land, on which no oil wells have ever been drilled. Along comes the Wildcat Oil Company to acquire some nonproducing acreage. The farmer, long on land but short on cash, willingly agrees to lease the land to the firm in exchange for a fixed sum per year plus a 12½% interest in any oil and gas revenues (called an overriding royalty). This is the usual share that landowners receive. Wildcat, then, owns an 87½% net revenue interest and a 100% working interest in the acreage. Net revenue refers to what chunk of the whole picture the firm owns. This figure also includes any overriding and straight royalty payments. Working interest, by comparison, indicates the percent of the total expenses the firm must pay. In other words, Wildcat Oil must put up 100% of the money to drill the prospect while receiving only 87½% of the revenues.

But Wildcat Oil doesn't have the in-house capabilities to test the geologic promise of this land thoroughly. The firm agrees to sell off another little chunk of its interest, let's say 7½%, to a geology firm in exchange for their testing the energy promise of the land. The geologic consultants decide that there is a very good possibility that a hydrocarbon pool exists under the ground, and Wildcat Oil decides to proceed. By now, Wildcat's interest has been effectively whittled down to 80%.

Wildcat starts contacting other firms, looking for other industry partners for the project. The small venture stock oil company finds three other eager partners who each receive a 25% working interest in exchange for spending 33% of the needed funds. This is known as a "third-for-a-quarter" deal.

In this case Wildcat is considered the prospect generator, and has "farmed-out" its interest in the land for a 25% carried working interest. The other three firms are said to have "farmed-in" to the prospect. Wildcat's only investment, then, was to buy the leasehold and perform the geologic background work necessary to convince the other three firms of the soundness of the project. By sharing the potential profit with others, Wildcat Oil has eliminated most of its monetary risk. The company's interest, though, has been whittled down to a 20% net revenue interest (25% of 80% = 20%).

Before we continue the sharing of this Overthrust land pie, let's go back a step. Wildcat Oil is a typical start-up oil exploration outfit. In other words, they're eager to tackle the world but they just don't have the money. Accordingly, the firm may seek others who are willing to put up the necessary cash. Institutional sources, such as bank trust funds and pension funds, have the money but don't care to take the risk of going into the oil business themselves. Typically, joint venture arrangements are formed between the small oil firm and a huge cash fund. The fund puts up the bulk of the money in exchange for a lion's share of the revenues. Simultaneously, the fund assumes most of the financial risk as well. This serves to fuel the small oil company's exploration efforts on a much greater scale than if the firm were forced to rely solely on its own resources.

Another source of funds for these start-up companies, as well as for seasoned companies, is the limited partnership. Put very simply, a limited partnership finances a particular exploration effort. The members of the investing public buy shares in the new limited partnership company. These persons are deemed the limited partners because their liability is limited to their investment. The oil firm arranging the partnership is the general partner and assumes complete liability. Typically, the limited partners put up 90% of the money and receive 85% of the revenues flowing back to the partnership. The differential goes to the general partner as a reward for managing the project. Besides the potential reward from the partnership, investors are induced to participate in the venture because of special tax benefits to be reaped from such an investment.

Let's get back to Wildcat Oil and their chunk of land in the Overthrust Belt. You'll remember that the firm was left with a 20% interest in the acreage. However, the firm still needed cash with which to buy the land and to cover other miscellaneous expenses. That's no problem, though: the company found a cash-rich partner who was willing to assume most of the risk in exchange for 75% of Wildcat's interest in all of its prospects. This effectively reduces Wildcat's net revenue interest in the project to 5% (25% of 20%).

You may say at this point, "Why should Wildcat Oil give up so much of the potential profits in the land?" Well, if you look back over the financing of this hypothetical situation, you'll see that the Wildcat Oil Company only put up the money to buy the acreage. However, the company pushed its land acquisition expense back onto its joint partner so that, in essence, they put up no money to receive a 5% carried net revenue interest in any oil that gushes out of this unproven ground.

One venture stock company that has been particularly creative and inventive in this area is the Hart Exploration and Production Company. Hart went public in late 1980 through the sale of four million shares at $1 each. In mid-January 1981, when the firm's OTC security was trading in the $4 range, the company signed a $20 million deal. A scant three weeks later, Hart capped this achievement with a $40 million arrangement. The $40 million Hart-Internorth-Hambros Bank partnership calls for Hart to receive a 3% management fee, regardless of the number of wells drilled or the success ratio. Hart President Fred Boethling said, "Hart, at minimum, stands to gain $1.2 million over the duration of the two-year program." Further, Hambros Bank puts up all of the money while Internorth is responsible for developing the geologic concepts. Hart then receives a 2% carried interest in any oil production resulting from its efforts. After costs have been recovered on the well—that is, payout—Hart's interest converts to a 4% carried interest.

Boethling spelled out why Hart Exploration is so very much interested in this arrangement. He said, "It gives us, a small company, tremendous acreage exposure." That's another one of those energy business terms. Boethling meant that his company, capitalized by the public with only $4 million, would be able to participate in $60 million worth of drilling ventures, with the time they spend as their only expense. Obviously, Hart's financial risk is greatly minimized in the venture as is the size of the potential rewards.[7] Hart is said to own a "gross" interest in each well discovered despite the fact that its "net" interest in each well amounts to only 2%.

This net/gross distinction carries over to two other areas of the oil business. Returning to our example of Wildcat Oil, the firm at one point owned an 87½% net revenue interest of 640 gross acres or 560 net acres (see Glossary). Of course, this doesn't mean the company could mark off 560 acres and call it their own. Rather, the firm owns an interest in the larger portion. Also, let's say that Wildcat, along with others, drills 100 wells on the property. The firm doesn't own a 100% interest in each of these wells. Rather, the company owns a 5% interest of the 100 wells. So, Wildcat owns five net wells or 100 gross wells. This same arrangement occurs in the sharing of oil production. If the 100 wells turn out 1,000 barrels of oil per day, Wildcat's net interest totals 50 barrels per day while its gross interest is 1,000 barrels per day.

The net/gross distinction is an important consideration. Before investing in a relatively mature company, be sure to obtain net figures of acreage, wells, and production. In the firm's annual report, the gross figures usually sit side by side with the net figures. Not always, though. If you think that you're buying into a company that's producing 20,000 barrels of oil per day, it is doubly important to check on the net sum. It could, and most likely will, turn out to be only a fraction of that figure.

The interest that a company retains also provides a very telling indicator of a firm's risk philosophy. If a company assumes 100% risk in return for 100% of the potential gain, then this suggests that the managers are very self-assured about their geological predictions. The firm, of course, may have earned the right to be so confident by virtue of its past performance. For example, Premier Resources Ltd., a ten-year-old seasoned exploration and production firm, retained a 71.25% working interest in the drilling of a Garfield County, Oklahoma, wildcat. If you didn't know anything about Premier's track record, you might be a little taken aback by the apparent risk that Premier assumed. But the Garfield County well, as it turned out, justified Premier's confidence in spades. The well produced 1,445 barrels of oil and 1.1 million cubic feet of gas per day initially. Premier, not content with just one bonanza, set out to drill a confirmation well. This well confirmed what they believed to be true—and how! The second well, drilled within the immediate vicinity, flowed 1,008 barrels of oil and 1.3 million cubic feet of gas per day. That's a considerable amount of energy. And because Premier retained such a large interest in the well, they should profit handsomely from production.

On the other hand, if the wildcat well had turned out to be dry, then the company would have borne the lion's share of the cost of the project. And all they would have had to show for their efforts and expense would have been a deep hole in the ground and a sobering experience.

Premier, a relatively established firm, could afford to take such a risk. In the first six months of 1981 alone, the firm participated in the drilling of thirty-five wells, twenty-two of which were producers. This brought Premier's gross well picture up to 260. The company also owns a huge gross land position, 253,194 acres. However, closer scrutiny of the annual report reveals that the net acreage position amounts to 81,325 acres, or 32% of the gross figure. It was very unusual for Premier to retain the 71.25% interest in the wildcat well and surrounding acreage. This is confirmed by the net/gross acreage ownership, which is far less.

Young, unseasoned venture stock firms, such as Hart Exploration, can't afford the risk involved in retaining such a large percentage. Hart, in order to reduce costs and risks, retained only a 2% working interest in the wells developed through the company's efforts. Granted, this practice won't generate tremendous revenues for the firm, but it does shield it from the downside, the dry hole. Young companies just can't afford such risk exposure.

In sum, the small, independent operator should take a smaller percentage of a very large picture as opposed to a larger percentage of a very small scheme. Tomahawk Oil & Minerals president David T. Laurence spells it out: "For small companies like mine, it's all risk and reward." Laurence commented that he "wasn't ashamed to go for the smaller wells with a smaller interest" because they offered less risk potential for the owners of his company. "I'd rather have five wells producing 10 barrels per day instead of looking for that one well that could produce 50."[8]

PENNY STOCK DOLLAR GLUT

Before getting down to the nuts and bolts of penny oil stock investment strategies, here's a study to whet your appetite. Gerald Schecter, an investment consultant, prepared a study that looked at all oil and gas issues coming to the public market between 1968 and 1979 in Colorado. His findings were impressive, to say the least. Schecter assumed that a $500 investment was made in each of the seventy-two companies. The total investment would have amounted to $36,000. By November 1980 the entire investment, if sold, would have yielded $693,156 exclusive of trading costs. Only one of the seventy-two companies was no longer in business.

Rainbow Resources and Energy Minerals were two of those companies that came to the public market. Rainbow originally sold shares for 50 cents. Later the company merged with NYSE-listed Williams Companies on a nearly share-for-share basis. Williams, in September 1981, traded for $27, representing nearly a 54-fold increase. Energy Minerals originally sold for 10 cents per share. The company moved from the OTC market to the American Stock Exchange, and in September 1981 sold for around $8.50, an 8,400% return on investment.[9]

Of course, not all of the energy issues have performed so spectacularly. But if all goes right, this book will point you in the direction of finding the potentially profitable firm. Irving Hale, vice-president of research of First Financial Securities, Inc., and the closest thing to a historian of the venture stock market that there is, has come up with a perceptive methodology for analyzing small oil stocks.

First you should consider whether you want to invest in "hope and potential"—a start-up company—or in a more seasoned one. The former is much riskier but has the potential for greater gains. Analyzing the two types of company calls for differing methods. Premier Resources, discussed earlier, is a relatively mature company with established production and reams of financial history. Hart Exploration, on the other hand, has only been in business for a few years and shouldn't be expected to be able to compete with Premier on the balance sheet. Similarly, Premier's shares are more expensive than Hart's.

WORTHY

Hale says mature companies, those in business for longer than five years, that "are worth their salt, have developed oil and gas production, cash flow from various sources, and reserves [of oil and gas]."[10] Many of these companies utilize reserve recognition accounting (RRA) to value their oil and gas reserves.

RRA attempts to place a dollar value on a company's in-the-ground assets. Here's why: normal accounting practices dictate that a company value its assets according to their cost of acquisition. For example, if a firm buys a desk for $100, then the asset value of the desk is $100. The same holds true for oil wells. For instance, if an oil well costs $300,000 to drill and the well is estimated to be capable of producing 20,000 barrels of oil during its producing life, then the asset's estimated true value is considerably more than the cost of developing the asset—i.e., drilling the well. Nevertheless, accounting practices call for the capitalization of an asset at its cost. If the price of oil is $35 per barrel, the estimated worth of the well would be $700,000, not the $300,000 spent to find the oil. Well, not exactly. This figure must be adjusted in several ways, such as estimating when the oil can be recovered and at what cost, before its true value can be determined.

This sum, though, doesn't take into account the time value of money. Readers will recall that the current selling price of a stock reflects the current asset value of the company plus some discounted estimate of future earnings for the company. The same holds true for oil well net revenues. The net future value must be discounted back to the present, at 10% per year,* to arrive at today's asset worth of the well.

The SEC, along with an accounting practices group, adopted the RRA method as a supplementary statement of accounting for energy firms back in 1978. The industry experimented with the method for several years before determining, in 1981, that the RRA estimates were too erratic. Accordingly, the RRA statement did not become a primary financial document, though it is still estimated and can provide you with a rough approximation of what a firm owns in the ground.

What's left, then, are the two traditional methods of evaluating a well on the basis of its costs. Either of the two accounting methods—successful efforts or full cost—is employed by energy firms to evaluate their wells. Successful efforts capitalize the costs of drilling on the balance sheet for only those wells that prove successful. Dry holes are written off as expenses during the current time period. This method tends to increase expenses and therefore reduce taxable income. Older firms that are already in the profitable category use this method to reduce tax liabilities.

* This particular discount rate is required for RRA estimations.

Full cost, on the other hand, assumes that to find gushers it is necessary also to drill dry holes. All expenses of drilling for both successful and futile wells are capitalized on the balance sheet, and any future production is charged off against the cost of both. Young companies that are already showing losses do not need to reduce tax liabilities. This method, as opposed to the other, tends to shore up their income statement by reducing expenses.

Both methods, though, really don't depict the true value of the oil and gas well. The wise investor will determine which method is employed by glancing at the financial statements in the back of annual reports. The reserve recognition accounting statements can usually be found in this section as well.

MATURE ENERGY COMPANIES

For older oil and gas companies, Hale suggests the following tactic for evaluating the worth of the firm relative to its stock's current selling price. First, calculate the company's working capital: subtract current liabilities from current assets. Subtract from this figure any long-term debts. Next, add in the acquisition cost of any nonproducing acreage, as well as any other assets of the company such as office equipment and so on. Be sure, though, not to include intangible assets, like goodwill. Noticeably absent from the calculations so far is an estimate of the worth of producing oil and gas properties.

Now, instead of adding the value of oil and gas properties from the balance sheet, arrived at through either full cost or successful efforts, add in the present value of future net revenues from proven reserves of oil and gas. Be especially careful to add in the *present value* and not the *future value*. Total up all of these figures and you have an estimate of that energy company's net equity.

As an example of this method, we will utilize an abridged version of Century Oil and Gas Corporation's 1980 financial statements, taken from the firm's 1980 annual report. First we determine the working capital (current assets less current liabilities). This totals —$56,479 (see Table 18). The second step is to add in other assets aside from Century's oil and gas properties. They total $58,738. Next, add in the value of the oil and gas properties, less the value of the producing properties, $1,004,952. This amounts to $1,007,211.

Now we flip to the RRA statements (see Table 19). The present value of estimated future net revenues from oil and gas properties amounts to $4,711,000. This figure should be added to the figure already calculated above. Thus, the estimated worth of the company is $5,718,211.

Take this figure and divide it by the number of shares outstanding. In this instance, we divided $5,718,211 by 4,053,838 shares to arrive at $1.41. Compare the per share value with the actual selling price of the security. If the two prices are relatively close, then you may have a good buying opportunity. More likely, though, the stock's price will be much higher. In evaluating the worthiness of a particular company, make comparisons with other similar companies.

Table 18

Century Oil & Gas
Abridged 1980 BALANCE SHEET

	Dec. 31, 1980
Current Assets	$726,296
Oil & Gas Properties—At cost using successful efforts	
Producing properties	$1,877,569
Undeveloped properties	652,244
Wells in progress	352,708
Total	$2,882,521
Less accumulated depletion and depreciation	492,125
Total	$2,390,396
Other Assets	58,738
Total Assets	$3,175,430
Current Liabilities	782,775
Stockholders' Equity	2,392,655
Total	$3,175,430

Table 19

Century Oil & Gas
Supplemental Schedule of Reserve
Related Information

Estimated Future Net Revenues
for Years Ending Dec. 31:

	PROVED RESERVES
1981	$ 916,000
1982	961,000
1983	903,000
After 1983	5,453,000
Total	$8,233,000

Present Value of Estimated
Future Net Revenues at:

December 31, 1980	$4,711,000

Here's another consideration that should be kept in mind. The stock's price is an estimate of current and future worth. For the energy company, you have already calculated the tangible worth of the firm. However, in the crazy world of oil and gas exploration, the company could just go out and turn one of their nonproducing properties into a bonanza. The $50,000 used to drill the well could result in a gusher, providing the firm with millions of dollars. Take a look at the company's track record. Does this event seem likely? It's all risk and there are no hard-and-fast rules. But by going through the quantitative and qualitative evaluations, you'll have a far better view of the stock you're considering.

BABY PENNY OILS

The field of energy exploration is rapidly becoming crowded. Overcrowded, in fact. Many who have worked for the majors are branching out to take part in the mad energy rush of the 1980s. Companies are formed and ten minutes later they go to the public investment pool with outstretched palms. On the balance sheet, they don't have much going for them. Hale says that "firms that have just come into existence obviously cannot be appraised" in the same manner as those companies already in the marketplace.

For these new companies, there are only two investment considerations: management's capabilities and the stock's selling price. Usually, when these new firms come to the public, their main selling point is the experience they have gathered while working for others.

Look at the capabilities and diversity of management. Along with the experts in the oil industry, is there someone on board with the financial competency to make the venture succeed? Are there people with experience in running a small business? And finally, does management have direct experience in the operating end of the oil business?

These considerations, obviously, are all qualitative—you can't quantify experience. Often, though, brokers will tout the fact that the managers have had over 100 years' collective experience in the energy industry. When you hear this, it should set off a little alarm in your mind that tells you to check further. There's no assurance that all of this experience wasn't obtained while working in the lube pit of a local gas station. For these start-up companies, the prospectus is a good place to find a short wrap-up of the managers' backgrounds.

Having said all of this about oil and gas companies, let me tell you a short story which apparently breaks all of the rules. Robert R. Spatz is president of Cheyenne Resources, Inc. From 1961 to 1976 he ran a restaurant in Cheyenne, Wyoming. Warren J. Hickman is vice-president of Cheyenne Resources and a practicing dentist with a degree in biological sciences from the University of Nebraska College of Dentistry. Lawrence E. Gill serves as treasurer of the company and is also owner-operator of Cheyenne's Deluxe Cleaners and Tailors.

Now pause for a moment, please, and ask yourself: if you had read this rundown in Cheyenne's early 1980 prospectus, what would you have thought? Despite the fact that the company had been in business for ten years (albeit without much activity), would you have invested your presumably hard-earned bucks, at the rate of $1 per unit, to buy a piece of an oil company run by a dentist, a dry cleaner, and a restaurateur?

You would have had a good thing on your hands if you had.

For one thing, by March 1981 the price had moved up to $10 per unit. The company's property acquisitions and production warranted its price relative to other similar energy firms. Although I have sandwiched together many of the more incongruous facts concerning Cheyenne, one thing is evident: each of these men had a great deal of experience in running a small business.

The second thing to consider is the stock's current selling price. In a hot market, after a new issue is cleared and begins trading publicly in the aftermarket, its price rises substantially and then falls back to a level above its initial offering price. Look at the current selling price of the security in relation to its original offering price. "If the multiple is far above that of other new companies to their offering price," Hale says, "the stock might be ahead of itself," and a correction—a decline—might be in the offing. Of course, in a down market a stock may open at a lower price than that at which it was originally offered. If this is the case and if the company is solid, you may be looking at a bargain. We'll table this discussion until the chapter concerning the price moves and patterns of a stock.

GRAY BLACK GOLD

The above considerations offer potential penny oil-stock investors plenty of food for investment thought. Let's move on to some grayer areas in the analysis of the worth of a company. The mere fact that a firm is in the energy business isn't enough on which to base an investment. The investor should look at what aspect of the energy business the firm emphasizes. Most energy firms specialize in one area or another of the industry. Some companies will lease nonproducing acreage, sit on it, and then turn over the land when there is a flare-up of interest in the acreage. This has led to tremendous gains for some because of the rapid growth in price of potentially productive areas. Other firms perform geological analyses of acreage and pick up interests along the way. An energy company, as a third alternative, could sit on the cash raised through its public offering and wait for other members of the industry to promote the land for a farm-in, "third-for-a-quarter" deal. Then too, there are the firms that specialize in organizing the actual drilling of the well. Finally, some firms own drilling rigs and will acquire an interest in a well by agreeing to drill for others.

In other words, the energy exploration firm can concentrate in any one area. All of the above-mentioned strategies have been a source of profit and growth for small energy firms. In reality, a firm will avail itself of a number of methods to gain interests in wells—performing geological work, buying undeveloped acreage, farming-in to a prospect, and so on. Determining what the company does best will provide investors with some angles for comparative investment shopping.

George O. Mallon, Jr., president of Mallon Oil Company, believes that serious energy investors should opt for the company with a great deal of experience in geological analysis. He adds some more details to the energy road map that we've already developed. He believes that a company's undeveloped acreage position is relatively unimportant. "Acreage," he says, "has never found oil. But good geology work has." Further, the acquisition of unproved acreage is very expensive, as there is no assurance that oil will ever be found on the land or that another firm will ever be interested in farming-in to the land. Mallon believes that, given a choice between two energy companies—one that emphasizes acquiring acreage and another that specializes in geological work—the investor's scale should tip toward the latter.

Another subject worth an investor's scrutiny is the success ratio. The potential energy investor will always hear talk of management's success in finding producing wells. As with all seemingly solid statistics, this is another one that should be closely examined. Tremendous pressure is exerted on young energy companies to achieve a high ratio between successful wells and number of wells drilled. Mallon counters that "the success ratio means very little and, in actuality, is a very dirty speedometer." He explains that "there are certain areas in the country where you can hit gas every time that you drill." However, in these productive areas, "you'll have to hold your breath for twenty years before you get your money back."[1]

A more valuable barometer for independent oil and gas firms is the estimated reserve level of its in-the-ground assets. While the engineered reserve estimates do undergo fluctuations, they provide an estimate as to the success of the energy firm. If the reserve estimates indicate that the firm has many millions of barrels of oil and billions of cubic feet of gas under its land, but its success ratio is only 5%, the firm is undertaking some very risky ventures. This strategy, though, could prove worthwhile for the firm.

OIL AND GAS ROUNDUP

In this chapter, I have laid out some of the ground rules of the oil and gas industry, as well as a number of factors that energy investors should consider. This has been accomplished through the use of examples as well as concrete suggestions for energy-company analysis. Nevertheless, one thing should have become evident: that the oil and gas exploration business is risky. You can reduce your odds by knowing what it all means, but you can't eliminate the risk.

As has been mentioned, the oil market was in a depressed state for most of 1981. The pervasive belief that there was an oil glut dealt a crushing blow to the major oil stocks; for the venture oils, it was almost suffocating. And when analysts discussed the logic behind the drop for the venture stocks, they couldn't find much to say. The chief concern for these companies isn't the price that they'll be paid for their product, but rather whether or not they'll be able to find oil. Nevertheless, it's important to recognize the volatility tied up in the oil stocks. Before you make an investment in a venture oil stock, look at the state of the world economy (i.e., OPEC's latest bellowings and actions—or lack thereof). This should give you a fairly accurate guide as to where the domestic penny oil stocks are going.

Investing in these stocks is as risky as the energy development business itself. As mentioned, there are about twenty to twenty-five variables that go into the formation and identification of an underground pool, only a few of which can be ascertained at the surface. The same holds true with venture oil stock investing. There are countless variables affecting the direction of an oil stock, only a few of which can be detected before venturing. Knowing these few oil company investment variables, though, is certainly better than just randomly buying stocks.

NOTES

1. William Stockton, "U.S. Needs Shot of Pride to Rev Up Lagging Technology," Denver *Post,* July 5, 1981, Sec. 2, p. 2.

2. "Economic Diary," *Business Week,* June 29, 1981, p. 16.

3. "Drilling Activity in North America During 1980," *American Association of Petroleum Geologists Bulletin,* V. 65 ⧣8, 1981, p. 1728.

4. Arville Irving Levorsen, *The Geology of Petroleum,* 2nd ed. (San Francisco: W. H. Freeman, 1976), p. 6.

5. Steve Lohr, "Why Hunt Oil? . . . Better Here Than There," Denver *Post,* August 30, 1981, p. 23.

6. Levorsen, p. 6.

7. "Internorth Deal Crowns Hart's Early '81 Harvest," *The Denver Stock Exchange,* March 3, 1981, p. 1.

8. Bruce McWilliams, "Tomahawk's Risks Become OTC's Reward," *The Denver Stock Exchange,* April 4, 1981, p. 8.

9. "Twelve-year Review of Oil and Gas Issues Reveals Big Returns," *The Denver Stock Exchange,* December 29, 1980, p. 5.

10. Irving Hale, "Picking Oil Stocks," *Colorado Business Weekly,* June 15–21, 1981, p. 10.

11. "A Passport for Investors Travelling to Oil Country," *The Denver Stock Exchange,* May 18, 1981, p. 6.

7

Mining: The Glimmer and the Glory

Mining companies come and go. Around the turn of the century, mining firms in the Rockies offered assessable penny stocks. Assessable issues allowed the mining firm to raise secondary venture capital by dunning their shareholders into either supporting company fund-raising efforts (i.e., investing more money) or giving all of their shares back. And, as often happens in the gold mining industry, many of these firms went the way of buggy whips and hoopskirts.

In the late nineteenth century, and again in the 1920s, the Rocky Mountain region was the center of a mining explosion. In each instance, though, crashing precious-metal prices eventually sated the mad hunger for gold and silver.

Today, once again, gold, replete with its promise of riches, is back on the shopping list. So are silver and strategic metals. From the East, West, North, and South would-be prospectors have flocked to the high country of Colorado, to the mother lode country of California, and to the great old mining districts of the Northwest with a glint of gold in their eyes. And it's the venture stock market that provides these modern-day forty-niners with their axes, picks, and shovels.

A leisurely drive through the Colorado Rockies vividly displays this revival of the mining industry. Miners in the process of reopening previously abandoned mines compete with tourists for parking spots in the old mining districts. Virtually all old mine shafts are being reexamined to determine whether or not enough gold remains to work them profitably. The economics of gold mining has altered even more dramatically than that of oil and gas exploration. In the 1960s, miners were lucky to get $35 for an ounce of gold. Today, while the price seesaws back and forth, it's safe to say that gold's price has exploded at least tenfold, if not twentyfold, depending on the current trend of the world market.

Consequently, many new gold and silver mining firms have entered the industry with the same age-old hope: striking it rich. A mining venture, in essence, requires four basic steps:

1) Finding an ore body capable of sustaining a profitable operation.
2) Staking a claim or buying the land rights.
3) Mining the ore in an appropriate manner.
4) Milling the ore into the desired substance.

It all sounds simple, but it's not. Mining for gold and silver is even more difficult than exploring for oil and gas. The chances of finding and developing an ore vein involve ten times the risk of drilling and completing an oil well. From concept to fruition, mining is a very risky and very expensive undertaking. The time involved in a successful mining development can be as short as three years or as long as ten years. Thus, wise managers plan for the company's cash needs should the development period have to be extended.

Typically a mining firm begins its venture by locating a potential mineral deposit—either previously undiscovered reserves or a closed mine. In seeking out the undiscovered reserves, the firm scrutinizes geological maps of the area to determine whether or not any anomalies—subsurface traps for the minerals—exist on the site. Next, the firm must stake a claim—that is, obtain the rights to explore for minerals on the land. Having accomplished this, the firm doesn't set to mining with picks and mules right away. Further testing must be done to confirm that the potential ore body is worthy of development. In this analysis, the company utilizes the latest geophysical techniques. If all systems are still go, then the firm obtains core samples—chunks of ore—from the vein. This defines the minerals present and the perimeters of the vein. Often eager young firms will jump into the actual mining of the earth before completing enough preliminary work to establish the probable wealth of the vein. This could mean that after expending much time and money, the managers will find that there wasn't enough of the precious metal in the deposit to warrant the heavy mining expense.

After completing preliminary work, many mining firms need further infusions of capital to get the project moving. We'll explore possible methods of financing later in this chapter. This taken care of, the firm must now decide upon the most cost-effective method of retrieving the ore from the earth. One method, open-pit mining, simply requires lifting gargantuan quantities of earth off the top of the vein. Another choice could be to dig long corridors into the earth and then line the resulting shaft. Still another method is called *in situ,* and essentially calls for the refining of the ore in the vein itself. The method the firm will use depends on the nature of the vein.

In addition, a mining operation finds itself heavily burdened with environmental and safety constraints. If open-pit mining is used, the firm must continually reclaim the land to protect the surrounding environment. Similarly, in an operation that employs shaft mining managers must remain vigilant to ensure the mine's safety. These regulations add another layer to a mining concern's costs.

Once the mine is uncovered or dug, it's just a matter of breaking up the rock and transporting it to the mill. If the company has a mill on site, this can be a cost saver. But if the company must transport the ore to another site for milling, additional expense is incurred and another layer of regulations become operative. For example, transporting ore over some federal and Indian lands is prohibited. The use of public roads for shipping ore requires an Environmental Protection Agency permit. But when they finally arrive at the mill, the tons of rubble are reduced to a more easily manageable form. The concentrate of gold and silver is then smelted into bullion.

In short, the whole process is very costly, very time-consuming, and burdened with regulations. If the firm simply reopens an old mine shaft, then much of the early exploratory work is eliminated. It is paramount that potential investors determine how much work is required to get the mine and the mill back into working order, as well as the length of time required before it can operate profitably. For mine reopenings and completely new mines alike, it is also important to determine whether or not the firm has a concrete strategic plan that will allow it to weather a long dry spell. If nothing more, this will alert the potential investor as to whether or not company management comprehends the particular requirements of the mining industry.

A. G. Foust, president of Minerals Engineering Company, sums it up best: "In oil and gas, if you make a discovery, you can get in quick and begin generating a cash flow. In mining, it's not that way . . . even if you make a discovery, it's still going to take a number of years to set up operations capable of generating money."[1]

The trump card in the whole affair of mining investment is the price of gold and silver. In the oil industry, analysts can make a worst-case assumption that the price won't drop, but instead will only stabilize. This is hardly the case with mining. Rapid and dramatic price fluctuations are par for the course in gold and silver prices and therefore for mining stocks. Between 1979 and 1981, gold's price plummeted from more than $800 down to the neighborhood of $400, and silver declined from upward of $50 to under $10. These almost vertical price moves wreak havoc on mining companies' attempts to estimate the profitability of their mines. We'll explore the sources of instability in the prices of precious metals and mining stocks shortly. But first let's go back up to the high country of Colorado.

UP ON CRIPPLE CREEK

As we drive through the Rockies, observing all of the current work on the old mining shafts, we come upon the historic Cripple Creek Mining District, west of Colorado Springs. This legendary town was the inspiration for numerous tunes written by miners lamenting their lack of good fortune. One who recently turned miner and hopes that he won't be singing those songs is Bradley Place, Jr.

Place, a stockbroker by trade, drove up to the old town in 1974. "I immediately fell in love with it," he said. Afterward he became interested in the mining industry because a number of his clients had recently gotten into gold-mining stocks. The run-up in gold's price that year caused a similar trend in the value of gold-mining shares. Place, no dummy, thought to himself, "Maybe I should get into this."[2]

So two of the three major ingredients of any budding business —an entrepreneur and a market—were present in 1974. However, procrastination, insecurity, and concern about the wife and kids all took their toll until 1977. Finally Place, believing he had talked enough and was ready for action, formed the Cripple Creek Gold Production Corporation and acquired the rights to 52 acres of land near the town. Now the only thing missing was money. So he sold 2.5 million shares of stock in the fledgling operation at 20 cents a share.

Place could not decide whether he should quit his job just in case the shaft caved in, so to speak. The decision was made for him. His brokerage house explained that he was either a stockbroker or a gold miner, not both, and gave him until eight o'clock the next morning to decide. By nine o'clock the following morning Place had hung up his three-piece suit for good and was on his way to becoming a rough-and-tumble, dyed-in-the-wool gold prospector.

Place hired several consultants to examine the feasibility of reworking the old Beacon Hill Prospect at a profit. The consultants gave Place the nod. But before Cripple Creek could start mining and milling, some major revamping of the site was called for. "The rudiments of a 25-ton-per-day milling structure were on the property," Place said. The building, which had been constructed in 1941, had succumbed to years of neglect. Another cranky old structure on the property was the mine shaft. To assure the safety of the miners, it needed major reconditioning, and 410 feet of the mine's shaft had to be relined before any mining could begin. Another necessity was the installation of a hoist and a large air compressor to be used to transport the gold-bearing ore out of the shaft. The property, which had not been mined in nearly forty years, was on its way to joining the gold rush of the 1980s. Place said they used a small gold deposit, uncovered in the mine, to try out the mill. This effort showed the company something else: it was undercapitalized. Their earlier projections apparently had not foreseen that their milling capabilities were insufficient. Therefore the company's capitalization through the penny stock market had been insufficient.

Place had already spent half a million dollars, supplied by the venture market, just to get the mine up to speed. And still not one cent in revenues had been generated. This need to revamp is typical of firms reentering old mines. Venture stock market historian Irving Hale adds that "while unrecovered ore may exist in many old mines, the tunnels and shafts often are flooded, which necessitates costly pumping."[3]

For investors looking at young mining firms, two chief factors are worthy of special attention: management's estimate of how much money is needed and the length of time it will take in order to make the mine operable. With these estimates in hand, you should then consult with others as to their reliability. Remember, all of this work must be completed before any revenues can be generated.

Cripple Creek obtained a bank loan to expand the milling operations to 100 tons per day. Still in need of more capital, the company entered into a joint venture agreement with another mining firm, exchanging land rights for much-needed cash. With this money, Cripple Creek expanded milling operations and during 1980 proceeded to process 600 to 700 tons of ore per month from the site. The ore generated 2 ounces of gold per ton.

This ratio, ounces per ton, is called the vein's mineralization. The mineralization of a firm's ore body establishes, in a very general way, the worth of the firm's interest. Let's say Cripple Creek owned the rights to 50 tons of ore. You might be led to believe, then, that the worth of the site was the amount of gold estimated to be in the ground, multiplied by the current selling price of gold. Far from it. For example, let's say gold was selling at $400 per ounce, thus you might conclude that the worth of the resource would be $4,000:

.2 oz./ton $\times$ 50 tons $\times$ 400/ounce $=$ $4,000

This doesn't take into account, however, the processing costs to recover the gold.

The next time a broker uses a mineralization figure to buttress a sales talk, find out what it will cost to recover the mineral from the mine. Also, find out what the world market price would have to be for the metal to be mined profitably.

Another chief consideration is the depth of the mineral zone. It makes a world of difference whether the ore body is located near the surface or whether it is deep down in the earth's bowels. This really wasn't a consideration for Cripple Creek or its investors because the mine shafts were already in place. For Extension Energy, a company we'll look at next, it's of paramount concern.

J. D. Schlottmann, geologist for Salt Lake City-based Extension Energy (despite its name, a mining firm), explained to me the potential and the problems of a company site in northern Nevada. The company uncorked what looked to be a mammoth zone of gold and silver. Schlottmann became aware of the site's potential while sifting through some tailings* left by miners who ditched the site in the 1940s; he discovered that it would be very profitable simply to remill the tailings. This led him to believe that greater fortunes could be found in the ground. The only problem was that the company would have to dig down 188 to 198 feet. To put this into a monetary perspective, Extension, at last report, sought an infusion of $6 million to get the ball rolling.

Another major concern for Extension was the lack of a mill on the site. As noted, Cripple Creek simply refurbished an old mill in order to reduce the unwieldly amount of ore (24 million to 28 million pounds per month) to a more manageable form. Extension was not so fortunate. Obviously the firm cannot truck that much earth to a faraway milling operation and therefore must construct their own mill. Accordingly, another item of concern to the potential investor is whether or not the firm has access to a milling operation nearby.

FINANCING THE GOLDEN GLIMMER

Mining is a risky business, and the path to the top of the ore heap is littered with more than a few mining firms' great dreams. The inherent risk often makes it difficult for would-be prospectors to capitalize their mining firms. As a rule of thumb, unproven mining firms receive the same cold shoulder from banks that other young companies receive.

This greatly limits their financing alternatives. Consequently many mining firms have turned to the venture market in search of funds. In the recent past the suppliers of these funds, the investors, have done very well. Cripple Creek stock, which originally sold

* The ore before it has been processed is termed the "heads"; the "tails" or "tailing" are what's left.

for 20 cents, hit a peak of $1 in 1980, but had settled back down to 75 cents as of this writing.

Another method of financing the mining operation is through joint venture agreements with other, larger firms. In these endeavors, the larger mining firm usually takes on the greater financial risk in exchange for the lion's share of any profits resulting from the work. But that's how little mining firms become bigger ones. Cripple Creek's Bradley Place explained that "There's always a big potential, common to the mining business, to lose a lot on a big deal." Place claimed that his firm was "more conservative than most. Rather than biting off more than we can chew, we feel the greatest success will come from generating deals and then keeping a piece of them." Sound familiar? Place persuaded American Stock Exchange-listed Standard Metals Corporation to finance another project of Cripple Creek's. And word has it that mining giant Homestake Mining Company is sending out feelers for possible participation in Extension's find in northern Nevada.

The concept of risk-sharing through joint mining ventures, however, is nowhere nearly as developed as it is in the oil and gas business. As elaborated upon in the previous chapter, cost- and risk-sharing arrangements are part and parcel of an oil investor's checklist; that is to say, the financing of oil ventures is a complex, relatively well-understood component of the industry. As Dermott Ross-Brown, president of Apache Energy and Minerals Company, has explained, "The oil and gas industry is far ahead of everyone else."[4]

The small mining firm completes the bulk of the exploration activities and then seeks a partner willing to finance the endeavor. There are, however, several major impediments. First, it is difficult to establish precisely the size of the ore body. The profitability of mining and milling the ore is therefore difficult to predict. This leads to reluctance on the part of major mining firms to expend the cash necessary to evaluate and develop the site fully.

Another stumbling block to joint venture agreements was described by the president of Lake City Mines, Michael W. Mac-Guire. He said, "I'd love a joint venture." But he claimed that the terms usually demanded by the larger firms are vastly unfavorable. "You get a 5% royalty, they take 95% of the action. They do it on their terms, put it on the back burner—ostensibly to be cautious, but in reality to get a free ride. Then, they get their money out before you do."[5]

The nature of the modern-day prospector himself may also retard the development of more joint mining ventures. Like the old-timers, today's miner likes to think of himself as an entrepreneur, a rugged individualist in need of nothing more than his hands and his wits. Bob Murray, mining attorney with Venture Analysis, Ltd., explains that these small mining concerns often feel they are giving up a little of themselves in order to join forces. "Little companies are awfully proud of their own little company. If an agreement is reached, it could be after a clash of egos. Somebody's got to be number two."[6]

THE TRUMP CARD

The vicissitudes of gold and silver prices dramatically affect the profitability (or lack thereof) of mining concerns, young and old alike. In the energy industry the price paid for products has tended to rise on a stable course. Only in 1981 was there a softening in the price of energy. Even so, the price didn't drop appreciably; instead, it simply made no further increases. Not so with gold and silver.

The market for gold and silver has been more volatile. As mentioned, in 1979 the price of gold ran up to more than $800 per ounce while silver ran up to $50. With equal contempt for logic, these prices dropped to $400 and $10. Anyone who bought at the high point obviously took a substantial loss. And for the presidents and the shareholders of mining firms, such price swings are vastly important.

All mining firms perform a break-even analysis to determine the price at which they can profitably mine their resource. Clearly, if the price of gold is $800 per ounce, their mining efforts will be a lot more vigorous than if it is $400 an ounce. Again, it's simple economics; what's profitable to mine at $600 an ounce may no longer be worthwhile at $400. Price hikes and subsequent collapses undoubtedly cause mining managers a great many sleepless nights. Even if the firm is very conservative and produces gold that can be mined for as little as, for instance, $150 per ounce, what guarantee is there that the market won't cave in? It's highly unlikely that gold will drop that low, but you can never tell. The potential of mining companies and their stocks is inextricably tied to the price of the metals they mine.

The future direction of gold's price is of considerable interest. Of course, there are just as many gold soothsayers as there are forecasters of the future direction of the stock market. However, we can lay out a broad overview of some influences on gold's price to aid you in determining the future direction of venture mining stocks.

Some observers have said that the trend in gold's price serves as an international mood barometer. When international tensions increase, investors and hoarders go into gold as a hedge against whatever economic calamity is brewing. When a socialist was elected president of France in 1981, the French franc dropped swiftly while the price of gold rose. When it became evident that François Mitterand wasn't about to nationalize the nation's industry overnight, calm returned, the franc stabilized, and gold's price declined.

A related source of price fluctuations are speculators' perceptions and interventions. While the world's economy may not be on the verge of collapse, various political hot spots cause speculators to believe that hoarders are about to enter the marketplace. Speculators buy gold in anticipation of an increase in demand and therefore in price. What happens then is that newspapers and analysts proclaim that the most recent actions on the world's stage precipitated the rise in price. It then becomes a reality as all of the players in the world gold game are busy second-guessing one another.

A more concrete explanation of gold's trend is found in interest rate levels. Speculators generally borrow funds with which to bet on the future direction of gold's price. The speculator estimates the level that the price of gold must reach in order for him (or her) to cover his borrowing charges and to make a profit. When the rates in the United States nudged 20%, speculators were driven from the market. One analyst said that speculators' actions add yet another layer of variables to gold's price. In early 1981, when speculators left the market, one of gold's price supports was eliminated.

Gold price and interest rates are linked in another manner. You'll remember that investments such as precious metals and interest-rate vehicles all lie at different positions on the risk-reward continuum (see Chapter 3). Gold moves fluidly between higher risk and highest risk while interest-rate securities, such as money market funds, are on the lower end of the risk spectrum. For example, as gold's price slumped through most of 1981 and interest-rate investments paid returns in the upper teens, money was taken out of precious metals in favor of interest-bearing assets. This, of course, dampened the price of gold even further.

What should be evident from this short discourse on gold price fluctuations is that gold's price is anything but predictable. As an investor you can nonetheless look to the current direction of gold's price in order to get a feeling—but only a feeling—of what mining stocks are going to do in the near term.

PROSPECTING FOR MINING STOCKS

As we have seen, price swings of mining companies' stocks are subject to an influence completely outside of the firm's authority: precious metals' prices. Most of the mining companies whose stocks you'll be considering are in business to uncover gold and silver. There are a few, however, that search for other metals. Another thing about mining issues: they're not as sexy as the oils. Mining is speculative in the truest sense of the word because no one yet has determined a foolproof method of finding gold. Unlike the oil industry, these firms will only participate in one, two, or maybe three mining ventures at any one time. And if a mine proves unworkable, that's usually the end of the road.

Mining for gold, though, doesn't carry with it the same sense of urgency, of national need, that oil exploration does. You don't hear much talk about "gold independence." The venture mining issues won't work their way up with the same vigorous frenzy as the oils. As a potential investor, you should be aware of this. On the other hand, you're not buying the entire market of mining stocks. Rather, you're buying into one carefully selected company. If the company can find gold, if management can retrieve the metal, and if the price of gold is high enough, your share of the mining company should appreciate dramatically.

Between midyear 1977 and the end of 1980, twelve metals and mining issues came to the OTC market from Colorado. Only one of those issues declined then, while the rest were selling at healthy premiums over their original offering prices. The average mining issue, in fact, had improved 350% by the final trading day of 1980.

However, mining winds blew cold over the next six months. A report conducted by *The National OTC Stock Journal* of the 13 new mining issues of 1980–81 concluded, "The chances are just about even that your stock would have gained or lost value" if you bought at the original offering price.[7]

We leave the subject of mining with a story about Minerals Engineering Company. Minerals currently rides a high crest as it considers going into production at its Creede, Colorado, property. Life hasn't always been so rosy for the firm, though.

The company was founded in 1948, before the uranium boom of the 1950s. In fact, the company was founded by one of the engineers from the Manhattan Project who had developed a form of the Geiger counter. A. G. Foust, current president of the company, said that they couldn't find much documentation of what the company went through back in the early days. But by 1960 the company had emerged as one of the world's leading producers of tungsten. Later, when the tungsten market "went to heck in the late 1960s and when Mexico expropriated the company's property," Minerals Engineering began to falter. To shore up the firm's poor financial health, company officials offered more shares of stock to the public. The prospectus for the offer announced that "the company has had serious problems and is presently insolvent."

In spite of this negative admission, Minerals raised some more money and made one more go of it. In 1974 the company went into production on the Creede property before establishing the reserve content of the earth. Because the price of silver was low at the time and because the reserves were less than expected, Minerals operated in 1975 "at a substantial loss." The loss was carried forward to 1976, at which time the company endured losses of more than $.5 million. All together, the company lost $1 million at the Creede property in three years. And, Foust said, "it wasn't that the potential wasn't there, it was just due to a premature production decision."

In January 1976 Foust was brought in to heal the rapidly failing concern. Foust knew the company had almost gone under twice and we all know the saying about three strikes. Foust, who was only thirty-three years old at the time, scaled down the work on the Creede property and negotiated a deal with Homestake Mining whereby Homestake would pay Minerals $300,000 per year for six years—a total of $1.8 million—to complete exploratory work on the Creede Formation.

"The biggest problem of young mining companies is the premature decision to go into production before ore reserves are established," Foust explained. He believed that all of the preliminary work was in place for the company to push forward conservatively on its two most promising prospects, the Creede Formation and the Creede Underground. An independent engineering report commissioned by Minerals estimated that the Creede Formation alone contained 3.4 million tons of ore with a silver content of 6.39 ounces per ton. The report stated, "The Creede Formation has the potential for profitable operations [so long as the price of silver is above $15 per ounce]." Additional drilling was scheduled on the property to reinforce this assessment of the reserve content of the mountainous terrain. Foust said, though, that "even with further drilling and testing, there is no assurance that additional reserves will be defined or that a production decision will result."[8] A production decision, of course, is management's approval to mine and mill the ore from the site.

One interesting comment about the preceding story: Foust knows that he's sitting on a healthy supply of silver. Nevertheless, the production decision still awaits further authentication of the reserve content. Another factor, not mentioned by Foust, is that at the time, silver's price was well below $15 per ounce. So, even though all of the silver's down there, mining it could prove uneconomical.

As a potential investor in a venture mining stock, you should pay attention to what the firm is doing and how long it has spent evaluating the property. Find out the price at which the precious metal must be in order for it to be mined profitably. Make certain that the company has reserve figures estimated by a reputable, disinterested party. Learn when actual production is scheduled to begin. For older mines, learn how much gold has already been excavated; this will indicate one of two things—either there's none left or there's a whole vein as yet untouched. Most likely, you're not a geologist and neither is your broker. Ask your broker to compile information on the site and scrutinize this information carefully yourself.

Here's another point worth considering. On an interview, I once was shown a piece of ore presumably exhumed from the mine. The geologist picked apart the ore and sprinkled part of it in his mine shoe.* Within a matter of minutes I began to see faint glimmers of gold sparkling in the sun. I remarked, "That's incredible." The geologist concurred. "Yes, it is incredible and we have a whole vein of the stuff." Now, I'm not doubting this crusty old prospector's integrity, but I, as a financial journalist, had absolutely no way of telling whether, in fact, the ore had come from the site. In addition, even if the rock had come from the area, it could just have been a gold-enshrined chunk the geologist showed to prospective investors. The point, again, is that without a geology background you might fall victim to deceptive attempts to sway you.

In other words, any mining investment is very speculative. Even if you do all of your homework and even if the company successfully evaluates the ore's potential, there's no assurance that the gold market will toe the line. On the other hand, if the firm is conservative and if the market is receptive, you could be in for the mother lode.

NOTES

1. Bruce McWilliams, "Minerals Engineering Conservatism Pays Off," *The Denver Stock Exchange,* May 11, 1981, p. 7.

2. Bruce McWilliams, "OTC Firm Prospecting in Legendary Gold Area," *The Denver Stock Exchange,* June 8, 1981, p. 4.

3. Irving Hale, "OTC Stocks Cover More Than Oil, Gas," *Colorado Business Weekly,* July 13–19, 1981, p. 18.

4. Jeff Smith, "Dogged by Problems, Mining Seeks Capital," *The Denver Stock Exchange,* August 31, 1981, p. 1.

5. Smith, p. 1.

6. Smith, p. 16.

7. "Mining Underwritings," *The Denver Stock Exchange,* August 31, 1981, p. 5.

8. McWilliams, "Minerals," p. 7.

* A device, similar to the prospector's gold pan, that enables one to separate the valuable from the worthless.

8

New Issues: Stock Rockets

"Buying new issues (especially in a bull market) is as close to a 'sure thing' as one is apt to find on Wall Street" or anywhere else for that matter, reports Norman G. Fosback, a respected Wall Street analyst and the editor of the stock market newsletter *New Issues*.[1]

New stock issues beat the market.

Nonsense? You've probably been told that outperforming the market is impossible, but twenty years of history testify that new stock issues *do* beat the market. There are a number of caveats, but we'll get to those later.

Disputing Fosback's bald assertion, *Venture* magazine, in an article entitled "Lean Times for Penny Stocks," announced the demise of the new issues market: "[By June 1981,] new issues began opening at a discount. Instead of subscribing stock at the initial offering and selling at a handsome profit the first day of trading, the smart investors found themselves waiting to pick up stocks in the aftermarket, where offering prices were dealt healthy discounts."[2] While the new issues market had declined relative to its high-flying days earlier in the year, *Venture* failed to point out that the average second quarter 1981 new stock offering stood 11% higher than its original offering price.[3] Moreover, during this time the Dow Jones Industrial Average was on its way down to a two-year low as uncertainty over President Reagan's economic program disrupted the market.

The Wall Street Journal and the New York *Times* also chimed in with financial establishment skepticism concerning the new issues market. The *Journal* stated, "Anybody investing in new issues today should be well aware that he could lose 50% of his money very quickly."[4] The *Times* cautioned investors that they could very well see their "entire investment [in new stock issues] evaporate." But the very next line contradicted this warning by explaining that "of the 74 initial public offerings of oil and gas stocks last year [1980], 96% gained on their initial offering price."[5]

In short, there's a witches' cauldron of controversy brewing over the wisdom of buying new stock issues. Nevertheless, it all boils down to the fact that by analyzing the issue and analyzing the market, you'll guard against losses and probably win. And while there may be temporary dips and swerves, new stock issues have beaten the market over the long haul. Let's look at the record.

RETURN ON INVESTMENT: THE KINGS

For the two-and-a-half-year period ending in December 1980, the top-performing new stock issue was an oil and gas firm, Oiltech, Inc. Underwritten by First Financial Securities, Oiltech sold five million shares at 10 cents each. Like many other energy firms, the company was just beginning its corporate life; it came to the public market with good management and a good outlook, but not much in the way of assets. However, market action demonstrated that this was one firm to follow. By March 31, 1981, Oiltech shares were selling for $1.94. Think what a $500 investment on the ground floor would have done for your portfolio's health! The firm went public in December 1978, and the March 1981 bid price of $1.94 reflects an annual growth rate of 257%. How does that compare with your passbook savings account or even with your money market fund?

Other big gainers during the time include:

LOCH EXPLORATION	UP 1838%
HLH PETROLEUM	UP 1817%
NEW WORLD COMPUTER	UP 1650%
DENELCOR	UP 1488%

As this list shows, the top performers are in the energy and high-technology computer business.

The darker side, represented by those new issues that dropped in value from their original offering price, reflects the inherent risk in buying new, relatively unproven companies. Pasta King sold 500,000 shares at $2 in September 1977. By March 31, 1981, all of those shares put together couldn't buy a cup of coffee. The company had plans to franchise take-out pasta dealerships, but soon discovered that America's junk-food appetite didn't include spaghetti. The firm couldn't break into the highly competitive fast-food arena and subsequently went bankrupt.

Other big losers for the period included:

NEOMED	—97%
MOUNTAIN HIGH	—95%
PHILLIPS CTRL.	—95%
MODERN ENERGY	—92%

I focus on the top gainers and the biggest losers to depict the range of risk-and-reward potential in buying new stock issues. This is not to say, however, that half of the issues go up while the remainder plummet—far from it. A recent study by Irving Hale reveals that "of the 213 new stock issues [emanating from Colorado], 171 were up over their offering price as of March 31, 1981, 40 were down, and two remained unchanged." In other words, 80% of the issues reacted favorably to public trading, 19% not so favorably, and 1% not at all. Only two firms underwent bankruptcy proceedings. Thus, two out of the 213 companies failed, or one third of one percent each year. Hale, estimating the bankruptcy rate for companies in the United States at 2% annually, concluded in his study that "an investment in new issues, so far, has been safer than starting your own business."[6]

A more comprehensive study by Roger C. Ibbotson and Jeffrey Jaffe in the *Journal of Finance,* covering the nation during the decade 1960–70, calculated that a new issue, on average, increased 12.8% above its original offering price during the first month of public trading. By the twelfth month of public trading, the average new issue grew 64.4%. Five years out of the starting blocks, the typical new issue appreciated 315% over its original price.[7]

In 1978 the stock market, as reported by the Dow Jones Industrial Average, was "virtually flat." Nonetheless, of the sixty-one new stock offerings made that year, two thirds sold for higher prices by the first month of 1979. If a fortunate investor could have invested $500 in each 1978 offering—including those that declined—his portfolio would have advanced a healthy 77% by the following January.[8]

GOING PUBLIC

Evidently there's some profitable magic in these new stock issues. To explore this synergy, we must first get to the heart of a new stock issue: its underwriting. Underwriting is the process whereby the company with big plans and the investor with a little risk capital are brought together by public stock offering. Knowing how this comes about is important if you are to understand the market. Furthermore, because so much enthusiasm revolves around these high-powered investments, the investor is well advised to know what's a good one and how to lay hands on it.

Going public, though, is not a simple process. The former editor of *The National OTC Stock Journal,* David Lewis, said, "The registration of new issues is a lengthy, expensive, and often a tortuous proposition, akin to going over the Niagara Falls in a gold-plated barrel. The trip might be bumpy, it might be painful, and, at the end, you might find either useless wreckage or a pile of gold."[9] In other, less metaphorical, terms, many advantages and disadvantages accrue to going public. To begin with, the company becomes more widely known, which should help it to obtain credit in the future. If venture capitalists believe that there will soon be a public market for the stock, the firm may be able to enlist their support during its pre-public days. Along the same lines, once the company goes public, the founders will eventually have a market for their shares. The major advantage of going public, of course, is that the company receives a huge inflow of cash.

On the other hand, registering a new public issue is a very expensive and time-consuming process. Often you'll hear company presidents complain that they spend more time organizing the offer than they do attending to the actual affairs of the company. In addition, fully registered companies are subject to federally mandated reporting requirements, such as filing quarterly 10-Q and annual 10-K financial statements. For small businesses, these disclosures are often onerous and may reveal sensitive information to competitors. Also, company presidents may lose some of their flexibility in running the enterprise. This is especially true in actions that require shareholder approval.[10]

WHO'S GOT THE FUNDING?

When the entrepreneurs we've discussed so far decided to go into business, they needed money. First, they dipped into their own pockets. Second, they asked the same of friends and associates. At some point, however, these oilmen, prospectors, and engineers discovered that they just didn't have the enormous sums of money required to realize their visions. They then hooked up with an investment banker. An investment banker, a misnomer of sorts, is really neither a banker nor an investor.* Instead, an investment banker is a financier, one who arranges for the infusion of investors' funds into ventures thirsting for money.

The investment banker doesn't arrange these deals out of some blind allegiance to capitalism; he fully intends to get a cut of the funds raised. The investment banker presents a menu of financing alternatives to the company and suggests which would be the most feasible and least costly. Usually the first method employed to raise funds is a private placement—the sale of corporate securities in the company to a small group of investors who are already well versed in the ways of the industry. Venture capitalists are asked to participate in the private placement. The venture capitalist, usually one well-heeled individual or a small company managing the funds of several small fortunes, understands the risks in these companies and is happy if two or three out of five investments prove out.

If, after the private placement, the company and the investment banker agree that the company is still insufficiently capitalized,

---

* The investment banker receives warrants as part of his remuneration for underwriting the issue and, therefore, is an indirect investor.

then they begin exploring other alternatives. The greatest obstacle to these young companies is usually a lack of enough money to operate successfully. This was the problem that Bradley Place and his Cripple Creek Gold encountered.

After more strategic huddling, the company and its financier might then decide that going to the public via an equity offering is their only hope. The investment banker could, and often does, serve as the underwriter.

Before deciding to underwrite the issue, the investment banker completes a thorough investigation. He must use "due diligence" to learn about the company. The reason is simple: before he can sell others on the company, he's got to be sold on it himself. And it takes a lot to convince the underwriter. The underwriting manager for a large broker/dealer says on this subject that "because of the rapid appreciation of these new stock issues, we've had a vast influx of companies to see us. We turn down ten for every one we'll even listen to." He continued, "If some guy comes in and says he's developed a microwave atomizer, we might yawn. But if that fellow flicks a button and disintegrates the office into smoldering ashes, then we'll listen."

Essentially, there are two types of underwritings: firm commitment and "best efforts." In a firm offer, the underwriters buy up all the shares and then turn around and resell the shares to investors. Naturally, this guarantees the company a sellout of the issue. With best efforts, the underwriter doesn't buy any of the stock; instead, the underwriter uses his best efforts to sell the issue. Most penny stock offerings utilize best efforts. Because there is no assurance that the stock will sell out, best efforts offers are riskier to the investor than firm deals.

Within this group, there are two subcategories: all-or-none and minimax. The all-or-none offering requires that all shares be sold; if this does not occur, the money is returned to investors and the underwriting has failed. The other arrangement, minimax, sets a minimum number of shares that must be sold and a maximum number that can be sold should there be great interest in the issue.

In the early stages of going public, the company and the underwriter negotiate the terms of the offering. Managers of the firm must decide how much capital they will need in order to get the revenues flowing. The constraint is obvious: there are limits to how much the investing public will provide. Once this total figure is arrived at, the company and underwriter then decide the price of the shares. In determining the price, they look at the market's recent performance. For example, during mid-1981, new stock issues costing more than $1 per share appreciated considerably less than stocks priced under that amount. Some quick corporate reshuffling took place and several deals were reoffered at lower prices. Concurrently, the number of shares offered was increased to make certain the company would raise the same sum.

When the 1981 slump hit, one firm was hoping to raise $3 million through the sale of three million shares at $1. Reconsidering, the company went back to the SEC and changed the offer to six million shares at 50 cents. The market apparently approved: when the stock, then priced at 50 cents, opened for public trading, it immediately shot to a higher price.

WARRANTS OF PLENTY

A variation on the theme of offering shares of stock is to offer units of securities. A unit consists of a set number of shares of stock, plus warrants to purchase more stock. A warrant is a contract allowing the holder to buy a certain number of shares at a certain price during a specified period of time. During that time, the warrant can be exercised to buy the shares at the preset price (provided an additional registration statement has been filed with the SEC), regardless of the current market price of the stock. By selling units, the company receives a lump sum up front from the offer and will receive additional funds later, when the warrants are exercised.

An example may serve to make this a bit clearer. On October 1, 1980, Valex Petroleum, Inc., sold two million units at $2 each. This raised $4 million for the company and its underwriter. Each unit consisted of two shares of stock and a warrant to buy an additional share. The shares were essentially valued at $1 each and the warrants were assigned no value, but enabled holders to buy one additional share of Valex for $2. You may be thinking, "What kind of deal is that? I buy shares for $1 and they give me this little coupon to buy more for $2 per share. Why would I ever do that?"

The warrants could have been exercised (provided the company filed an additional statement) between June 1, 1981, and October 1, 1982. On August 19, 1981, you, the warrant holder, could have bought a share of Valex for slightly more than $2.38 on the market or you could have exercised your warrant for $2. If you chose the latter, you then could have turned around, and immediately sold this share for $2.38 and pocketed a tidy profit.

On the other hand, instead of going to the trouble of buying and then reselling the share, you could simply have sold the warrant. Warrants trade on the market just like shares; when Valex reached $2.38, the intrinsic worth of the warrant was 38 cents. You proved this yourself by exercising the warrant for $2 and then selling at the market price, $2.38.

At that time, the warrant itself sold for 81 cents. Thus, your profit would have been a little over twice as great had you simply sold the warrant. A warrant's price is based on two theoretical concepts. The first is its intrinsic value: the difference between the current selling price and the exercisable or "striking" price. The second, clearly more esoteric, is the premium. Determined by the marketplace, the premium is the collection of investor perceptions on the future of the stock. At 81 cents, the price of Valex warrants suggested that investors and speculators believed that the price of Valex common shares could go as high as $2.81. Time is of the essence, however; as the expiration date draws closer, the possibility that the stock will rise diminishes, and therefore the premium attached to the warrant also drops.

Trading in warrants offers investors greater potential for profits and losses than investing in shares. For example, Valex Petroleum shares sold for $2.13 in July 1981 and the warrants sold for 56 cents. By August, the price of both the stock and the warrants moved up. On a percentage basis, though, the growth of the warrants was much more impressive (see Table 20).

Let's look at two hypothetical investors—one who bought the shares outright and another, a more speculative investor, who bought warrants. Within a month's time the shareholder's position advanced 12%. Not that there's anything wrong with a gain like that, but the trader who bought warrants reaped a 45% gain. The leverage potential of warrants should now be obvious.

While I have chosen a positive example of the potential of warrants, you need to be aware of several other factors. They're a two-edged sword: if the stock depreciates, the downside risks with warrants are just as great as the possible rewards. A loss of 10% on the common shares can be magnified into a 50% loss on the warrants. If the premium attached to the warrant is too high initially, it's possible that when the stock price jumps the warrant won't budge. And, finally, if the value of the common share dips below the striking price of the warrant (e.g., if Valex shares drop below $2), then the warrant becomes worthless.

Table 20

Valex Petroleum Shares & Warrants

Month	Shares	WARRANTS Market Price	=	Intrinsic Value	+	Premium Value
July 1981	$2.13	$0.56		$0.13		$0.43
August 1981	$2.38	$0.81		$0.38		$0.43
Percent Change	+12%	+45%				

Companies that are going public will offer units including warrants, instead of just shares, for several reasons. The primary reason is that warrants provide the issuing company with more money (through the exercise of the warrants) after the initial offer is complete. If the company does well, the stock price will move up, the warrants' striking price will be reached, and management will receive another influx of capital. Furthermore, the offering of warrants provides investors an additional incentive to buy that particular issue.

SEC CARE

Once the underwriter and the company agree on the terms of their stock offering, they submit a registration statement to the Securities and Exchange Commission. The initial proposal must include a description of the company's business, the transactions between the company and its officers, current capitalization, the market for the company's product, its properties, and the plan for distributing its securities. In the registration statement, the firm must state clearly any possible risks such as a lack of operating history, a lack of profits, adverse economic conditions, dependence upon key personnel, or any other factor which, in subsequent years, could possibly affect the company.

The SEC insists that these risk factors be set forth prominently in the registration statement. The registration statement is, in essence, the prospectus for the offer, although it does include additional material. When the company submits the registration statement, it may also print a number of prospectuses in order to generate interest in the investment community. These preliminary prospectuses are called "red herrings," a term that stems from the fact that investors are advised, in red ink on the front page, that the prospectus has not yet been cleared by the SEC.

Upon receipt of the registration statement, the SEC scrutinizes it very closely. The agency tries to make certain that all information relevant to the investment is fully disclosed. However, they do not make a judgment as to the soundness of the offer. Rather, the officials just want to make sure that all pertinent information is printed in black and white for all to see.

The reason for the SEC's determination is quite simple. In the 1920s, many small investors were misled and defrauded by unscrupulous operators in the securities business. From this experience grew the concept that potential investors need to be told everything pertinent to the issue before they invest.[11] Indeed, when the SEC gives its nod, it does not "approve" the issue, but rather "clears" it. The officially cleared registration statement is deemed the "final" prospectus.

While the SEC holds its magnifying glass up to the registration statement, the company and the underwriter get ready for the big day when they can begin selling the stock. One of the preliminary steps is the organization of the underwriting group (for firm commitment offers) or the selling syndicate (for best effort deals).

SELLING THE HOT STOCK

Most penny stock deals sell millions of shares on a best efforts basis. The underwriter could take it upon himself to sell all of these shares. If he tried, though, he would most likely fail. The underwriter contacts other broker/dealers to aid in the sales effort. If the market is buoyant, it's usually no problem to persuade other broker/dealers to join the selling group. If the market is soggy, it's more difficult to find others to help sell the offer. Linking up, though, lessens the underwriter's financial risk. These broker/dealers and the underwriter all join forces in a temporary joint venture, called a selling syndicate, whose sole purpose is to sell the best effort new stock offer.

Around the time of the SEC clearance, the managing underwriter will hold what's called a "due diligence" meeting for members of the selling syndicate. At this meeting, the brokers who will sell the issue exercise due diligence to ascertain pertinent information about the company.

In addition to SEC registration, the new issue must be registered with state securities agencies. Some states require the issue to undergo a stringent process called merit review, which attempts to ascertain the worthiness of a new stock offer. Some states are very rigid and allow very few young companies to sell their stock through the initial offer. Others are not as restrictive. But in any case, once the security has been approved for public sale by the appropriate state authorities, the issue is said to be "blue-skyed."

Within three days of the clearing of the issue, the underwriter and the other members of the selling syndicate begin selling it. At this time the red ink disappears from the border of the prospectus and the final clearance date is printed at the bottom in black ink. The sale of the issue must be completed within a specified period of time, usually ninety days.

From the time the registration statement is first submitted to the SEC until ninety days after it has been cleared, company officials, the underwriter, market makers, brokers—the whole crew—are not allowed to make comments about the company that are not included in the prospectus. This is known as the quiet period. During this time, any major changes to the company must be reported to initial and subsequent investors via an updated prospectus. Usually the company prints up stickers stating the changes and affixes them to the final prospectus, an action known sensibly as "stickering."

After the quiet period is over, sellers of the security can be a little more relaxed in their discussions of the company and its stock. SEC regulations and ethical considerations, though, still require that no misleading information be disseminated about the company.

For hot new stock issues—those expected to perform well in

the immediate aftermarket—shares are apt to be scarce, as the interest in the issue far surpasses the number of shares available. The managing underwriter allocates shares to the members of the selling group based on past practices, prior performance, and personal contacts.

As we've seen, the average new stock issue does very well on its first day of public trading. After the first month, the gains begin to diminish. Accordingly, many traders try to unload their stock on the first day. But if everyone tried to sell, the tremendous supply would be met with sluggish demand and the price would surely drop. To ensure that the price doesn't crash through the floor, the managing underwriter and the selling group enter the market to "support" the price of the shares by buying up shares being sold. Obviously, this can be a very expensive effort. A gentleman's rule in the industry says that members of the syndicate will support their allocation of the new issue. If the house fails to do this because of a lack of capital or for some other reason, the support effort falls to the other members of the syndicate and ultimately to the managing underwriter. The underwriter and other members of the group aren't going to look favorably on the member that dumps all of its allocation back into the market during the first few days of trading, and that house will probably be snubbed when the next new issue is underwritten.

Initially, the issue's success depends upon the amount of support the underwriter can generate for it. The company has already presented itself in the prospectus and, because of quiet-period restrictions, cannot release information that has not been solidified lest it affect the stock. After a time, though, increases and decreases have more to do with the company's achievements than with any active support from the selling team.

THE BIG BUCKS THEORY

Earlier in the chapter I summarized a study showing that of 213 new issues coming to market from 1977 through 1980, 177 were up. Eleven of these, in fact, had appreciated more than 1,000%.

Centennial Petroleum, Inc., was one of the biggest gainers. Centennial was well staffed with noted oil-field hands, landmen, and geologists—in short, the makings of a very professional outfit.

The company sold 35 million shares at 10 cents on November 4, 1980. The issue received national attention and opened at 80 cents, but it didn't stop there. Before the dust settled, Centennial had hit $1.40. This meant that at $1.40 per share, the market valued the worth of Centennial Petroleum at approximately $91 million (including the original financiers' stock). And the company sold shares to the public totaling only $3.5 million.

At the time, I interviewed Steven James, thirty-one-year-old president of Centennial, and he told me emphatically that his company was simply not worth *that* much. He was quick to add that if all of the assets, tangible and intangible, were added up, maybe the company had that much potential. But currently, on the balance sheet, "No way." This again reveals the strange market psychology that often overwhelms common sense. Let's look at why.

An economist friend of mine examined a list of recent stock offerings and was awed by their appreciation. He remarked, "Well, they're obviously undervalued." When I asked why, he responded that "markets always tend to move towards an equilibrium point. If all of these stocks move up, then it indicates that they were originally priced below their true market value." Before I could stop him, he continued, "For example, if the price of a pound of hamburger was set at 20 cents, everyone would flock to the market, but this wouldn't cover the producer's costs. On the other hand, if the hamburger cost $10 per pound, the costs would be covered nicely, but no one would buy any. If the price settled at, say, $2.50 per pound, everyone who wanted hamburger and was willing to pay for it could buy, while the producers would recover their costs. This is equilibrium price. At that point," my economist friend concluded, "the market clears and everyone— buyers and sellers—is happy. But with these new stock issues, they're obviously undervalued."[12] Once again, economics offers a commonsense explanation that runs counter to common practice. But he did raise an interesting point: Why do these new issues all seem to go up? To answer this question, we need to look from the perspectives of the interested parties: underwriter, company, and investor.

The underwriter earns his reward in two ways. First, he gets a cut of the proceeds, regardless of the price per share. Typically, this amounts to 10% of the offer. J. Daniel Bell & Company, which raised $4 million with the Valex offer, received $400,000 up front.

Second, the underwriter receives warrants to buy the stock at a later time. These warrants are priced slightly above the offering price and usually enable the underwriter to buy shares equaling 10% of those sold to the public. J. Daniel Bell & Company received warrants to buy an additional 400,000 shares at $1.20. Thus if the price rises to the striking level, the underwriter is guaranteed another healthy profit from the offering. And as we've seen, a stock has a greater potential of reaching this level or higher if it was underpriced originally.*

Undervaluing new stock offers also tempts other broker/dealers into joining the sales effort. If they view the issue as potentially profitable, they too will want to participate. The aftermarket support required for a hot new issue is considerably less than for those issues that float along at their original offering price. When a stock shows signs of dipping below the initial price, massive aftermarket support could be required. If the original price is set below the market value, however, the issue will rise to its market and will not require tremendous outlays of capital on the part of the selling syndicate. Finally, if the issue performs well, the underwriter will be able to attract other quality companies that are looking to be underwritten.

Norman Fosback, the fellow who's so bullish on new issues, concludes that "the underwriter's self-interest in underpricing a new issue far outweighs any interest in maximizing proceeds to the selling company."[13] This certainly seems true, but what about the company? After all, if the company's shares rise from 10 to 20 cents, wouldn't the company have been better off to price the issue at 20 cents, thereby doubling the proceeds from the offering? If it were as simple as that and the company could be assured of selling the issue, then the answer would be yes. There are a number of reasons, though, why undervaluing the security is also in the company's best interest.

The company needs to market the stock issue in the most competitive manner. This holds especially true for best efforts offerings where a sellout of the issue is not guaranteed. If all of the

---

* "Underpriced" and "undervalued" refer to the stock's relation to other stocks in the market and not necessarily to a share's net tangible worth on the books.

10-cent issues appreciate immediately while the 20-centers open flat, investors will want to buy only 10-cent stocks and stay away from the 20-cent deals. Obviously a start-up company is greatly hampered if the issue doesn't generate the funds promised by the underwriting. Fosback said, "A sellout is most easily achieved and the proceeds most certainly obtained when the issue is priced at a recognizable discount from the existing market prices of comparable securities."[14]

The company also needs to maintain a friendly relationship with the financial markets. When a firm returns to the market in the future, investors will be pleased to reinvest if, on its first outing, the stock turned in a superior performance.

Thus the company also benefits from undervaluing the price of its securities relative to the rest of the market. For obvious reasons, investors who buy the original offer also enjoy rewards from the undervaluing of the security. If the investor knows that the security is undervalued and that the price will go up once it is released, then he will do his best to obtain shares. He won't be alone, either. As has been stated, for hot new issues, the interest in the stock far overwhelms the supply. Those who could not originally buy the stock try to buy in when the stock first starts trading. Demand for the stock still outstrips the supply and the price keeps surging forward.

I have painted a fairly bright picture of new issues. The reader should recognize that a decline is just as likely as a gain if the market is sluggish or if the support team isn't wealthy enough. The underwriter tries to guard against this possibility by undervaluing the stock in the first place. Nevertheless, some new issues do open at a lower price than when originally offered; this is known as "opening at a discount."

To protect your portfolio from such a debilitating experience, you must dissect the offering's prospectus and then look at the market. Accordingly, we pick up those topics next.

NOTES

1. Norman G. Fosback, "Bonus Reports," *New Issues: The Investor's Guide to Initial Public Offerings* (Fort Lauderdale: The Institute for Econometric Research, 1979), p. 6.

2. Jerry Ruhl, "Lean Times for Penny Stocks," *Venture,* September 1981, p. 12.

3. "Aftermarket Performance of 2nd Quarter Underwritings," *The Denver Stock Exchange,* August 31, 1981, p. 6.

4. Jill Bettner, "Penny Stocks, New Issues Are Still the Rage; Risks, Fraud Charges Don't Deter Investors," *The Wall Street Journal,* March 30, 1981, p. 40.

5. Douglas Martin, "Buying New Issue Oil Stocks," New York *Times,* March 29, 1981, Sec. 3, p. 13.

6. Irving Hale, "A Survey of Colorado-based Underwritings: July 1, 1977–December 1, 1980," paper presented to 1981 Eastern Finance Annual Meeting, Newport, Rhode Island, April 1981.

7. Roger C. Ibbotson and Jeffrey F. Jaffe, "Hot Issues Markets," *The Journal of Finance,* V. 30, #41, and Roger C. Ibbotson, "Price Performance of Common Stock New Issues," *The Journal of Financial Economics,* V. 2, #3, both cited in Fosback, p. 6.

8. Fosback, pp. 5–6.

9. Caryn Frye, "For the New Investor," *The Denver Stock Exchange,* April 20, 1981, p. 4.

10. United States Securities and Exchange Commission, *Q&A: Small Business and the SEC,* pp. 1–2.

11. U.S. SEC, p. 1.

12. Thomas Seale, interview conducted by the author in Los Angeles, December 1980.

13. Fosback, p. 4.

14. Fosback, p. 4.

9

The Prospects: Hitching Your Portfolio to the Right Rocket

Ahh, the prospectus. The president of a large penny stock brokerage house at one time called the prospectus "the most interesting of documents."[1] Well, I beg to differ, sir; these documents range from the simply tedious to the downright soporific, but there's no doubt that they should be considered before investing in new stock issues. The prospectus is the only authorized vehicle through which new stock issues can be sold. The problem with prospectuses, though, is they contain distracting information that tends to disorient the uninitiated. Even for those who have spent years scanning prospectuses, unearthing the crucial details can take a considerable effort. But the prospectus can tell you a great deal about the company and about its stock's short-term prospects in the marketplace.

If you have never read a prospectus (and even if you have read one, but for a nonventure stock deal), flip to the back of this book and telephone one of the brokerage houses listed there. Request that the house send you a prospectus, preferably one for an issue that has already gone effective and is sold out. When you receive the brochure, you'll be able to analyze it in the ways suggested below.

As mentioned earlier, the prospectus is the main portion of the registration statement and must disclose all relevant data about the company and the offering. Special emphasis is placed on details that could adversely affect the company and therefore your investment. Often, potentially positive information is not included in the prospectus lest it mislead people into thinking the firm is definitely going to succeed when there is no way of knowing for certain whether or not it will. The investor should keep this in mind when reading through a prospectus. As one broker said, "If you didn't know this [the prospectus' negative slant], you'd read through a prospectus and never invest because it makes the company sound like a pile of garbage."

Typically the prospectus is divided into several sections explaining the company and its offering. On the first few pages, there is a summary of the business, a summary of the offering, and some of the more pertinent risk factors. Following these summaries are various definitions that the lay investor needs to know in order to understand the business, a more detailed list of risks, and information about how the offering will affect the capitalization of the company. The booklet also provides a detailed summary of how the company plans to spend investors' money in addition to a discussion of the managers' backgrounds.

Before beginning to analyze each of these sections, there are several areas especially worthy of your careful attention. First, look at the management. Whether or not the company succeeds is based almost entirely on the abilities of these individuals. Second, determine how much of the managers' money has been invested in the company. After all, you're being asked to invest; it's worth it to find out if management has put its money where its mouth is. Similarly, find out the dilution of your share from the price that you paid. (We'll discuss what dilution is and what it means to your investment shortly.) All these are important considerations.

The first page of most venture stock prospectuses proclaims the offering—the numbers of shares to be sold and their price, the name of the company and its underwriter, and two warnings. The first warning is that investors who cannot sustain a complete loss of their entire investment should look elsewhere. Second, the prospectus announces that the SEC has not approved or disapproved the offer nor has it evaluated the company or its officers.

PEPI PROSPECTS

Piezo Electric Products, Inc. (PEPI) was a new stock offering made June 2, 1981. The front page of its prospectus explained that ten million shares were offered at 50 cents each, with 5 cents of each share devoted to cover the underwriter's commission. The underwriter was OTC Net. The SEC caveat and disqualifier mentioned above were also included.

We'll use PEPI's prospectus as an example of a new issue. PEPI, a high-tech concern, plans to manufacture a product capable of using piezoelectricity to transform mechanical energy into electrical energy and vice versa. (We'll explain soon what piezoelectricity is.) Prior to SEC clearance, the underwriters generated tremendous interest in the issue. On the first day of public trading, more shares of PEPI were bought and sold than of any other OTC security in the country. Certainly there were more people interested in buying PEPI than selling, as the price more than doubled, up to $1.03. During its first month of public trading, PEPI consistently ranked among the top ten most active stocks and its price shot up to more than $1.56. If you had invested that now-familiar $500, your investment would have been worth $1,560 in less than two months' time.

Upon opening any prospectus, you'll find the prospectus summary. One or two pages present a description of the company, the planned use of the proceeds, relevant risk factors, and selected financial data. The prospectus summary of PEPI was no different from any other.

After this tantalizing glimpse, the prospectus gets down to business. Various definitions peculiar to the industry are given. You should glance over the list and refer back to it once you get to the heart of the prospectus; this is especially important for high-tech issues. After investing in oil or gas or mining securities, you'll gain an understanding of the terminology. Every high-tech company, however, is different and the jargon is peculiar to each subfield. For instance, you're probably wondering (as I was) what piezoelectricity is. Here's the definition given in the prospectus:

Piezoelectricity: A property of certain crystalline minerals (especially quartz, tourmaline, and rochelle salt), which, under certain conditions, develop electric polarity or produce a flow of electricity when subjected to pressure.

BRING ON THE RISKS!

Once past the definitions, you turn to the section detailing all of the risks that could possibly affect the company and your investment. Generally, these risks fall into three categories: those specific to the company, those particular to the industry, and those related to the company's soon-to-be-publicly-traded stock.

The first risk factor for the typical venture stock company is that it hasn't been in business for very long. The risk here is straightforward—there's no assurance the company will ever get off the ground. In the PEPI prospectus, this risk is explained thus: "The company was organized on December 17, 1980 [only six months prior to its public emergence]; it has conducted no operations and has minimal assets. . . . The company is in the development stage and its operations are subject to all risks inherent in the establishment of a new business enterprise, including the problems, expenses, and delays frequently encountered in connection with the development of a new business."

The second risk, also commonplace in many venture stock offerings, is that the firm may find that it needs additional financing to complete the proposed endeavor. The risk here lies in the possibility that the firm may not be able to secure capital in the future. PEPI plans to use the $4.5 million raised to fund all of the start-up work necessary to begin generating revenues. The founders, two scientist brothers named Henry and Eric Kolm, plan within two years to produce four products using the principle of piezoelectricity. If they are unable to produce and then market these products within that time, they may need more money.

The third risk, like the other two, is fairly common. This one explains the firm's dependence upon the chief executive officers. The prospectus spells out how crucial the managers' efforts are and how seriously the company would be disadvantaged if they were to leave. Most of the companies you'll consider for investment are small businesses, operations in which one or two people are usually the entrepreneurs, the dreamers. Such a company, naturally, would face real hardship if one of them were to leave.

However, the prospectus makes it sound as if their departure were imminent. Obviously, it isn't or else they wouldn't be trying to make a go of the venture. Make sure, though, that the company has an employment contract with the founders of the firm. PEPI has a five-year employment agreement with the Kolm brothers for their services.

The fourth risk factor is again specific to the company. The prospectus states that PEPI lacks patent protection for its products. For the four proposed products, two patent applications had been made and investors were assured that applications would be filed for the remaining two. However, there's no assurance that the patents will be granted.

For high-technology companies, there should be firm contracts to ensure that the concept or invention remains within the firm. One solar company had the misfortune to see its proposed product leave with one of its employees. The firm did not have a contract to assure that the invention would stay even if its creator decamped.

The possibility of a conflict of interest between the company and its managers' outside interests is always a risk that investors should consider. In PEPI's case, it turns out that the Kolm brothers already own another company called Kolm Associates. PEPI planned to spend $400,000 from the offering to pay Kolm Associates for the rights to the four piezoelectric products. The prospectus asserts that a conflict of interest could arise in the future because of the close dealings of PEPI and Kolm Associates.

Potential investors in this issue as well as in all venture stock offerings are well advised to study the prospectus closely to learn what precautions have been taken to avoid any trouble of this kind. This particular prospectus also elaborated another risk that investors should consider. The Kolms are experienced in the field of "scientific research and technological development." These men are scientists, not businessmen. The prospectus warns, "In order for the company to make a successful transition from its development stage to commercial operations, the company will require additional personnel with particular experience in marketing, finance, administration, and quality control." We learn from another risk factor that Eric Kolm previously served as president of a corporation that manufactured piezoelectric products, and that

that company dissolved in bankruptcy in 1976. Investors must watch the balance sheet and income statements closely and sell out quickly if PEPI seems to be experiencing the same calamity as that which befell Kolm's earlier company.

These types of risk factor are common to all venture stock offerings, and should always be considered; whenever a question arises, such as the potential for a conflict of interest, further scrutiny of the prospectus is warranted.

MAJOR CONCERNS

The second subgroup of risks is those common to the industry. There is a noticeable absence of these in PEPI's prospectus. The reason is simple: there is no piezoelectric industry—that's what the Kolm brothers want to develop. For other high-tech concerns, the usual risk is whether or not there is a market for the product and whether the company will be able to obtain adequate supplies.

In the energy business, those risks particular to any given company are similar to the risks already mentioned for any start-up company. Risks to the industry are very predictable. First and foremost, exploring for oil and gas in and of itself is very risky. We've already devoted considerable attention to that aspect and need not discuss it further. Other common risks include difficulty in obtaining drilling rigs and leasehold acreage and the financial burden of complying with environmental regulations.

Here's another energy prospectus warning that should be taken with a grain of salt: "There is no assurance that future domestic legislation or world events will not significantly and adversely affect the company's operations." Sure, this is a risk factor, but what other industry in the country can claim that "future domestic legislation or world events" won't affect its profit and loss statement?

Mention is always made of OPEC's dominion over the price of oil. Several energy company prospectuses proclaimed, almost in unison, "The price of oil is set by a complex interplay between decisions of the Organization of Petroleum Exporting Countries (OPEC), federal regulation, and other market forces." Is there anyone who doesn't realize this already? Investors in new energy issues should anticipate disclaimers such as this in the risk section; it's how the game is played.

YOUR RISKS

The next category of risks is those that the investor might face in trading the security. The founders and early financiers of the company usually own large quantities of shares, variously called "letter stock," "rule 144 stock," or "restricted stock." If one of these insiders unloads a large block of his stock onto the market in one fell swoop, this could crater the price of the particular security. To prevent such a debacle, insiders must accept certain restrictions. They cannot sell their stock for at least two years and in addition, they are limited as to the number of shares they can sell during any three-month period. Despite these precautions, an insider could sell a major portion of his holdings through the prescribed 144 rules, a move that might have a devastating effect on the stock's price. This is particularly true in the thin venture stock market and we'll see why in the next chapter. Investors must take care to be aware of the possible effect on the market of future rule 144 sales.

Finally, the prospectus warns investors that the price of the stock may go down from its initial price and that investors must realize that they might lose money, possibly even their entire investment. While this hasn't been true for the vast majority of new stock issues, there are exceptions. Remember Pasta King, whose shares dropped from $2 to 0?

Also, bear in mind the story of Tri-Ad Energy before you blunder blindly into the next new stock issue that comes along. Tri-Ad Energy, a New York firm, went public in the first quarter of 1981, selling two million shares at $1.25. By mid-June, the company's assets had been quietly removed from a bank account and the president was nowhere to be found. The stock subsequently was forced to stop trading.

I have explained some of the more common risk factors in great detail because they're important. You should also remember, though, that many of the more negative aspects are brought to the fore while other more positive aspects remain in the background. In other words, take the risk factors with a bit of informed skepticism.

DILUTION

At the beginning of this chapter I suggested that investors in new issues look specifically at the dilution factor and at management's financial input into the offer. Now is the time to take up those subjects.

PEPI sold shares to the public for 50 cents each. This price, however, did not reflect the underlying book value of the shares. Rather, the price was arbitrarily set by negotiations between PEPI and OTC Net, the underwriter. The actual worth per share is calculated by dividing the company's assets and the proceeds from the offering by the number of shares outstanding.

$$\frac{\text{(Former Book Value} + \text{Net Proceeds of Offer)}}{\text{Shares Outstanding After Offer}} = \frac{\text{New Book Value Per Share}}{}$$

PEPI insiders paid $437,832 to receive 24,664,000 shares. Public investors, on the other hand, paid $5,000,000 to receive 10,000,000 shares in the company. Now we are at an important stage. The company's original financiers made an investment totaling $437,832 to get the company moving. Further perusal of the financial documents clarifies who invested the money and how many shares they received. From the Material Transactions section, you can determine whether or not management has actually invested in its own company.

The original investors invested $437,832 during its prepublic days, but PEPI whittled this amount down to $252,853. The net proceeds from the offering amounted to $4,258,000 (the total raised less expenses and commissions). Thus, the asset worth of the company after the offering was $4,510,853 and the per share worth was approximately 13 cents.

$$\frac{(\$252,853 + \$4,258,000)}{34,664,000 \text{ (shares)}} = \frac{\$4,510,853}{34,664,000} = 13 \text{ cents}$$

Public investors paid 50 cents to receive a share of the company, which was valued on the books at 13 cents. That's what is meant by dilution. In percentage form, the public investors in PEPI incurred a book loss of 74%.

Book Value After Sale — Offer Price
Per Share   Per Share $\times$ 100 = % Dilution

. Offer Price Per Share

$$\frac{\$0.13 \quad - \quad \$0.50}{\$0.50} \times 100 = -74\%$$

Early investors enjoyed an immediate book appreciation of 12 cents on their shares. The amount of dilution is mostly symbolic, since a stock's price seldom dips below book value. And when it does, this is usually in the rare instance of liquidation.

The insiders, through owning 24 million shares, controlled 71% of the company. By comparison, the public received 29% of the company. Typically, the early investors and managers will retain control of the company. If the company sells more than 50% of the total number of outstanding shares, this assures investors that there are relatively fewer restricted shares (insider stock) outstanding. In addition, it suggests that management is not overly worried about losing control of the company through shareholder-initiated actions. Some companies will sell more than 50% of their total shares to the public as a further inducement for investors to purchase the stock.

You should be aware of these factors—or rather, of the market's view of these factors—before investing in a stock. Nothing is absolute in the securities business, however, and Piezo Electric Products certainly proves that. Public investment was diluted 74% and investors gained an interest in only 29% of the company. Nonetheless, the market's faith in the Kolm brothers and the support efforts of the underwriters were strong enough to propel the stock up threefold in less than two months.

SPENDING THE MONEY

The company you're considering has raised a lot of money, usually amounting to millions of dollars. What it plans to do with all this capital is described in the Use of Proceeds section. As a rule, the prospectus details the intended use of these funds over the next year or two. The uses of the proceeds are divided into various categories—office expenses, executive salaries, travel, marketing costs, production costs, and so on. A good method of putting this all in perspective is to divide the various sections into subgroups. Place all of the administrative expenses, salaries, and other costs not directly related to production in one group and total the sum. Second, determine what portions of the proceeds are to be used for the company's intended business, e.g., mining for gold or drilling for oil. Find how much is being devoted to marketing and to research and development, if it's a high-tech concern. Finally, you should calculate the ratio of each group to the total amount raised. This puts the uses of the funds in a more readily-comprehensible form. In short, you should ascertain whether or not the intended use of funds coincides with what the prospectus says the company plans to do.

After scanning prospectuses for a time, you'll begin to get a feel for a "correct" allocation. Remember, the SEC doesn't approve or disapprove of the offering: they just try to make certain that all pertinent information is included.

FINALLY, THE BUSINESS

The offering is designed to jet the company off in a spectacular way. Accordingly, the next section of the prospectus explains just what the planned business of the company is. It details the company's prior pursuits, future plans, and special industry considerations. Usually this is the most interesting part of the whole booklet. In relatively readable form, this section sums up the numbers, the charts, and other data already encountered. Close perusal of the Business of the Company section pays off.

For high-tech concerns, this section will describe what the company has accomplished to date, how long the anticipated development period for the product is, what the future marketing plans are, and what might be possible impediments to reaching this goal. In addition, this section provides an overview of the company's proposed product in a form that's understandable to lay investors.

In PEPI's prospectus, the section gives the history of piezoelectricity, a scientific report analyzing the potential of piezoelectricity, potential applications of the product, and also patent considerations. Here too you'll find a description of the background of the company—why and when it was formed, the number of employees, contracts for the company, and other similar data.

Before I had read this section of PEPI's prospectus, I was completely in the dark about piezoelectricity. By reading the business section, I learned something about piezoelectricity as well as learning what the Kolms had planned.

For energy and mining companies, much the same type of information is included in the Business of the Company section. Typically it also includes maps and written descriptions of land the company already owns. Many times, pages and pages of the document will present exhaustive maps of the company's developed and undeveloped oil and gas prospects. While these add color to the otherwise uneventful prospectus, a large number of maps means nothing more than that the company has acquired acreage. You should not be swayed into believing that these maps all represent production (i.e. revenues) unless, of course, they *do* represent producing wells. Remember, there is no assured method of finding the exact location of oil and gas deposits. Even if the maps show a number of producing wells near the company's land, there's no guarantee that the company's land also will produce.

In addition, you should not be influenced by the fact that the major oil companies own wells in the immediate vicinity. Often brokers will boast about a company's land position, saying that Exxon (or one of the other majors) owns all of the acreage surrounding the site. You should ask yourself why Exxon didn't buy the rights to the land if it's so good.

The company's planned area of emphasis is also elaborated upon. For energy firms, this emphasis might be on drilling, completing geologic acreage, buying undeveloped acreage, and so on. Similarly, a mining prospectus will describe the mineral the firm is in search of, where it intends to find it, and how the company plans to finance the work. In short, the business section will provide you with an easy-to-read summary of the company's big plans for the future. The point is to make sure it coincides with what the firm said it planned to spend money on.

MANAGEMENT, MANAGEMENT, MANAGEMENT

The managers. This is the section that you should read particularly carefully because it details the backgrounds of the individuals who must achieve the goals laid out for the company. The work histories of the board of directors are given in ten or eleven sentences. If a company plans to develop a product using computer chips, it's crucial to the success of the company that the managers be experienced in the field. If an oil and gas company plans to emphasize wildcat drilling, the managers ought to have years upon years of geologic experience on which to draw in order to make sound judgments. For a mining firm, you should see if the managers are crusty old prospectors or lawyers who predict the price of gold will rise.

In essence, you need to be a detective and fit together all of the clues we have been discussing in order to decide whether or not they go together to make a good case for investment.

Another factor to consider is how many of the members of the board and how many of the officers will be working full time for the company and how much they are being paid. Often a company will assemble a galaxy of industry stars as members of the board, but only one of them actually plans to work for the firm. This isn't necessarily bad, but it should be taken into consideration. Similarly, look at the salaries the board members are drawing. If the salaries appear high, this isn't necessarily a bad sign either; it doesn't mean that the company won't achieve its objectives. Nevertheless, this money won't be spent on furthering the objectives of the company. I know of one underwriting where half of the funds raised were allocated to the salaries of three members of the board. The company may succeed, but you have to stop and ask yourself, "Do I want to invest in a company where 50% of my money is paying a couple of salaries for a year?"

Compared to the sections so far described, most of the rest of the data in a prospectus is not nearly as important. Nonetheless, you should flip through the rest of the brochure to learn if the company has any legal suits pending against it, to unravel the details of the underwriting, and to look at other similar factors.

The prospectus should be read before investing. It is estimated that only one in ten investors even glance through it and only two in one hundred understand what they read. You already know more about new issues than the majority of the investing public. Nowhere else will you be able to gain as much information about an investment and its prospects. The prospectus will tip you off as to how much hope you're buying and how much actual worth. Use this knowledge and be aware of how the market reads this information, and you'll profit.

YOU READ THE PROSPECTUS, NOW READ THE MARKET

I bought Energy Oil, Inc. as a new issue in mid-1981. I read through the prospectus. The company appeared solid with a staff of trained geologists and financial experts, and in addition, the company already owned rights to several producing properties. Six million shares were sold at $1 each and the underwriting was managed by Chesley & Dunn, Inc. I thought the market would react favorably to the solid offering. On the first day of public trading, Energy Oil dropped to 81 cents. What happened?

New stock issues don't exist in a vacuum: their movement is influenced by the general state of the market. Therefore, you should also look at the market's trend at the time in order to gauge the appreciation potential of a new stock issue.

For instance, new venture stock offerings that were cleared in the final quarter of 1980 appreciated on average 98% by March 1981. The pot cooled immediately thereafter. For first quarter 1981 venture deals, the average appreciation of the issues amounted to only 41% by that June. What happened to Energy Oil, a second-quarter 1981 new issue, is a case in point.

Energy Oil suffered from three major weaknesses, undoing any hope aroused by the prospectus. First, the underwriter, Chesley & Dunn, was a new brokerage house and couldn't generate enough support to uphold the issue during the stock's first few days of trading. Consequently, speculators who tried to sell during the first few days of trading took losses.

The second problem with the new issue was that the offering was too large and the shares were priced too high. Energy Oil offered 6 million shares for $6 million in a market that already looked bearish.

Finally, the oil stocks had fallen out of favor with the market, which at the time just wasn't interested in a new oil and gas issue. These three problems caused Energy Oil to strike out in its first

Table 21

Fourth Quarter 1980 New Issues

Company	Initial Price	Bid Price, 3/26/81
Mining		
American Gold Minerals	$0.50	$0.53
Moritz Mining	2.50	3.00
Mountains West Exploration	.10	.28
QED Exploration	.30	.68
Southwest Resources	1.00	.68
High Technology		
BSL Technology	4.00	6.24
Intl. Remote Imaging Sys. (IRIS)	1.00	2.50
Luther Medical Products	1.00	1.93
Oil and Gas		
American Public Energy	7.00	6.50
Aspen Exploration	.60	1.25
Bellwether Exploration	5.00	5.12
Centennial Petroleum	.10	.90
Deca Energy	7.00	11.25
Energy Production Company	1.00	1.00
Hart Exploration	1.00	4.75
Merit Energy	2.00	3.62
Parallel Petroleum	2.00	5.50
Parrent Oil and Gas	.25	.59
Regent Petroleum	.10	.31
Royalty Development	1.00	2.18
Score Exploration	.10	.40
Seville Energy	1.00	1.37
Shannon Oil and Gas	1.00	3.75
Tomahawk Oil and Minerals	.10	.43
Valex Petroleum	2.00	4.61
Woodbine Petroleum	1.00	1.75
Other Industries		
Housing Industries of America	.50	.37
Livestock Financial	.50	.15

few days of public trading. Of course, it's easy to pick out these factors by hindsight and, so far, I'm wiser, not richer, for the experience.*

Once you've read the prospectus, consulted with experts, and decided that the company would be a solid investment, it's time to look at the market. You need to decide whether or not buying the issue through the original offering is your best strategy. If you believe there is little market interest in the issue, your best approach is to wait until the stock opens for public trading, and buy it then. Of course, the wisdom of this latter strategy depends upon whether or not the stock opens at a discount.

Below are two lists of recent offerings. The first list presents fourth quarter 1980 new stock issues at their offering prices and then at their trading prices three months later (see Table 21). The second list contains the same information for companies that went public in the first quarter of 1981 (see Table 22). A summary sheet breaks down the offerings by industry, thereby depicting the average appreciation for each sector (see Table 23).

These new-issue tables provide some interesting and potentially profitable hints. They depict the fickleness of these instruments, but they also offer an indication of the appreciation potential. After examining a company itself, you should look at the industry's recent performance. During the fourth quarter, oil and gas issues turned in the most spectacular showing, followed by high-tech, mining, and other issues. During the following quarter, however, high-tech beat out oil and gas for the first position as a result of the alleged oil glut. These facts suggest that, on a statistical basis, the high-tech issues had a greater potential for appreciation than did the oil and gas issues.

Mining stocks came in third during the fourth quarter of 1980 and last during the first quarter of 1981 because (1) mining is not as glamorous as the other two areas and (2) the price of gold and especially of silver was slumping. This isn't to say, however, that mining stocks don't do well. Investors who bought Mountains West Exploration—which shot up 180%—will certainly attest to this. On the whole, though, mining stocks' average appreciation

---

* However, I persevered and held on to the stock. By the end of 1981, Energy had discarded its market gloom, and grew to $1.44. So, I had a 44% as yet unrecognized gain. Maybe I will be richer for the experience after all.

Table 22

First Quarter 1981 New Issues

Company	Initial Price	Bid Price, 6/17/81
Mining		
Intermountain Resources	$ 0.25	$ 0.18
High Technology		
Data Law	3.00	2.00
Engineering Measurements	3.00	3.37
Genetic Engineering	5.00	11.25
Intl. Institute of Applied Tech.	1.00	1.25
Synthe med	1.00	2.00
Oil and Gas		
Acadia Petroleum	.10	.15
Balboa Exploration	.10	.25
Dallas Oil and Gas	.10	.18
Impact Energy	.20	.28
JM Resources	.25	.35
Lyric Energy	.10	.21
Target Oil and Gas	.25	.25
Tri-Ad Energy	1.25	1.00
Uintah Energy	.50	.28
Viable Resources	5.00	2.50
Western Oil and Mining	.10	.19
Other Industries		
Burst Products	100.00	300.00
Energy Dynamics Intl.	.50	.37
Float to Relax	.10	.03
Grease Monkey Holding	.15	.06
King of Video	.15	.31
Spectrum Communications	.10	.12

of 60% (at a time when the overall average issue went up 132%) reveals the slower growth rate of these stocks.

The general category stocks didn't fare as well as those in other areas. They're not as sexy and not as easily comprehended. These issues represent many different industries and call for entirely different concepts. As a result, brokers don't mount the same big sales effort and, consequently, the stocks don't do as well. This isn't to say that there aren't special situations where these issues do very well. Nevertheless, this is one additional consideration you should add to the mental checklist of things to look for in buying a new issue.

When your broker calls to suggest a new issue, he is required to send the prospectus. Read it with care. Then look at the market. In general, how are new issues doing? Next look at comparable issues—same size, same price, same industry. How did those similar stocks perform in the immediate aftermarket? This should give you an indication—but only an indication—of how well you can expect your issue to do.

Table 23

New Issues Performance
Fourth Quarter 1980 and First Quarter 1981

Industry	Average After Three Months of Public Trading	
	4th 1980 Issues	1st 1981 Issues
Mining	+60%	−28%
High Technology	+100%	+46%
Oil and Gas	+178%	+33%
Other Industries	−48%	+28%
All Industries	+132%	+32%

SOURCE: "Aftermarket Performance of Recent New Issues," *The Denver Stock Exchange,* March 30, 1981, p. 5 and June 22, 1981, p. 5

Another good indicator of a new stock's potential is the underwriter's past performance. Ask your broker to send you a list of the underwriter's recent issues. If most of them are up over their original price (as will be the case for some houses), this, of course, is a very good sign. Conversely, if the underwriter has a spotty record, you might conclude that he cannot develop the needed support or that he is not a very good judge of quality companies.

Remember, new issues don't exist in a vacuum; market forces can downplay even the best of issues.

HITCHING UP YOUR PORTFOLIO

In good times, new issues are all the rage and a very scarce commodity. They are primed for energetic movement from the start. Consequently, demand shoots upward for these issues while the supply remains relatively fixed. For instance, Centennial Petroleum offered only 3.5 million shares at 10 cents. Prior to its SEC clearance, Centennial was described on the street as *The Issue*. Talk ran high and demand ran even higher as venture investors begged, borrowed, and possibly stole to obtain shares of the new issue. Within a month's time of its effective date, continual investor jockeying pushed Centennial up to $1.40.

During times of high demand, obtaining such shares can be quite difficult. Cocktail party conversations revolve around surefire methods of getting the new issue. The first step is to talk with your broker. However, if the house he works for is not a member of the selling syndicate or underwriting group, it may be very difficult to pick up the issue. For this reason, some venture stock enthusiasts open accounts at a number of brokerage houses in order to have access to more new issues.

If your broker does work for a member of the syndicate, your chances are better, and if he's a big producer of the house, your chances are better still. The house doles out its allocation to its best brokers and the brokers dole out their allocations to their best clients. Sometimes it may be in your best interest to find one of the newer, hungrier brokers. They will sell you the new issue in the hope that you'll become a regular client. As a good client, you shouldn't drop the allocation back in the broker's lap on the first day of public trading. While you may make some money, the odds are that you won't be offered any of the next hot new issue that comes along. In the industry, these traders are referred to as "in-and-outers." Finally, no matter how scarce a new issue may be, a broker cannot require you to buy another stock as a requisite for selling you the new issue. This is tantamount to stock manipulation, it is illegal, and you should find another broker immediately if your broker tries to push you to it.

Another tactic you can employ to obtain a new issue is to call the managing underwriter and attempt to persuade one of the brokers there to sell you the issue. Because the firm is managing the offering, their allocation of the issue will be larger than that of other members. You must convince the brokerage house that you're truly interested in doing business with the house, because otherwise they'll look at you as nothing more than a fastbuck artist, what the industry calls "a new issues whore."

Norman Fosback suggests that if you can't find a broker willing or able to sell you a new issue, then you should call the company issuing the stock. Explain to the president or an officer of the firm your interest in the company and your inability to buy the stock. Also, explain to him that your interest in his company is sincere (which means that you'll have to read the prospectus, at the very least) and that you don't plan to dump the stock on the market when it begins to trade freely. While the president himself cannot sell you the stock, he may aid you considerably in securing shares through the underwriter.

These are several possible ways to obtain shares of a new stock issue. The best way, of course, is to maintain a good working relationship with your broker; you'll be rewarded accordingly.

In this chapter, we've looked at new stock issues. Sometimes, they perform very well; other times, not so well. But with the tools you've acquired, you should be able to gauge your risk and evaluate the odds. And then it's just a matter of hitching up your portfolio to the right rocket.

WRAP UP

In this section, we've looked at the four primary areas of the venture stock market: high-tech, energy, and mining stocks, as well as new stock offerings. Our primary purpose has been to suggest a methodology you can employ to analyze these issues specifically and any penny stock in general. Let's sum up some of the factors that must be taken into consideration before you make any venture stock investment decision.

A primary concern is the industry itself. Learn the constraints which every similar company faces. Also, ask yourself if the company is trying to break into an industry controlled by two or three giants or entering an industry with thousands of similar-sized firms. If it's doing the former, then it may not have a chance.

Once you've examined the industry, you can focus your attentions on the company itself. For many of these start-up firms, you cannot rely on the traditional stock market gauges: they just won't work. Often, you'll be forced to use management's own forecasts for the future. First, find out when work will commence on the company's primary endeavor. Second, determine how long the firm will be in the start-up stages and how long management believes it will take for funds to begin flowing into the company's coffers. A related question is whether the firm already has enough capital to reach that point or whether it will have to return to the financial markets for a new infusion of money.

Then you're ready to ask the big question: when does management believe the company will begin showing a profit? Talk to others outside of the company about realistic answers to this question. Once the market gets past its initial fever over the issue, the only way a stock's price can increase in the long run (at least in theory) is if the company's asset growth warrants an upward move. Often rumors may spark a temporary run-up, but once the rumor subsides, the price settles back down. In other words, it is essential that the company soon begin taking in more than it's paying out.

Another point that cannot be stressed enough is the necessity of looking at the firm's management. This can be accomplished in several ways: the prospectus will include this information and as mentioned, a roundabout method is to look at the balance sheet and income statements. Wise managers plan for consistent asset growth and for short-term cash needs.

These considerations can be applied to any industry. For example, the cable and solar industries were not mentioned in this section even though both have been focal points of venture stock market interest. The solar industry is currently in a holding pattern. Many might disagree, but the short-term prospects most definitely do not point to profits. Around the time of the OPEC embargo, solar penny stocks were all the rage, but the great hope faded as soon as it became known that solar collectors weren't about to replace the local utility any time soon.

Another popular venture stock industry is cable. Everywhere you go these days, there's talk of cable television and its breathtaking, limitless possibilities. But before investing in the next cable company that comes your way, learn the basic ingredients of the industry. For instance, all cable firms incur heavy front-end costs to lay the groundwork. These firms typically need a lot of money right away and suffer big losses in the early days. Furthermore, the small cable company faces stiff competition from several very large, well-established firms. This is the kind of information you should seek about any industry.

By learning of the industry's constraints, you can formulate intelligent investment questions. And once you've deciphered the industry, it's just a matter of applying common techniques to analyze the company itself.

NOTE

1. Bruce McWilliams, "For the New Investor," *The Denver Stock Exchange,* June 22, 1981, p. 3.

PART THREE
SOARING

10

Tracking Your Trades

When venture stocks move, they move rapidly: they'll either sky-rocket or tumble. Afterward, they settle back into quietude, building for the next big explosion. When they move again, it'll be with lightning speed. You need to be ready and technical analysis is the best preparation.

At the risk of belaboring the obvious, let me emphasize the over-riding importance of buying stock low and selling it at a higher price. But lying behind this simple dictum is an unspoken assumption: that you can determine what is a "low" price and what is a "high" price. Buying low and selling high isn't as easy as it might sound.

Technical analysis is the flip side of fundamental analysis. In the securities business, those who adhere to the latter method are called "fundamentalists," while those who believe in the former are called "technicians." Technical analysis posits that buy and sell signals aren't seen in earnings reports, oil well discoveries, and big sales contracts. Instead, these signals can be discerned from a stock's recent price moves, from its buy and sell figures, and from relationships between current and past selling prices. The strict technician believes that all information relevant to a company—including truth and rumors—is already reflected in the current selling price of its stock.

One analyst said, "The true technician locks himself in a room and pays no attention to any news—political, economic, or cor-porate—because he believes the market already knows this infor-mation and has taken it into account."[1] The technician watches and charts price trends primarily because he believes that what has happened once will happen again, and that a trend continues until some force causes it to change. We'll see what this means shortly.

SPECULATING VERSUS INVESTING

Essentially, there are two ways to make money in stock markets: investing and speculating. Investors buy stocks based on the underlying value of the company while speculators may well ignore the value aspects of a company if a quick profit appears in the offing. Some contend that speculation (that is, buying one day and selling a short time later) is the only way to make money in the penny market. I disagree, as will those who bought Rainbow Resources for 50 cents in 1969 and sold out in 1981 at $46.80. Money can be made in this market both through speculation and through investment.

Because of the relatively unsophisticated state of the venture market, very few use the tools of the technician to calibrate the timing of their trades for the greatest profit. Those venture market investors and speculators who use these charts will be one step ahead of the rest. This market is incredibly volatile, and missing a sell signal could result in a substantial loss or, at least, the loss of a potential gain.

"The stock market," claims Dun & Bradstreet analyst C. Colburn Hardy, "is rooted 85% in psychology and 15% in economics."[2] I would suggest that for the venture market the psychology factor should be nudged up to 90%. Hardy says, "Everyone who wants to be a successful investor should understand technical analysis."

Technical analysis, though it is primarily a speculator's tool generating buy and sell signals in a precise mathematical fashion, can also serve the investor well. Using fundamental methods, you have chosen a company worth owning; now the only question is when to buy. Technical analysis will help you time your trades for the moment of greatest profit. But before we delve into the fascinating world of stock charts, a word of caution is in order. Stock charts depict the past buying and selling history of a stock. Some who use charts, however, become overconfident about the chart's predictive powers—and pay handsomely for their overconfidence.

Underlying stock price predictions is the theory that history repeats itself. Analysts look at the variables that came together in the past when the price of the stock rose. When these variables all coincide again, the analyst makes a prediction based upon the past. There's always the possibility, though, that some completely unexpected event will render the forecast invalid. It is, therefore, wise to remain somewhat skeptical about forecasts that are derived solely from stock charts. The more conservative among technicians believe that you can't make forecasts from the charts, but that they simply describe, in very accurate terms, current price actions. In addition, a stock's chart can help illustrate how various stocks react to different overall trends in the marketplace.

CATCHING THE PATTERNS

Your broker has already made several suggestions about stocks that are worth buying, and you have studied the annual reports. You decide to invest, but when? If all you can find are the high and low bids for the year, or for the past several years, this is better than nothing (annual reports and Form 10-Ks usually contain this information). If you know the stock is currently selling for close to its yearly high, there's a good probability that it's due for a drop (that is, a correction). I stress probability because there's no indication that the stock won't reach even higher levels. However, you need a chart of the stock's price in order to determine whether the stock's price is moving upward or whether it has been descending.

For finding the best time to buy a New York Stock Exchange security, you could just call up your broker and request that a chart be sent to you. This isn't the case with venture OTC stocks because your broker isn't likely to have a chart of the recent selling trends. He could probably recite recent highs and lows, but he couldn't give an exact history.

Nevertheless, you shouldn't give up on using a chart because your broker doesn't have one. Several services chart venture stocks, and you could subscribe to one of these. You could also construct the chart yourself.

Making a chart is an easy matter. Simply get a sheet of graph paper and make it a daily exercise to sit down with the newspaper and find the previous day's bid and asked price of the securities you're interested in. Each day, place a point at the bid price and another at the asked price. Below that day's prices, record the trading volume. (For OTC stocks, the volume figures are always given in hundreds.)

On August 4, 1981, for example, Advanced Monitoring Systems's quote appeared in papers across the nation in the following form:

AdvMsy   313   8   8¼   ———

This denotes that 31,300 shares of the stock changed hands on the previous day. The indicated bid price paid by market makers was $8, while the asked price was $8.25 (exclusive of commissions, mark-ups, or mark-downs). No change was reported for the bid between this and the previous day, as is denoted by the dash at the end of the quote.

After a month, you'll have a fairly good idea of the stock's current trend. By connecting the bid and asked prices with a line, you can see, in visual fashion, the spread on the security (see Chart 3). If the spread widens, this points to dwindling interest in

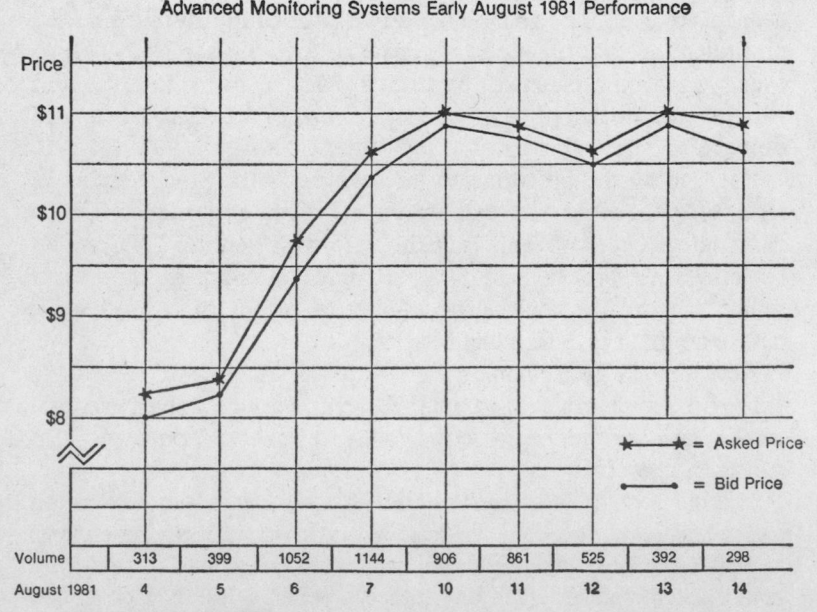

Chart 3
Advanced Monitoring Systems Early August 1981 Performance

NOTE: Volume figures in 100's.

Source: National Over the Counter list, August 4 - 14, 1981

the stock and if the gap narrows, the opposite is true. The volume figures should confirm what the spread and the price direction are already telling you. That is, if the volume figures are steadily increasing, the spread should be narrowing and the price should be upward bound. (There are, however, exceptions to this rule and we'll look at why shortly.)

MAKING SENSE OUT OF THE CHART

With your chart, you can begin to see patterns in the price trends of the stock. There are several further manipulations of the dots and bars that can serve to solidify the trend. First, pencil in a trend line along the tops of the prices. The line is a straight line and should not connect with every point (see Chart 4). Don't draw the trend line across the entire graph unless the trading has been in a relatively narrow zone. The trend line establishes the direction of the stock's price and should not encompass dramatic changes as these represent changes in the trading zone of the stock. We can already begin to make tentative investment prescriptions from this line. If the company's stock price is on the way up, it is a candidate for buying. If the trend line is pointed downward, don't buy, because in all likelihood the trend will continue.

For Advanced Monitoring Systems (whose NASDAQ calling card is AMSI), the trend line continues from early January through the middle of March (see Chart 4). As the stock is declining, the trend line parades along the top of the bid prices. In mid-March, the stock's price jumped appreciably. This calls for a new trend line. This new trend line is sketched in, starting in mid-March, and running through June.

To add another dimension to the chart, draw in a second trend line along the bottom section of the bid prices (see Chart 4). Taken together, these two lines form a channel. The bottom line is referred to as the support level and the top the resistance line. Within the trading channel, the stock seems to resist breaking through the top line. Similarly, the stock never dips below the support line; it remains within the current channel. When the stock's price penetrates one of the trend lines, upward in this case, it calls for the drawing of a new channel.

Channels are basically a speculator's tool. The speculator buys

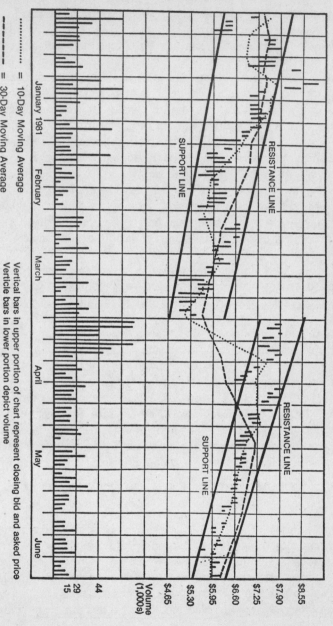

Chart 4
Advanced Monitoring Systems (AMSI)

············· = 10-Day Moving Average

– – – – – = 30-Day Moving Average

———— = A trading channel, formed by trend lines

Vertical bars in upper portion of chart represent closing bid and asked price
Verticle bars in lower portion depict volume

Reprinted with permission of The Denver OTC Stockline

a stock when its price is at the low end of the channel and sells when it reaches the high side; the gain, while small, can usually be reaped within a few days. Investors, too, should use channels to aid in buy and sell decisions. After all, it's better to pick up those few extra fractions of a point than to pass them up.

As the graph shows, the stock will trade in a narrow range until some force precipitates a break from the channel. It is often impossible to foresee from the chart alone what might spark such a jump. (For example, in mid-March, when AMSI rose to a new, higher position, there was no indication from the chart that the move would occur.) After a stock trades above the resistance line for several days, it is said to have penetrated the channel, and a new, higher channel line is drawn.

Another method of detecting trends, this one more mathematical in nature, is to construct moving-average lines for a stock's price. Moving averages are another way to verify the current direction of a stock. For the extremely volatile venture OTCs, a 10-day moving average and a 30-day moving average are usually most useful.

A moving average does just that: it averages out the price of a stock during the time period it covers and then moves. For the 10-day moving average, the price of a stock over the last ten days is added together and then divided by 10, providing the average price of the stock during the last ten days. On the eleventh day, the same calculation is made, adding the most recent day's price and discarding the first day's price. Thus, this new figure represents the new 10-day average stock price (see Table 24).

Table 24

	1st	2nd	3rd	10th	10-Day
10th: Day	Day's Price +	Day's Price +	Day's Price . . . +	Day's Price ÷ 10 =	Moving Average

					New
11th: Day	[(10th Day Moving Average × 10) +	11th Day's Price	− 1st Day's] ÷ 10 = Price		10-Day Moving Average

The price of AMSI's stock jumped from the $5 range up to nearly $8 in mid-March, but the 10-day moving average did not reach that level for several days (see Chart 4). The 30-day moving average moved up even more slowly. Until the price remained at a higher level for several days, the average still factored in the prices from the period when the stock was at the $5 level. Another tentative technical strategy is derived from the relationship between the moving averages and the current stock price. If the moving average is on its way up and a majority of the daily stock prices are above this line, then the stock is indeed on its way up, a good candidate for buying. The converse holds true as well—if the stock's daily price is below the moving average line and the moving average is losing altitude, then it's not a good time to buy.

DECIPHERING VOLUME

The daily buying and selling of a stock—its trading volume—presents yet another barometer by which to measure a stock's current price direction. Up to this point, we've simply looked at the direction of the price and at the price level. No mention has been made of what forces the price of the stock to move in one direction or another. This is where volume comes in. The number of shares that change hands represents the omnipotent forces of supply and demand. Very simply, when demand for a stock outstrips the current number of shares available at a given price, the price rises to induce more shareholders to sell their stock. Conversely, when current shareholders desire to unload their security to a market uninterested at the current selling price, the price drifts lower until an equilibrium is reached.

Stock market theory holds that the price of a stock will move to where the market (that is, the investors) believes the price should be. The move, however, is not along a straight path. Rather, the price bumps along, edging up a quarter and then back down an eighth, until it finally settles. A stock's price is in a constant state of flux as investors change their opinions as to the correct price. As the price moves toward its equilibrium level, other new forces influence the stock. The price then moves again until its new correct level is found.

OTC market makers act as intermediaries in this process and exert a stabilizing influence on rapid price fluctuations. Whenever an investor enters the venture marketplace desiring to buy a security, he'll buy the stock either directly or indirectly from a market maker. Conversely, when he sells, he sells either directly or indirectly to a market maker. The market maker moves the price up or down to reflect the interest, or lack thereof, in the security.

Market makers do not, however, exercise monopoly control over the price of the stock. If the market maker receives many phone calls from the trading desks of other OTC houses looking to buy a particular issue, he begins to move the price up. However, at some point he'll stop receiving phone calls because the price is too high. Accordingly, he'll move it down a notch to see how much interest that price generates. Every market maker is in competition with other market makers in attempting to pay the lowest bid and to receive the highest asked prices. In the final analysis, then, it's you and the multitude of other venture stock investors who influence the way in which a stock's price moves. And it's the volume figures, the amount of buying from and selling to market makers, that depict these forces.

Let's take this out of the theoretical realm and look at a concrete example (see Chart 2). In early January 1981, AMSI sold in the $7 range. Daily trading volume, at that time, averaged around 20,000 shares daily. Over the next two and one half months, the daily volume dwindled. Concurrently, the stock's price slithered down to the $5 range. You'll note that the price decline wasn't a straight line but a zigzag, moving from side to side of the corridor formed by the resistance and support lines. Nevertheless, the volume faltered and the price reflected this. Investors lost interest in acquiring any AMSI for their own portfolios. Consequently, any sale that occurred forced market makers to lower their price. Market makers are always required to buy a minimum number of shares and, in this case, they weren't too happy about it, because they couldn't turn around and sell the stock.

In late March, volume swelled. This suggests one of two things: either a large holder (or a multitude of smaller investors) came into the market and dumped upward of 40,000 shares of AMSI, or one big investor (or many smaller ones) came into the market to buy. The price actions will tell us which it was. The price vaulted back up to the $7 range; buyers entered the marketplace, and interest was once again sparked in the stock as trading volume remained in these new higher ranges for several weeks. Eventually, interest and therefore volume diminished as the price began declining once again.

Rising volume tends to produce even more trades and greater volume. Investors across the country see the growth in the daily volume figures and become more and more interested in the stock. For this reason, the volume figures and the changing levels of volume are important technical indicators. In a sense, volume acts as publicity for the stock.

The penny stock market is composed of a great many individuals, people like yourself, who do not trade tremendous numbers of shares. Consequently, there is not much depth in the marketplace to insulate a security's price from the effect of big sales. Relatively small buys can force a stock's price to move up dramatically. Patricia Dreyfus, in an article entitled "Secret Soarers from A to Z," claimed that "many of these companies [low-priced stock companies] offer outstanding opportunities for profits to investors—as well as some risk, for their thinly-traded stocks tend to be more volatile than shares of the largest corporations bought and sold on the New York Stock Exchange."[3]

Dr. Del Hartley, an economist and one of the few technicians of the venture stock market, notes, "there's no liquidity on no volume."[4] In other words, selling when the market is at a low ebb is likely to perpetuate the forces that lowered the price in the first place. On the other hand, if you should sell out a stock position when market activity is fierce, then there should be no problem in finding a willing buyer for your security at a good price.

In this market, millions upon millions of shares aren't traded on a daily basis, primarily because huge institutional funds don't invest. On August 4, 1981, Piezo Electric Products' stock (whose prospectus we looked at in the last chapter) enjoyed the highest trading volume in the OTC market. On that day, 267,000 shares were bought and sold. At the same time, New York-listed Conoco, in the throes of a takeover, traded 1,838,300 shares. More than six times as many shares of the top-volume New York stock were bought and sold than of the most actively traded OTC security. (Occasionally, though, the top OTC stock's volume will beat out the volume leader on the Big Board.)

AMSI's price move in March resulted from the trading of only slightly more than 50,000 shares. The price paid was between $5 and $7. Thus, at most, only $350,000 (50,000 shares $\times$ $7) in trading forced the price to move. By comparison, if that amount had been spent on Conoco, it would have accounted for slightly less than 3,800 shares—less than 1% of the shares traded of Conoco's Big Board stock.

UPS AND DOWNS

Rising volume coupled with rising prices suggests that investors consider it likely that the stock will continue to rise. They want to buy in and take advantage of the rising price. Obviously, this is a good sign.

On the other hand, if the price rises while the volume dwindles, this is a sign for caution. In the thin penny market, a big buy can thrust a stock's price upward. But when investors don't have much faith in the price continuing to move, they don't buy and so there's little volume. Accordingly, as soon as market makers appreciate this fact, the price will move down, a correction, to compensate for the general lack of interest.

If the volume rises but the price declines, the stock is on its way down. Investors and speculators try to unload their holdings before the price drops further, while market makers resist having to buy up the shares and continue to lower their bid prices.

The final scenario is a declining price at a time of dwindling volume. Investors are reluctant to part with their security because of an underlying belief that the stock's price should be higher. Another way to interpret this, of course, is to suppose that many investors are holding onto losses and are hesitant about selling out, hoping instead that the stock will resurrect itself. But that's just a hope and not a certainty.

Here's an added bit of intrigue for the volume mystery. Inside stockholders, the original financiers of the company, own restricted securities, which cannot be sold until two years after they have been purchased. In addition, insiders are restricted as to the number of shares they can sell during any three-month period. Sometimes an insider will sell off some of his holdings, thus causing the volume to swell for a day. This isn't necessarily a sign of renewed market interest in the stock. You should be aware of this and wait to see if the volume figures remain at a higher level for several days before seeking the causes behind the swell in volume.

Insiders, of course, can also buy large amounts of stock. They are required to provide information concerning these transactions to the SEC as well, and their trading activity, reported in several newspapers, is sometimes a precursor to company developments.

TECHNICAL OUTPUT

Technical analysis provides venture stock investors with a useful tool, but nothing more. It can suggest which are better times to sell and which are better times to buy. Note that I didn't say the best times to buy or sell. If you try to buy at the lowest price or sell at the highest, you'll inevitably miss that moment and fail. The stock's price chart can tell you when the direction changes, but only after the fact, not before.

Often, investors are swayed by belief in the stock chart as a mathematical soothsayer and mechanistic certainty. The charts simply describe the current actions. The stock market doesn't work like a clock, as the chart itself has certainly shown.

However, the charts can point to market timing strategies that can "save money by preventing too-early buying and by avoiding too-late selling."[5] The rule of thumb here is to sell when the trend is down and to buy when the trend is up.

NOTES

1. Bruce McWilliams, "For the New Investor," *The Denver Stock Exchange,* April 6, 1981, p. 4.

2. C. Colburn Hardy, *Dun & Bradstreet's Guide to Your Investments,* 26th ed. (New York: Lippincott & Crowell, 1981), p. 57.

3. Patricia Dreyfus, "Secret Soarers from A to Z," *Money,* July 1981, p. 50.

4. Dr. Del Hartley, interview conducted by the author in Denver, July 20, 1981.

5. Hardy, p. 69.

11

The Right Choice: How to Pick a Venture Stockbroker

In early autumn 1981, *The Penny Stock Newsletter* reported that "the third largest OTC brokerage in the country [M. S. Wien and Company] closed its doors September 10, shocking its friends and competitors." Wien served as a major wholesaler of OTC stock for many years and had recently branched into the area of lower-priced securities. The *Newsletter* commented that just a month earlier, "John Muir & Company, another prominent underwriter of low-priced issues, was closed down by the Securities Investors Protection Corporation (SIPC) after the 71-year-old firm [the firm's assets] dipped below the SEC net capital requirements."*[1]

When these two firms shut their doors, it caused considerable inconvenience to their clients. The SIPC protects the assets of clients in just such events up to certain maximum levels.† While the

---

* Federal security law requires brokerage houses to maintain a certain ratio of indebtedness to liquid assets, called the net capital requirement. When the market declines, brokerage houses' securities drop in value and therefore their assets dwindle. If the firm is not cautious, the value of the assets drops below the required level. In this event, severe penalties are imposed.
† SIPC guarantees client accounts up to $500,000, of which up to $100,000 can be in cash.

clients could rest assured that their funds were safe, the closings caused a delay in the transmission of sales confirmations, of stock certificates, and of checks. Furthermore, the clients were forced to find other brokerage houses. You have enough to worry about in the stock market without added concern about your brokerage house's stability. Obviously, you must exercise extreme caution in selecting a brokerage house and a registered representative (or more colloquially, a broker).

A broker will execute your buy and sell orders. But more than that, your broker will be your main window on the penny stock market. Because this market is still in its infancy, information concerning these stocks is far from ubiquitous. *The National OTC Stock Journal,* and *Barron's* only occasionally feature stories on the companies in the low-priced stock market.

Your venture stockbroker will present various investment alternatives along with counseling. He'll suggest those stocks that he believes are poised to shoot up and those that he expects to increase at a steady rate. He will not, however, make the decisions —that's up to you. Many successful venture stock investors began their investment careers by following their broker's advice to the letter. As they became more experienced, they analyzed the issues themselves, but at first they listened very closely to their brokers. The stockbroker you choose can be as important as the investment decisions you'll finally make.

FINDING THE RIGHT ONE

John Plumb has spent much of his life teaching soon-to-be brokers how to become registered reps at his Investment Securities School. He says, "Many people will shop extensively for a $200 suit, but will utilize the first broker that they come in contact with."[2] Plumb urges those new to the market to shop around, to talk with various brokers, and to get a feel for the situation before finally settling on one individual.

There are essentially two ways to find a broker. Jim Scott, author of *How to Make Money in the Penny Stock Market* and a broker himself, suggests talking with friends and associates.[3] In this excursion, you shouldn't limit yourself only to your well-heeled friends; this market has introduced security investing to many who could not afford to invest in New York stocks.* From these referrals, you can learn the names of various brokers as well as something about their track records.

The second method of finding a broker is through random selection. In Appendix A of this book, there is a list of penny stock brokerage houses. Find one close to you and give them a call. Avail yourself of the toll-free numbers or call collect, if necessary. Brokerage houses are always looking for new clients and will be more than happy to cover the initial expense. Instead of calling a nearby brokerage house, you may want to call one in Denver or Salt Lake City. Because these cities are the focal points of the current explosion, there's something to be said for having a broker where the action is. One broker who happens to work in Salt Lake City said, "The brokers in this area are in constant contact with the management of many penny stock companies and have a better feel for these companies' situations."

The same concept holds true when investing in some of the regional exchanges, which we explore in a later chapter. However, the whole venture stock market is exploding, and low-priced issues now emanate from New Jersey, New York, and Florida, among other places.

When you call a venture stock house, explain to the receptionist your interest in learning more about the market and possibly investing. The receptionist will route your call to the house's broker of the day. In some firms, all the brokers take turns answering questions like the ones you're about to pose. In others, only the newer or less-productive brokers answer routine questions.

When your call goes through, tell the broker that you've never invested in the venture stock market before, and that you might like him to be your guide.† Most likely, he'll be very enthusiastic. He's sure to ask how much you plan to invest. Be honest. Whether it's to be $300, $500, or $5,000, be straightforward; you

* For example, while I worked in Denver, my car mechanic and the woman who cut my hair were both avid investors. They were anything but wealthy. When I began graduate school in Philadelphia a short time later, many fellow students began seeking penny stock market advice. And everyone knows about the legendary budget of a graduate student.
† I refer to brokers as male during the course of this work, but in fact there are a considerable number of female brokers, and they are as confident, competent, and intelligent as male brokers.

want to develop a good relationship with this person and you shouldn't start out on the wrong foot. Talk with the broker for several minutes about his current recommendations for your money and the reasoning behind these selections.

Any time the broker uses words or concepts that you're not familiar with, *stop him and ask for clarification.* Remember, this person will be working for you, not vice versa. If you decide to work with this broker, you'll be paying money for just this service. Many a new investor, for fear of sounding stupid, has let a broker ramble on for several minutes and has failed to understand a word of the conversation. In these instances, the investor and the broker have both wasted their time.

At the end of the conversation, the broker may ask you—or pressure you—to buy one of his recommendations. Here's another firm rule: *Don't.* Ask him to send you materials on the companies that he suggested, material such as the most recent annual report, quarterly financials, and press releases. When you receive these, you can verify for yourself the broker's contentions about the worthiness of the firms. I repeat: *don't invest on the first phone call.* You may eventually invest in the broker's suggestion anyway, but your understanding of the market will grow and your chances will be that much better if you do all your homework.

After making several phone calls to various brokerage houses, you'll get a feel for the vocabulary and basic attitudes of venture stockbrokers. You'll also begin to discern differences in their styles. One or two of them were probably very persuasive. A third, while not as persuasive, seemed to have all the facts. And yet another may have even been a bit bumbling. Stockbrokers aren't a faceless group of men with three-piece suits and three-piece attitudes—they're people like anyone else. You may feel confident about one and completely cold toward another.

The two primary things to consider when selecting a broker have nothing to do with the broker's track record. First, you need a broker with whom you can develop a good rapport. Second, the broker must be honest—and you must *believe* that he is honest. While you probably cannot expect to develop a working relationship with a broker on the first phone call, after several calls, you'll begin to see patterns emerging.

If you can talk with the broker in person, you'll find this is a far better way to develop an understanding. When you're in the offices of the brokerage house, look around. Do you feel comfortable? Some brokerage houses maintain the image of Tiffany's, while others are more like a K-Mart. Don't be deceived: both houses may run up tremendous profits for you and both may channel you into losing stocks. The point is to be comfortable with the brokerage house and the broker's style.

While talking with your potential broker, inquire as to whether the brokerage house has any SEC-filed suits settled or pending. Even though the house may have won the settled suits, dispute isn't a very good sign. Also, ask the broker about the house's net capital standings; you don't want to start investing with a house that's on the verge of financial ruin and it's just better not to have to worry about such things if the answers can be had for the asking.

BROKER BACKGROUND

The explosion in the penny market in late 1980 caused numerous heretofore uninterested people to become stockbrokers, which happens every time the economics of a particular industry improve dramatically. Consequently, there are many people selling stock who probably should be doing something else. To become a broker requires no college education. The average broker does nothing more than pass a test administered by official agencies. (A cram course is offered, specifically designed to help people pass the test.) One broker, derisive of the training of his brethren, remarked that the stockbroker might have a "peripheral knowledge of the business from his daily activities plus his reading of reports and newspapers, and he might have an extra measure of common sense. But, by and large, he does not have to know a great deal to do what he does."[4]

While making your search, ask each potential broker about his background and about any special characteristics that might qualify him as your broker. Be prepared for the sales pitch. In a similar vein, ask him how long he's been a broker; if he's been around a while, he probably has a large number of clients, which might mean that your small account won't get much attention. On the other hand, if he's new to the industry, he probably won't have as many accounts, but he won't have as much experience either. It's a trade-off: you can retain the broker who is well-seasoned but might not pay much attention to your small account, or you can hire the green kid who will pay attention.

This brings us to another point. When you're just starting out in the venture stock market, your account will be small. If your broker produces for you, though, it won't be small for long. You should recognize that some brokers—probably most—are more inclined to pay attention to their larger accounts; it just makes economic sense. Nevertheless, you'll be providing the broker with commissions and you can demand attention as well. On your initial round of phone calls, you won't be able to tell whether or not the broker will actively follow your account. This is something that can only be learned over time.

When you select your broker and decide to jump into the market, he'll begin by asking for seemingly personal information that is required to open your account with the firm, which will be similar to the questions you might be asked if you applied for a department store charge account (e.g., Where do you bank? What's your social security number? Are you a U.S. citizen?). There will also be questions about your personal worth, the purpose of which is to ascertain your financial suitability to invest.

Once you have purchased a stock, you need to send your check to the brokerage house quickly; the money must be in the house's hands within five working days of the date the trade was executed.

After you make the initial investment, you'll undoubtedly scan the newspapers on a daily basis to see how your stock is doing. If you followed the suggestions from the previous chapter, you'll already be charting the price performance of your stock. Make it a point also to follow the other stocks that the broker suggested but which you did not buy. By doing this, you can gauge your broker's ability in a broader manner—and for free. If the word on the street is that penny stocks are pushing forward with amazing rapidity, but your portfolio, as recommended by the broker, is only poking along, this could be a sign that your broker is, shall we say, less than wise. Broker teacher Plumb makes this analogy: "If the average car is getting 20 miles per gallon, but your car only gets eight, then it's time to trade it in."[5] The same holds true with brokers.

Your broker works for you. And even if the account he handles for you is small, you deserve some attention. If you receive nary a phone call from him, either to make further suggestions or simply to inform you of your portfolio's health, it's time to have a little talk. If overall the portfolio has been profitable, then you'll have to decide whether it's in your best interest to retain the particular broker, or whether someone else could have done better for you.

After you have found a broker and effected several trades, your understanding of the market and of your broker's style will grow considerably. You'll know whether your rapport with him is good or bad. A common complaint against brokers—good and bad alike—and one you'll probably share, is that they only recommend that you buy, buy, buy and never advise you when to sell. Here's why: if a stock you purchased is up, you certainly don't want to bail out because it could always inch up a little bit higher. And if it dips from the high, there's always the possibility that it might return to its previous high position. And you sure don't want to miss out on that.

Brokers want you to make the best possible profit, of course, but they find themselves between a rock and a hard place in making sell recommendations. If, after the broker counseled you to sell, the stock continues to climb, you may well say to yourself, "That louse, why did I ever listen to him in the first place?"

Conversely, if the stock price falls below the price at which you purchased it, you'll be very reluctant to sell. Even if you decide you've made a mistake, it's only human nature not to want to part with it at a loss. Hope springs eternal in investors, and brokers are hard put to suggest getting out at a loss. This is especially true if they recommended the stock in the first place. In addition, if the broker recommends that you sell a stock, and you take his advice, only to find that the stock turns right around, you may think to yourself, "That louse, why did I ever listen to him in the first place?"

WHAT YOU PAY

The broker's lifeblood is commissions. Any time you enter the market to buy or sell a security, you'll incur a commission (or mark-up or mark-down). The one exception is when buying a new stock issue, in which case the issuing company pays the commission. When you sell the issue, however, you'll pay a commission. The price level of the commission is always a matter of controversy and sometimes of ill will.

The commission is nothing more than the charge for work done by the brokerage house and your broker. While it may seem to you that all the broker does is fill out the confirmation slip, his work is actually far more extensive. Furthermore, the commission helps to cover the cost of operating the brokerage house five days a week, eight hours a day. To run a brokerage house is a very expensive affair.

Your broker attempts to stay on top of the trends of the market and abreast of the activities of the companies so he can make the best recommendations to you. The commission covers the cost of this research in addition to the operations charges for the transaction.

The amount charged for commission is not always evident on the confirmation slip that you receive as a record of the transaction. In the event of an agency trade—where the house acts as a broker and contacts another brokerage house to buy the security —the price paid in commission is filled out in the appropriate box on the confirmation slip.

The commission box is left unfilled for a principal trade. Of course, this doesn't mean that in a fleeting moment of charity, your broker decided not to charge you for the transaction. Instead, the house, acting as a dealer, dipped into its own inventory to find the stock. The house marks up the price of the security from the going market price. The commission, in this case, is the difference between the current market price and the price you paid.

The same holds true when you sell your stock to the house's account. The house is said to mark down the going bid price when buying the stock. In this case, the difference between the current market bid price and the price paid to you reflects the house's commission.

Now that we've looked at the mechanics of commission fees, let's turn to the hazier subject of what you actually pay. The amount a broker can charge—either through a commission or a mark-up or mark-down—is not fixed by law. The only qualification is that the charge must be "fair and reasonable." Obviously, there's much room for disagreement about what is "fair" and what is "unfair." The Securities and Exchange Commission, in determining what constitutes a fair rate, looks at a number of different factors: whether or not the broker has violated his fiduciary responsibility with regard to the client, whether or not there is evidence of indiscriminate buying and selling, as well as a whole host of other largely qualitative matters. The National Association of Securities Dealers (NASD), the self-regulating arm of the Over the Counter industry, also maintains no strict schedule and, again, requires broker/dealers only to charge what is "fair and reasonable." The NASD, though, offers a guideline for the level of a justifiable commission, 5%. Brokers are advised, but not required, to tack on a 5% surcharge to agency and principal transactions. Most houses charge a minimum fee for any trade. This fee will be encountered when you start out with a $500 investment. These minimum fees range from $25 to $40 and even higher. Because initially you'll be trading in small sums, you should add in the amount of commission to determine the break-even point for your investment.

For example, if the asked price of a stock is $1 and you buy 500 shares, the total cost to you would not be $500. Remember, the house adds on the commission (say, $25), so you bought 500 shares for $525. Thus, the price-per-share cost was $1.05, not the asked price of $1:

ASKED ⅍ OF COMMISSION   TOTAL COST ⅍ OF COST PER
PRICE SHARES CHARGE   SHARES SHARE
$1.00 × 500 + $25   = $525   ÷ 500 = $1.05

In order to recoup your initial investment, the bid price must move to a level covering your total purchase price plus the added commission to sell the security. Assuming the same $25 commission charge, the bid price has to be $1.10 for you to break even with your investment:

TOTAL PURCHASE COMMISSION   ⅍ OF   SELLING
COST   CHARGE   SHARES PRICE PER SHARE
$525   + $25   ÷   500 = $1.10

Once the minimum charge is reached for a transaction, the rest is negotiable. For a sale of $100,000 worth of securities, the total commission paid will be greater than for the $500 purchase. On a percentage basis, though, it will be much lower. For smaller trading, the commission could amount to anywhere from 5% to 7% and upward, while on the larger sales it could be as low as 1% or 2%. Strict guidelines do not exist. Even though many houses follow the New York Stock Exchange Commission book, the broker can charge as much as he likes, as long as it is "fair."

Most brokers only charge the minimum house fee if the sale resulted in a loss for the client's account. However, brokers often believe it fair to charge up to 10% of the cost if the sale resulted in a hefty gain for the client's account, especially when the broker recommended the stock. When you talk with brokers on your initial search, ask them all, point-blank, about their philosophy concerning commissions as well as the house's minimum transaction charge.

With principal trades, where no commission appears on the confirmation slip, determining the commission becomes a bit trickier. The NASD, in calculating the percentage charge that is tacked onto a principal trade, uses the market makers' highest bid and lowest asked price. While I worked at *The Denver Stock Exchange* newspaper, a woman called with a very vexing problem. She read the quote for a security that she owned in the previous week's edition. The bid price in the paper was $1.20 and she was quite pleased because she'd purchased the stock for a dime. She called up her broker and instructed him to sell, assuming she would receive nearly $1.20 per share. She was flabbergasted when she received the confirmation slip, *sans* commission figure, informing her that she sold for 80 cents per share. She quickly calculated the difference between the apparent market price and the marked-down price that she received:

Price Received	Market Price	Market Price	Mark-down
[($0.80	— $1.20	) ÷ $1.20]	× 100 = −33%

She inquired, "Does that seem fair, does that seem reasonable?" I replied, "No," and suggested that she have a heart-to-heart talk with her broker. That failed to clear up the matter and later she contacted the SEC. While the woman enjoyed a tremendous gain, even at 80 cents, the mark-down of one third was unreasonable.

Difficulty over commissions and mark-downs can be avoided altogether. Before you begin actively trading with a particular broker, ask about his philosophy concerning fees. This way, you'll know what to expect. When you make a transaction—either to buy or to sell—ask the broker what he plans to charge. Presumably, you'll avoid the consternation of the woman who sold out at 80 cents when the market was $1.20.

ETHICAL CONSIDERATIONS

The venture stock market has been characterized by detractors as just "a bunch of quick-buck hype artists." While this is far from true, there are undoubtedly some individuals who engage in shortsighted activities, but hypesters can also be found trading in New York stocks. You can avoid them by searching conscientiously for a decent brokerage house and a decent broker.

Some brokers will say to their clients, "Just follow my advice, don't pay any attention to the companies, and you'll profit." If you have a dislike for research and you trust your broker's word, this may prove a profitable strategy. For some it has worked.

It has been the point of this study, though, to give you a good working knowledge of the venture stock market and the types of companies you'll find in the market. You should want to investigate companies that are potential investments, though at first you may feel as if you're traipsing through a dark forest at night. The broker is there to guide you, to focus a flashlight in the right direction; ask him to send you company reports and prospectuses. After a time, the stock market will become clearer and you'll be able to find your own way. Then, while your broker will continue to be your eyes and ears, he won't be your stock market mind.

Through comparing your stockbroker's comments with the actual data in reports, you'll be able to see whether or not he has been straightforward with you. As observed earlier, honesty is the prime consideration in selecting a broker. The good broker will back up his sales pitch with facts, statistics, and solid analysis of the stock's price movement. This is especially true in the venture market where facts often blur into mere potential. Some brokers may claim to have completed all of the research, calculation, and incantation necessary to see that the stock's price is going to rise. If you trust your broker and believe in his ability, that might be all you need. On the other hand, you are paying him for the service of providing information to you, and it just might turn out that professional obfuscation is just a mask behind which to hide his lack of research on the company.

The most common complaint received by the NASD against brokers concerns violation of the ethical conduct rule. The NASD has a simple rule requiring that brokers and their registered representatives "observe high standards of commercial honor and just and equitable principles of trade." The vague phrasing of this clause brings forth complaints based on questionable recommendations and actions of brokers. If you believe your broker has out-and-out lied to you or has misled you in any way, you can file a complaint. A safeguard against this occurrence, of course, is an understanding of the market and a knowledge of what can and cannot happen.

One example of a violation of this ethical conduct rule is "churning." Churning refers to the constant turnover of a portfolio, based on broker recommendations, without much attention to its profitability. For example, a broker might recommend that you move into a stock one day and then out the next; the only one to benefit is the broker himself. Actual churning can be difficult to detect. If the market is in a slump, the broker may only be suggesting what he believes to be the proper course of action. But if after several months you add up the value of your portfolio and determine that you've paid more in commissions than you've actually made, this could be a sign of churning. You can guard against this possibility, though, by not agreeing to buy every stock that your broker recommends but only buying the ones you have researched yourself.

Another common complaint against brokers is the use of fraud, manipulation, or deception to sell a certain security. Leo M. Loll and Julian G. Buckley, in their seminal work *The Over-the-Counter Securities Markets,* describe several violations of the ethical conduct rule. They explain that setting up a fictitious account so as to place an order that would otherwise be illegal is against the rules; buying and selling in a discretionary account over and above the authorized limit; and sending confirmation slips to customers in hopes of causing them to accept transactions are also violations.

A variation on this theme, which is very common in the venture stock market, is as follows: the broker leans over, his eyes dart around, and he whispers, "Something big's about to hit." This is hype. Legal restrictions require that any information concerning dramatic changes in a company's well-being—either good or bad—be dispersed in a broad manner. If a broker should happen to stumble onto information that could affect the stock's market, it is illegal for him to release this information to selected clients. This doesn't stop many venture and listed brokers alike from leaning over and whispering, "Something's looming on the horizon but I can't reveal it to you." Usually, this statement is completed with a suggestion to buy.

While penny stocks often rise on the rumor and fall on the news, many penny stock market investors do buy on their broker's whispers. Sometimes it works, sometimes it doesn't. By law, though, the broker cannot reveal the unreleased information to you. Consequently, the sentence uttered in hushed tones may border on the illegal.

Loll and Buckley give some examples of the sort of comment that your broker is not allowed to use as part of his pitch:

> "We will refund your purchase price if you wish to sell out when the market value is below the purchase price."
>
> "This security will be issued in one week. Give me your order [and your check] today, before the allotment is sold out."
>
> "Get in on the ground floor. I know the price of this security will double in three months."[6]

In reference to the final comment, Robert Davenport, regional administrator of the SEC for the Rocky Mountain region, once said something that makes a lot of sense about a broker who asserts that a stock is going to double or triple in a month: "How the devil does he know? He doesn't," Davenport continued, unless some manipulation is planned.[7]

If your broker states in absolute terms that some stock will appreciate to a predetermined level, it's time to find another broker. He can make a general prediction, such as that the stock will probably move up. But just remember, he can't know for certain unless some manipulation is planned.

One apparent case of stock manipulation took place in mid-1981 with Chipola Oil's new stock issue. The stock was underwritten by Investment Bankers, Inc.—their first and last issue. Chipola offered 20 million shares at 10 cents. Between June (the clearance date) and a month later, the stock shot up to $1.20. Investment Bankers cornered the market on Chipola by buying up the existing shares and by not allowing clients to sell. The underwriter then jacked up the price because it was the only market maker holding any shares. Demand far exceeded supply because there was no supply. Subsequently, the SEC filed suit and the company was eventually liquidated. This is an extreme example and is far from common practice. Nonetheless, it is one example of how a stock can be manipulated.

Again, you can guard against being deceived, defrauded, and manipulated by understanding the market and by cross-checking the facts provided by your broker. If you believe that your broker has treated you unfairly in a legal sense, talk with him. If that doesn't clear up the matter, you can file a complaint with the local NASD office. The complaint is filed by sending a letter detailing the suspected violation. The NASD will route the complaint to the District Business Conduct Committee (composed of broker/dealers from the same region) as well as to the brokerage house in question.

The brokerage house has fifteen days to respond to the complaint. If the house fails to reply, the committee assumes that the house is guilty as charged. On receipt of a response, the committee reviews the allegations and the response in order to decide whether or not the matter warrants further consideration. If the complaint is considerable, hearings are scheduled. The client and the house present their cases at this hearing and the District Business Committee judges whether or not the brokerage house has, in fact, violated the NASD's rules. If the committee decides against the house, they can impose penalties of varying severity. The mildest punishment is a reprimand and possibly a fine. On the other hand, the house and the particular broker could be expelled from the NASD, effectively ending their work in the securities business. Though unavoidable at times, the process is onerous and unpleasant and should be avoided if at all possible.

WHAT TO EXPECT

Obviously, you do not want to get involved in a situation that calls for filing charges against your broker. In any event, the action certainly will not be profitable for anyone. Potential complaint situations can be avoided by:

1) Understanding the operations of the venture stock market.
2) Developing a rapport with the broker.
3) Knowing what to expect and what not to expect from the broker.

We already have examined, at considerable length, the first two concerns. You can expect your broker to treat you honestly and fairly. He must give advice that he believes will eventually lead to profits for your portfolio. He must offer suggestions that fit snugly into your own investment strategy. For example, the advice given to a speculator in venture stocks would be altogether different from that given to a long-term investor, which means you'll have to explain to your broker your own investment desires.

If you want to trade in and out of stocks on a short-term basis, which is fun and exciting, let the broker know. Conversely, if you want to invest and hold your stocks, tell him this. See that he notes this information on the back of your account card.

The securities broker, by law, is required to evaluate the financial suitability of an investment for his client. The broker must examine the client's net worth before making investment suggestions. For example, the investment of a pensioner's entire assets into a venture stock would not be advisable or suitable. On the other hand, for a working person who understands the risks inherent in the market and who invests only a small percentage of his total assets, the investment may be entirely suitable. Remember, you could lose your whole investment or a substantial portion of it. The broker must evaluate your financial situation and make suggestions within these parameters.

You might expect the broker to make short-term strategy suggestions. Because the broker lives off his commissions, it's to his advantage if you continually buy and sell. Exaggerated forms of this develop into churning. The fact remains that it is in the broker's interest for the portfolio to turn over, but it may or may not be in your best interests. You must weigh his suggestions with an understanding of this inherent self-interest on his part.

You cannot, however, expect the broker always to be right. The registered rep is only human. A broker may make a suggestion with the best of intentions and the best available understanding of the company, and the stock may still turn out to be a dog. If this should become a chronic problem, though, it's time to turn elsewhere. "If the average car is getting 20 miles per gallon, but your car only gets eight. . . ."

In short, you can expect an honest, dedicated individual, but for the best results, do your own investigation as well.

NOTES

1. Jan Prince, "Paper Crunch Dealt M. S. Wien Final Blow," *The Penny Stock Newsletter,* October 1, 1981, p. 21.

2. Bruce McWilliams, "For the New Investor," *The Denver Stock Exchange,* December 25, 1980, p. 5.

3. Jim Scott, *How to Make Money in Penny Stocks: The Ultimate Solution to Participating in the Growth of America for the Small Investor* (Annandale, Va.: KS Enterprises, 1979), p. 15.

4. Ray Dirks, *Heads You Win, Tails You Win* (New York: Bantam Books, 1980), p. 34.

5. McWilliams, p. 5.

6. Leo M. Loll, Jr., and Julian G. Buckley, *The Over-the-Counter Securities Markets,* 3rd ed. (Englewood Cliffs, N.J.: Prentice-Hall, 1973), p. 307.

7. Bruce McWilliams, "SEC's Davenport: Some Pressing Issues," *The Denver Stock Exchange,* April 6, 1981, pp. 10–11.

12

The Big Winners:
How to Become One

How to win in the market . . . there's a vexing question if there
ever was one. What's the secret? Alas, there's no pat answer.
Some of you will win—and win big—while others won't do so
well. You can hedge your bets, though, as did the big winners
whose stories we look at in this chapter.

Dick Regan has made a lot of money in venture stocks. He
began investing in 1977 while still in graduate business school;
armed with his MBA textbook methods of security analysis,
Regan thought smugly, "I've learned how to do it and now I'm
going to go out and make a killing." He found a venture stockbroker and explained to him his desire to invest $8,000. The bro-
ker began suggesting some potential investments for Regan, and
the headstrong MBA candidate began asking the traditional investment questions: "What are these companies' debt-to-equity
ratios? Do they have any working capital? And what are their
PEs?"

The broker, somewhat surprised by this interrogation, replied,
"Those things don't matter in the penny market, just follow my
advice." Regan was taken aback, but he invested nonetheless and
it proved a wise move: within six months, Regan's initial $8,000
investment had grown to a little over $25,000.

Dick Regan is one of six successful investors we'll look at. And
while each of them has a different strategy, there are several common threads running throughout. First, all of the investors found

brokers whom they could trust. If they didn't trust one, they found another. Second, they've found that the market experiences tremendous swings and that safety lies in diversifying their portfolios and in holding good stocks. And finally, they all had a lot of fun in the venture stock market. Now let's go back to Regan's story.

FROM PLUNGER TO PROFESSIONAL

On his first foray into the market, Regan bought shares of Burton-Hawks, Phoenix Resources, Columbine Energy, Fremont Energy, and Universal Fuels. Except for Universal Fuels, his investments did quite well. All of his commitments were in the oil and gas industry, again except for Universal Fuels, which was in uranium production.

During the latter half of 1977, Columbine shot up from 17 cents to $2.25; Burton-Hawks climbed from $1.12 to $5; and Fremont Energy nudged $2.50 after Regan bought it for $1.50.

Universal Fuels had grand plans to explore for and produce uranium. Regan bought the stock for $3.50, before Three Mile Island shook the industry. In the accident's aftermath, the stock sunk to $3 before Regan bailed out. He correctly surmised that the fading future of the nuclear power industry didn't bode well for his uranium holding.

About his first venture stock experience, Regan said later, "I didn't even pretend to understand the oil and gas industry or the goings on of the penny market." He added, "I also learned that something else was going on. The fundamentals didn't seem to matter." Regan wasn't sure what the driving force of the market was, but that didn't matter—he was making a lot of money. "I trusted my broker completely. Often, my broker would call to sell me a new issue. He didn't even know anything about the company and I didn't even want to see the prospectus—I would just buy it. The market was overheated back then."

Since those days, though, Regan's been burned several times. He's wiser now, too. In September 1980, the penny stock market started revving up again. "Why, you could almost buy a new issue for a buck and then sell it for three bucks three hours later." During later 1980, the market made a small fortune for numerous small investors, but when the market teetered in the beginning of the following year, many got creamed. Regan warns potential investors to look at the market they're buying into; he believes that the truly wise investor shouldn't jump in head first, as he did several years ago. The market's getting smarter now and investors are scrutinizing the management and the companies instead of blindly stumbling in. He also cautions investors about rumors. He bought a mining stock, whose name shall not be mentioned, at $1 per share. Rumor had it that:

1) The stock was to be listed on NASDAQ.

2) The Coors family (of brewery fame) was taking over the company.

3) The ore content of the company's holdings amounted to sixty-nine ounces of gold per ton.

All of these rumors turned out to be false, the stock dropped by half, and Regan sold out and dumped his broker. This experience hardened him and he adopted a more skeptical attitude about the market. He believes that you can't go on rumor alone; in an informed market, there's no substitute for careful research and reliable information.

Regan has faith in the market, though. So much so, in fact, that he has begun his own venture stock charting service, The Denver OTC Stockline. His technical prescriptions are generally keyed to the volume figures. He emphasizes that this market is not broadly held because huge pension funds and other institutional sources of capital do not support the market. Sometimes a big chunk of stock will be sold by an insider; Regan believes that investors should watch the ensuing days' volume figures to determine whether or not this has occurred. If volume drops back down, this suggests that the price probably won't start leapfrogging upward, despite one day's big jump in volume.

For Regan, the strategies outlined above have paid off well in good times and even better during the bad times.[1]

$500 TO $18,000

In the summer of 1980, Beth Cooke, a reservations clerk for Continental Airlines, decided to become financially independent of her husband. At the time, a friend was urging her to get into the venture stock market. So finally, in July 1980, she plunked down $500 to buy a new oil and gas issue, Ridgeway Oil, although she knew nothing about investing in stocks. She bought 5,000 shares for 10 cents apiece, and when the stock first began trading in the aftermarket, it shot up to 35 cents. "Boy, was that fun—I made $1,250 in a matter of two and one half hours," she said later about her initial plunge.

Next, she bought several other new issues. Cooke opened accounts at several houses to increase her chances of getting new issue shares; her new brokers offered these shares in the hope that she would become a regular client. By the end of 1980, she had turned her $500 into $18,000. When the market heated up, she explained, "You didn't have to work at it."

After accumulating a healthy profit in the venture market, she became curious about investment strategies and about how stock markets work. One of the keys to building up an asset base, she learned, is to diversify your holdings. Accordingly, she took some of her venture stock market profits and bought commercial real estate, which, unlike the sagging residential market, subsequently took off. One year after her initial $500 ante, her stock market portfolio was valued at $15,000 and the real estate at $10,000.

While still a true believer in the venture market, she knows that it is given to very volatile fluctuations, so she spreads her risk by investing in other situations less subject to big swings. But she still enjoys taking chances. "It's fun. When you invest in a start-up oil company and they strike oil, you feel that you're partially responsible. And you own a very small percentage of it." She commented, "The New York market's just not for the small investor. And with today's inflation, you just have to take some of your money and gamble."

Cooke relies primarily on her broker to analyze the new issues for her and she has been very, very successful. Her secret has been to look for a broker whom she trusts, and she's gone through several of them in her short stock market career. She said of one: "He urged me to buy a dime deal and then to sell out at 12 cents, which I did." Later, she calculated that she wound up paying more in commission than she made on the transaction. She ditched that broker pronto.[2]

SCOTT'S EXPEDITION

Jim Scott's an army man. His mannerisms, his bearing, and his gravelly voice all point to a man who has spent years in uniform. In 1980, however, he turned in his dog tags to become a full-time venture stockbroker for Chesley & Dunn, Inc.

He explained his involvement in the venture stock world:

> My own investment career began in 1961 with the purchase of a mutual fund. During the subsequent nine years, I experimented with many forms of investing—all of which benefited my stockbroker the most and me the least. I bought and sold OTC stock, AMEX stock, NYSE stock, and several mutual funds. . . . My willingness to experiment led me to the penny stock market. Beginning with the first cautious purchase of $540, I have netted over $95,000 in slightly more than eight years. I sincerely believe that the penny stock market is the last place that the average investor can make a small fortune.[8]

Scott, obviously, is enamored of this market. Let's look at his early investments and some of the precepts that he has developed for successful venture stock investing.

He was introduced to the market during a visit to Denver in 1971. A stockbroker convinced Scott to invest $540 in a start-up oil and gas company, Energy Minerals, at 18 cents per share. He was skeptical about buying such low-priced shares in a company that operated on a shoestring, but his broker convinced him that the firm's management was aggressive and that its low-priced stock wouldn't be cheap for long. Scott invested, reasoning that "oil and gas is energy and energy development can't be bad." The stock hung on at that level for several months, but by June 1971, Energy Minerals had started to move and Scott was ready for more.

His broker suggested that he buy into another small oil and gas firm, Burton-Hawks. He bought 10,000 shares at 16 cents, for a total investment of $1,630 (including commission).

Both stocks stagnated for the remainder of the year, but as January 1972 began unfolding, the Dow Jones Industrial Average was moving to what proved to be a cyclic high. Scott's stocks began to shoot upward. Burton-Hawks reached $1.68, and believing it couldn't go any higher, Scott sold out for $16,830. He was incredulous; he had netted $15,200 on the investment. The following month, he sold out Energy Minerals at 96 cents, adding $2,309.50 to his portfolio. Since then, Scott has seen both magnificent gains and big losses over the years, but overall he is ahead by $93,000, a more-than-respectable amount.

Scott has come up with three basic tenets for venture stock market investing that, he says, have helped him considerably. "When you decide to buy or sell a stock, be absolutely certain that *you* are making the decision. If you have the slightest doubt about the transaction, don't do it." Scott, like others, notes that one unsettling characteristic of stockbrokers is that they never recommend when to sell a stock, but they're always eager to have you buy more. He cautions that the only time a broker will actually recommend that a stock be sold is when the capital is going directly into another stock. If you have attacked the venture market intelligently—learned about the company and learned about the market—it should be less of a problem to decide when to buy and sell and when to sit tight.

Scott's second key to penny stock trading is to buy only shares selling for under $1. He explains, "Penny stocks that reach a dollar are to be sold, never bought." He suggests that 10-cent stocks that reach a dollar may be overpriced. If this is the case, a severe correction may be in the offing. However, this rule doesn't hold if a stock has been out for a number of years and during that time has traded in the range of several dollars.

Scott's third tenet relates to any investment—New York and venture stocks alike: be patient. The venture market jolts around at amazing speeds and then cools off for several months. This has been the pattern over the last decade. When Scott bought the shares in Energy Minerals and Burton-Hawks, they didn't move for six months. But instead of losing patience, he held on for another six months after that; then, they shot for the sky and Scott's faith was justified.

Scott bought 30,000 shares of Chaparral Resources for an adjusted price of 13.75 cents per share in mid-1973. You'll remember Chaparral from the first chapter as the company that had to cope with the largest oil well fire up until that time and that later dug one of the deepest wells in the Rockies. Scott sold out when the stock doubled at the end of 1973. He made a profit, but if he had persevered and waited patiently until early 1981, he could have sold his shares for more than a half-million dollars.

Patience pays off. If you have thoroughly investigated a firm, you'll be aware of its underlying fundamental strength, which will someday shine through on the quote sheets of newspapers. If a solid stock is down, it's just a matter of time before the stock market corrects for its nearsightedness.

MR. PR AND DR. DENTIST

Everywhere Bob Schulman went in 1978, it seemed that all that people could talk about was their latest penny stock profit. Schulman, who works as public relations director for Frontier Airlines, joked that "at work and in suburbia, the normal talk changed from sex and religion to the penny stock market." By 1980, the chatter had become more intense and more persuasive. Schulman, a skeptic until then, finally asked himself, "Why not?" He decided to take a fling and contacted N. Donald & Company. At the time, investor attention was focused on Centennial Petroleum, a new energy issue. "So, I took a whopping $500 and bought 5,000 shares of the new issue." He later sold part of his holdings when the stock hit 90 cents and the rest at $1.20, earning between eight and eleven times his initial stake. Schulman, who deems himself financially conservative, said, "I couldn't believe what had happened. I was hooked."

Schulman had never invested seriously before. After that fateful December, he bought many new issues (among them Merit Energy and J.M. Resources) as well as aftermarket stocks (among them Ridgeview Oil and Polaris Resources). At one point, his initial $500 accumulated an unrealized gain upward of $10,000. During 1981, though, the worth of his portfolio had diminished to $4,000. Schulman invests solely in oil and gas issues: "It's like owning a little piece of OPEC—every time the oil-producing nations jack up the price, the oil and gas stocks are going to do well." He has bought numerous issues, but says that owing to the demands of his job, he just doesn't have the time to do his own research and therefore relies fairly heavily on his broker.[4]

Dentist Russell Casement learned about the venture stock

market from a patient of his, J. Daniel Bell. When the dentist wasn't at work on his client, Bell was at work on the dentist, extolling the virtues of the market. Finally, in 1977, Casement decided to give it a whirl. He'd invested in New York equities before, but really knew very little about investing in the pennies. With Bell as his broker, he decided to risk $20,000. At first, he invested in three companies and "nothing very much happened for about a year thereafter." On his broker's advice, he traded out of these securities into several high-tech stocks, including Optelecom and Applied Medical Devices. At that point, things really began to cook.

Several of the stocks appreciated two and three times while another shot up sixfold. Casement said, "As the market got hot, it didn't really seem to matter what I positioned myself into . . . it was kind of like throwing darts at a board." He bought $4,500 worth of U.S. Minerals at 10 cents and sold off portions when the stock reached $1, $1.40, and $1.75. He follows his stocks on a daily basis, saying, "You get a feel for where it's going after a while. When it takes a run, it behooves you to take a profit and get back in [into the quality] companies later."

When he first began in the venture market, he listened exclusively to Dan Bell's advice. Later, he retained two brokers from other firms as well. He found this a profitable strategy because he could bounce one broker's suggestion off the other two. After four years in the market, Casement, like the other investors we have looked at, is thoroughly committed.

He no longer blindly accepts his broker's decisions and makes his own instead. Some of them have been wrong: he bought U.S. Energy for $33 a share and sold out when the stock plummeted to $12. His loss was approximately $20,000. Even with his reasoned approach, he still doesn't read the prospectus. He said that "reading the prospectus [is] one of the dumbest things I ever did" because it contains so much negative information. "I read Denelcor's brochure [prospectus] and thought 'no way could I ever invest in this.'" Denelcor turned out to be one of the venture market's top performers since 1977.

Casement doesn't pay any attention to rumors either. He says that there are so many of them that it's impossible to tell which are based on actual fact. "There's always big talk of takeovers, incredible discoveries, or tremendous contracts." He's made it a rule, albeit not a steadfast one, not to buy on rumors. He'd rather stick to the facts.[5]

ON THE CUTTING EDGE

Terry Freeman's been through the mill. He started out with blue chip stocks and lost. Then he began shorting stocks at the end of the 1974 rout, and lost. Moving into options, he again suffered shattering losses. It wasn't until Terry discovered penny stocks that his luck changed for the better. Let's look at his tale.

Freeman worked in San Francisco as a film editor. He never inherited any money and began investing only with his wages. In fact, when he began his investment career, he was earning only $200 a week. These minimal financial resources are important to Freeman's story, as is the fact that his success didn't come overnight, but rather after he had suffered tremendous losses.

Even though he characterizes himself as relatively cautious about his personal financial affairs, he calls himself "a madman investor." Freeman saves his money to feed this seemingly insatiable appetite for investment and speculation. One other characteristic is worth reiterating: his perseverance.

In 1974, an associate of Freeman's suggested to him that it would be a good idea to buy government bonds and gave him the name of a stockbroker who handled such securities. The stockbroker told Freeman to send a check and they would try to acquire the bond. Freeman withdrew $10,000 from his savings account and sent in the money. A week later, the stockbroker called back and said, "Sorry, we didn't get it, but there'll be another auction in a few weeks and we could try again."

Freeman replied, "Well, we *could* try again. But you're a *stock*-broker; what does that mean?" The broker happily explained, and suggested several stocks. Freeman agreed to buy $2,000 worth of U.S. Homes and Kaufmann and Broad, both New York-listed. Keep in mind that Freeman knew absolutely nothing about investing in equities; he bought those stocks and others on his broker's advice alone. Before long, Freeman had all but forgotten his government bond and had his $10,000 positioned in various stocks.

He doubled his investment from the first two stocks, but that was the end of it. During the latter part of 1974 and early 1975, the stock market endured its worst crunch since the 1930s. Freeman's holdings were sliced in half. In his words, "I panicked. I had no feeling for stocks and was totally vulnerable."

Attempting to calm his distraught client, Freeman's broker said "Terry, your problem is that you're swimming upstream. You should be shorting."* Freeman subsequently closed out his long stock positions (taking a loss of $5,000) and thought, "O.K., buying stocks didn't seem to work out, let's try this short selling."

The novice investor was in for another shock. He began selling positions he didn't own—a month before the market hit rock bottom. When buying stocks outright, the most that can be lost is 100%. However, when selling short, there is no theoretical limit as to the amount that can be lost if the stock appreciates. Freeman knows of this firsthand. "I started getting margin calls at work. First, I had to come up with $700 and then—the next day —$900, or else the house would close me out of the positions." Once again, half the money he had invested was lost.

Now Freeman was desperate: "I didn't have much capital left and I needed to get it back, and fast." His broker introduced him to the idea of trading options. Options are short-term warrants enabling the holder to buy a stock at a preset price during a preestablished period of time. Freeman lost money on his long positions thanks to a market decline. He then lost money on his short positions when the market climbed sharply. Freeman started moving what was left of his funds into options; underlying this investment was the assumption that the market would continue to rise. Instead, the market digested its recent gains and drifted into a plateau. Freeman saw all of his options expire worthless.

"I was totally depressed," he says of that period—and small wonder; over the course of the year, he had managed to lose $17,000.

After Freeman's disaster, he lay low for over a year. He figured that he'd had enough investing to last a lifetime. Then he was sent to Denver to edit a news clip. A cameraman there started talking about penny stocks and explained to Freeman how he had pur-

* Short selling or "shorting" means to sell a stock you don't own, hoping to buy it back at a lower price. The speculator "borrows" the stock in order to sell it before he actually owns it.

chased a stock for a dime, sold it for 20 cents, and made a neat $1,000. Freeman's eyes lit up, and he thought to himself, "Maybe this is the answer to my predicament." The cameraman said, "Why don't you go see my broker? He works for Blinder, Robinson & Company."

Once again, Freeman was about to enter an investment area about which he knew nothing. But this foray turned out to be profitable. His broker at Blinder, Robinson suggested a $500 investment in Solar Controls and another $500 in Scientific Exploration. Solar Controls doubled within three weeks and Freeman sold out his position. Scientific Exploration didn't move and later dipped lower, but Freeman held on to it. "Winnings you can always pocket, but it's so much tougher to sell at a loss because you always think the stock will resurrect itself," he says, like others we've already encountered.

Buoyed by his rapidly-earned profits, Freeman was primed and ready to go once again. "Let's play some more," he thought. "I made money on a solar stock and because of the energy crisis, solar is probably the wave of the future. Let's stick with the solars." In late 1977 and early 1978, he bought up a number of solar stocks, such as Solar Development, Soltrax, Solarcell,* and Solar Energy Research.

Then something went awry. No one else seemed to be buying solar and the stocks were going nowhere. The analysts claimed this was because it was wintertime and no one was thinking of solar. "But," they said optimistically, "just wait until summer." The analysts also explained that solar wasn't cost-effective. "But just wait until Congress passes the solar tax credit; then these stocks will make a run." Summer came and went, and still nothing happened.

The analysts then changed their tune. "Just wait until winter when people start paying their utility bills." Winter and the tax credit both passed and still no action. Finally, in late 1978, the solar industry found itself under a cloud: some of the firms in the industry filed for bankruptcy. Upon reevaluation, Freeman decided that he "should stick to the traditional oil and gas stocks."

He began buying into penny energy stocks. His first venture was with Colt Oil, in which he invested $1,000. Six months later, he turned it over for a gain of $300. He bought other energy

* Solarcell, despite its name, manufactures insulation.

stocks, such as Burton-Hawks, Bronco Oil and Gas, and Columbine Exploration. By this time Freeman, turned off to the New York market, was ready to play the pennies full time.

He made twenty-five trades in 1978 (see Table 25). Looking back, he commented that 1978 was a relatively slow year for the venture market. He gained a mere $500 on his short-term trades (those made within a year) and lost $641 on long-term trades (stocks held for at least one year before being sold). Thus, his yearly net figure was —$141.

But despite his loss, Freeman was hooked. "It's so much fun. I make money, I lose money. But I feel so much more involved in this market than I did with my New York stocks."

Before continuing with Freeman's tale, let's look at his records for 1978. Consistent record-keeping is a mundane yet important facet of playing the venture market. Systematic records show you where you've been and what gains are needed to ensure profits. Remember, when you buy at the asked price, the bid price must appreciate to the asked price's former level (and that doesn't even include commissions).

Accurate records also should be kept for tax purposes. Capital gains made on stocks bought and sold within a year's time are fully applicable to an investor's income. For long-term gains, however, only 40% of the profit is applied to ordinary income. Short-term losses reduce ordinary income by the amount of the loss, while long-term losses must be sliced in half before deduction from ordinary income. Accurate records of transactions will simplify the late-night tax figuring sessions commonly encountered just before tax day.

By late 1978, Freeman began entering other venture stock arenas. He laughs about one of the investments, Beef & Bison Breeders, Inc. This firm planned to market beefalo—a hybrid between beef and buffalo. Freeman thought, "Here I am, Mr. Visionary, buying into a new technology that could prove to be the wave of the future." He bought 1,900 shares of Beef & Bison for $10,171. He didn't wait, though, to learn if he was correct in his assumption about the future; instead, he sold out shortly thereafter for $12,678.

During 1979, he bought into Key International Films, a film distribution company; PureCycle, a water purification firm; and a few other concerns. He concentrated on the high-tech and energy

Table 25

Terry Freeman's 1978 Stock Transactions

Company	Number of Shares	Bought For:	Sold For:	Gain (or Loss)
Securities held one year or less: short term				
Solar Dev.	2,500	$ 778	$ 873	$ 95
Soltrax	9,400	2,109	1,220	(889)
Solarcell	1,700	564	593	29
Solar Energy Research	4,000	523	478	(45)
Mountain High	650	650	908	258
Colt Oil	5,000	1,003	1,298	295
Denelcor	250	250	560	310
Computer Automation	100	2,146	2,373	227
Burton-Hawks	500	659	653	(6)
Solar Controls	8,600	4,539	3,086	(1,453)
Marine Nutritional	1,250	938	1,123	185
Federal Energy	7,500	1,256	73	(1,183)
Pan Am	100	733	664	(69)
Western Airlines	100	920	835	(85)
Charter Co.	200	1,039	958	(81)
Mohawk Data	100	695	741	46
Entropy Ltd.	5,000	2,303	840	(1,463)
Key Intl. Films	20,000	2,000	2,998	998
National Paragon	200	962	491	(471)
Polaris Oil and Gas	8,000	2,163	1,038	(1,125)
Solar Industries	15,000	1,500	7,267	5,767
Advent	800	6,783	5,920	(863)
Securities held for more than one year: long term				
Bronco Oil and Gas	2,000	643	92	(551)
Columbine Exploration	1,700	530	440	(90)

fields, relying heavily on his broker for investment suggestions. It was Freeman, however, who made the final decisions. He says that much of his buying was based largely on superficial data, such as the company's name or logo. He also notes that he began to be able to discern when his broker was truly hot on a stock and when the broker was suggesting a stock only because his brokerage house was backing it. Freeman's seemingly unacademic method of selecting stocks is not as off-base as it sounds at first. Some stocks in the venture market receive considerable touting from brokers, while others that are not very sexy or that are in unglamorous industries do not benefit from this attention. And without the sales pitch, the trading volume of the stock remains low.

About his own investments, Freeman says, "I was making money and I didn't know why. It seemed as if the market had a mind of its own. When I had money in the New York market, I watched the news wire and the economic forecasts. When the news was good, the market went up, and when the news was bad, the market went down." But regarding the penny market, he says, "It didn't seem that any of the usual economic forces had any impact. If anything, the market runs on the daily rumor mill."

In February 1979, Freeman's broker introduced him to new stock issues. Freeman said, "New issues, what are those? New issues, old issues, I don't care, I just want to buy at a quarter and sell out at 50 cents." His broker offered him shares of Credo Petroleum at 10 cents. A week after public trading began, he acquired additional shares; all told, he spent $5,874 to acquire 47,233 shares of the fledgling oil and gas company. His investment rose in value until, in April, he sold out through five separate sales for a total of $8,408. He had generated $2,534 in a matter of two months with Credo.

In 1980, the market became super hot and Freeman did tremendously well. Over the year, he only made thirteen trades, and he notes that this in itself may have been one of the reasons he did so well. He didn't move in and out of stocks; instead, he waited for a stock to make a run before selling. His investments were heavily weighted in energy (see Table 26), but his largest gain came from his holdings in Sci-Pro. There, he netted $12,647, buying 27,500 shares at 10 cents and then selling for nearly 56 cents. All of Freeman's gains during the year would be classified as short-term with the exception of the sale of Sci-Pro; his only loss, $250, was in Loch Exploration.

Freeman's tax liabilities for the year's venture stock income are calculated as follows: first, find the net figure for short-term gains and losses. Second, add in 40% of the long-term capital gains. (If he'd had any long-term losses, these would have first been subtracted from the long-term gains.) This sum, $22,000.80, is applied to Freeman's ordinary income for tax purposes (see Table 27).

Table 26

Terry Freeman's 1980 Stock Transactions

Company	Number of Shares	Bought For:	Sold At:	Gain (or Loss)
Securities held for less than one year:				
Winco Petro.	10,000	$1,000	$ 4,644	$ 3,644
Basic Resources				
International	100	1,278	1,394	116
Biofuel	10,000	1,000	2,747	1,747
Interactive	10,000	1,000	5,647	4,647
Sunbelt Explor.	10,000	1,000	3,854	2,854
Denver Explor.	2,000 units	500	800	300
Cheyenne Res.	2,000 units	4,631	7,125	2,494
Loch Explor.	5,000	2,750	2,500	(250)
Storm King Mines	800	800	1,020	220
Ridgeview Oil	2,400	504	648	144
Search Natural				
Resources	300 units	360	1,386	1,026
Securities held for more than one year:				
Sci-Pro	27,500	2,750	15,397	12,647

Freeman continues to invest in the venture market. He purchased insider stock in three companies, helping them get to the point where they could make a public stock offering. One of the firms went bankrupt, resulting in a loss to him of $5,000. For $20,000, he bought 500,000 shares in the other two firms, which subsequently went public. While he is restricted by federal regulations as to how many shares he can sell at any one time, the total $20,000 investment had a market value of $225,000 by late August 1981. Freeman had earned a hypothetical return of 800%

on his money, even including the $5,000 loss. As we pointed out at the beginning of this tale, Freeman has been involved in a number of different investments. In all likelihood, if he had investigated his early ventures more carefully, he would not have suffered such severe losses at the beginning. Nevertheless, he has made the really big gains only through the penny stock market, where he has experimented with numerous venture stocks. His conclusion is that success lies in diversity and patience.[6]

Table 27

Freeman's 1980 Venture Stock Gains
Tax Liabilities

SHORT-TERM GAINS	$17,192.00
SHORT-TERM LOSSES	250.00
NET SHORT-TERM	$16,942.00
LONG-TERM GAINS	$12,647.00
LONG-TERM LOSSES	0
NET LONG-TERM: 40% OF LONG-TERM GAIN	$ 5,058.80
NET NET-GAIN ADDED TO ORDINARY INCOME	$22,000.80

WINNING!

How'd they do it? These investors came to the market without much venture stock knowledge and managed to parlay their inexperience into really big gains. It was more than just luck, and you can do it too. These investors developed an intuitive feel for the market through actual trading activities. And, with the strategies we've examined in hand, you're already way ahead of where these investors were when they began.

They came to the market with very different backgrounds; nevertheless, several factors are the same for each. Let's take a look.

At the outset, they all relied heavily on their respective brokers. After they acquired some experience, they began making their own decisions, but at first decisions essentially were made by the stockbrokers. This is why it is crucial to find a broker that you can trust.

Your broker also will be your prime source of rumors. If you have friends in the market, they too will pass along the latest rumors. In fact, if your paper-carrier invests in the market, he could be another source of this hearsay. You should be very careful, though, about buying on any rumor. Here's why:

1) By the time you hear the rumor, everyone else may have already heard it, thereby running the price of the stock up. You could end up being the "greater fool."

2) The rumor may have been blown so far out of proportion as to make it completely irrelevant to the actual company news.

At first, buy only on a company's fundamentals. After hearing a few rumors, you'll begin to get a feel for their general nature. Furthermore, you may be able to differentiate between those possibly based on fact and those that emanate from some devious or wishful stockbroker.

Susan Rueler, who as a new investor turned $500 into $10,000 over the course of two years, echoes some of the other investors: "My brokers never tell me when to sell—that's always my own decision."[7] We've heard it before; it's important to understand this about brokers. If you want to buy another stock, they'll be glad to recommend which stock to sell. However, if you plan to pull the money out of the market altogether, their lips are likely to be sealed. But in defense of brokers, they too become caught up in the excitement and often believe that a stock could go a little higher.

Frank Cappiello, in *The $2 Window on Wall Street,* argues that investors in low-priced stocks should only consider investment in rising industries. Cappiello's advice is based on the fact that, regardless of how solid a certain company is, the stock will probably be overlooked if the market does not favor its industry.[8] And an overlooked stock doesn't go anywhere.

The investors we've looked at all put their money in rising industries. When the oil glut infected the market, for example, many investors' attentions strayed from start-up oil and gas companies to other areas where there was more activity.

100% GAINS—WHAT TO DO WITH THEM

Max Bowser, who publishes an imaginative little newsletter called *The Bowser Report,* advises followers to sell their venture stocks (which he calls mini-priced) once they have (doubled) in price. He says, "There are few mini-priced stocks that keep going up, up, up—after they have doubled in price."9

Again, this is sensible advice for two reasons. If you sell after the stock appreciates 100%, you'll have made money. Second, as we've seen over and over, the venture stock market's moves are very volatile. When advances are made, many traders come into the market and take their profits. Subsequently, the price moves back down. Bowser says:

> So, you buy a mini-priced stock and eventually it doubles. Then, two things happen. First, you have a feeling of elation. It's like winning first prize at the local bingo game. Next, inevitably, comes the delightful thought, "Well, if it went from $3 to $6, what's to prevent it from going to $9? Anyway, I'll just hold on and see how much more it goes up."
>
> Of course, every day you grab the paper and eagerly turn to the stock tables. Maybe it does go up some more. The odds, though, indicate that most of the time it will go down. Maybe to $4. And that's when you promise yourself, "If that son of a gun goes back to $6, I'll sell for sure." But again, the odds are that it won't go back. It'll probably retreat some more and you've missed your chance.10

Despite these sensible statistical reasons to sell after the stock doubles, you probably will be reluctant to do so. In this situation, follow the strategy of selling off half of your investment and sitting on the remainder. You recoup your original investment and the rest of your position is essentially free. Accordingly, you won't be as emotionally attached to the investment.

The disadvantage to this strategy, of course, is that it limits your profit potential if the stock should continue to rise. Stocks with that much horsepower are usually new issues. You'll have to look at the recent performance of similar new issues to determine the potential for that kind of move, but that's something you should be doing anyway.

As we saw when we discussed stock charts, another indicator worth watching is the stock's daily trading volume. This will give you a feel for whether or not there's much general market interest in the security. If shares only trade sporadically, the market, as a whole, is bored with the security. If you try to buy such a stock, it might tip the demand/supply scales upward and force up the price to you. Similarly, if you try to sell these shares to an uninterested market, the price could drop. Again, an overlooked stock . . .

When a company first goes public, it sells shares to public investors but probably retains the lion's share for insiders. Learn how many total shares are outstanding in the public's hands; this figure is called the "public float" or just the "float." A smaller float encourages more volatility—both up and down—for the stock, because fewer shares influence the supply/demand equilibrium. A larger public float, in percentage terms, guards the stock's market against the possibility of big blocks of stock being dropped.

MARKET MATH

Diversity has been another source of profits for the investors we have examined. If you start with $500, you will probably be limited to buying shares of only one company. On the other hand, if you're starting out with a greater sum, or if you acquire more money to invest, you can start to buy a number of venture stocks. The advantage in diversifying is evident through simple mathematics: if you buy $500 worth of each of ten different companies and one of your holdings goes up 450%, this erases 50% losses in the other nine stocks. In any one stock, you can only lose 100% of your investment, while your gains can be several hundred percent or more in others. By diversifying, you spread the risk—an extremely prudent strategy to follow in the venture market.

Initially, your venture portfolio probably should not exceed 10% of your personal assets. After investing for some time, of course, you can increase this amount. But at first, it's best to follow the venture market's golden rule: don't bet the rent money.

Stock market analysts concur that it is imperative for the investor to have clear-cut goals. "Goals?" you say, "I just want to make money." But there's more to it than that. Some venture stock players are rampant speculators who move into a stock one day and out the next, profiting on as small a move as a quarter of a point. Other investors prefer to find solid companies and hold them.

Personally, I believe in investing in this market. The outsider, one who does not have a direct connection with the market, cannot accurately time daily trades. If you start with only a small sum, most gains will be whittled away by commissions on in-and-out trading.* Cappiello concurs with this assessment. "Don't trade in and out [of venture stocks] on a short-term basis," he says. "That way, you'll get out of the winning stocks before they have a chance to move and you'll be spending too much on commissions."[11]

In other words, you must be patient with your investment. The mere fact that a stock is priced low doesn't automatically mean that it is speculative and will zoom up 500% in a matter of minutes. Bowser says, "More money has been lost in the stock market by impatient investors failing to allow a situation to develop [that is, allowing a stock to appreciate]."[12]

Think back to the investors discussed in this chapter. Sometimes they bought a stock and nothing happened. Then, all of a sudden, the stock took off. Patience rewarded these investors and it will reward you as well. This isn't to say, however, that certain stocks are not simply dogs and will never perform. If a stock is really that bad, then sell out at a loss and chalk it up to experience.

Once you find a broker, discuss with him your stock market goals. The broker, of course, will be more than happy if you're trading in and out because this means more commissions for him. Nevertheless, if you consider your investment to be a long-term investment, make this clear to your broker. Be absolutely sure he understands.

The final piece of advice is to have fun. The venture stock market could make you a fortune, but if you can't stand the thought of possibly losing your investment, don't invest. This market is interesting, perplexing, and spectacular; view it as a challenge and as something to have a little fun with. Above all, remember these two adages: on the one hand, nothing is a sure thing; on the other, nothing ventured, nothing gained.

NOTES

1. Dick Regan, interview conducted by the author in Boulder, Colo., July 1981.

---

* For instance, if the house charges a minimum fee of $35 on your $500 investment, this amounts to 7% of your money. Only 93% of your money will be working for you.

2. Beth Cooke, interview conducted by the author in Aurora, Colo., September 1981.

3. Jim Scott, *How to Make Money in Penny Stocks: The Ultimate Solution to Participating in the Growth of America for the Small Investor* (Annandale, Va.: KS Enterprises, 1979). p. 1.

4. Robert Schulman, telephone interview conducted by the author in Denver, July 1981.

5. Russell Casement, interview conducted by the author in Denver, August 1981.

6. Terry Freeman, interview conducted by the author in San Francisco, September 1981.

7. Susan Rueler, telephone interview conducted by the author in Philadelphia, October 1981.

8. Frank Cappiello, *The $2 Window on Wall Street* (Summit, N.J.: Dow Beaters, Inc., 1981), p. 15.

9. R. Max Bowser, "How to Make Money with Stocks $3 a Share or Less," *The Bowser Report,* May 1981, p. 3.

10. Bowser, p. 7.

11. Cappiello, p. 64.

12. Bowser, p. 2.

13

The New Wall Streets

The OTC market isn't the only place where venture capital investors can prospect for mother lode stocks. Three stock exchanges, each specializing in mining and energy stocks, offer monetary rewards—and risks—unheard of on the major exchanges.

Specifically, the Vancouver Stock Exchange, the Spokane Mining Exchange, and the Intermountain Stock Exchange (in Salt Lake City) have enjoyed a strong resurgence in volume and price over the last five years. The forces behind the growth in these exchanges are the same as those for the venture OTC market: entrepreneurs needing risk capital and small investors seeking to get ahead. The Vancouver market is made up primarily of oil and gas stocks while the other two exchanges' principal draw is mining stocks.

Speculative isn't the word for the trading on these exchanges. Highly speculative is closer.

Jim Fortune, a Colorado Springs businessman, knows of this first hand. He bought 5,000 shares of Butler Resources at 60 cents per share. The firm, a gold mining company whose shares trade in Vancouver, owned a chunk of land in the Bell Mountain area of Nevada. The company merged with American Pyramid Resources, another Vancouver company, resulting in a 2:1 reverse stock split for Butler. A short time later, Fortune sold out for $6.50 (adjusted to reflect the stock split). His profit amounted to 983%.

Fortune enjoyed similar Canadian success with Cold Lake Resources, another Vancouver-traded security. He said, "I bought it at 10 cents and sold out for $2.50." Fortune owned several thousand shares of this hot little performer, and when he sold out, he'd realized a tidy 2,400% gain.[1]

CAREFUL

While the appropriately named Fortune's profit amounted to a considerable sum, the downside risk is equally substantial. You are forewarned that steep run-ups and precipitous drops are very much a part of this wild and woolly speculative arena. The stock that drew far and away the most attention and notoriety to the Vancouver Stock Exchange was March Resources, Ltd. This energy company's closing price in 1980 was $4.63. Six months later, the stock's price had moved as high as $31.50. The big run-up was fueled by talk that the firm was sitting on a huge oil find.

In a June 1981 article entitled "Canada's Oils: How Much Is Hype?" *Business Week* claimed, "Unless March [Resources] and a group of related companies can quickly convert drilling prospects into earnings, some investors and regulators fear that the speculative bubble may soon burst, threatening a horde of new investors in the small, hot Canadian oil stocks."[2] By August 1981, March had plummeted to $7. There were still no confirmed reports on the well that had prompted the stock's high-wire act. When—or if—the news finally does come out, it's likely that March won't move at such a rapid pace.

Henry Huber, who writes a newsletter about the goings-on of Canadian venture stocks, comments, "Speculation loves mystery; that is, what might happen. Once the facts are fully known, the sell-off occurs."[3]

The Vancouver Stock Exchange, site of fast and furious trading activity, has enjoyed spectacular speculative growth. Five years ago, a scant one million shares traded daily, but by late 1981, the daily trading volume had more than quintupled. This exchange has operated since the 1920s but only recently has it enjoyed this rejuvenation. The catalyst behind the growth is the same as for the U.S. OTC market: an urgent drive to uncover oil and gas resources. Many small companies, including some based in America, have sought the capital-producing capabilities of the exchange. Frank Underhill, a Canadian market maker, claims, "Vancouver is now the center of risk capital for the whole world." He backs up this claim by saying that "several hundred new oil and gas and mining issues have been brought public in Vancouver in just the last several years."[4]

There are several ways in which Americans can participate in this excitement. You could contact a broker who owns a seat on the exchange. Then, to execute your trade, you would simply call your broker, who would transmit the instructions to the firm's floor agent. This method is advisable because such a broker has direct contact with the market and knows the rumors, the facts, and the current market interest in a particular Vancouver issue. Alternatively, you could contact a brokerage house in the United States that owns a seat on the exchange. Several of the major houses have agents on the floor to execute trades. In this instance, you've utilized an American house to buy a stock in Canada.

Or you could buy a stock through your own NASD-registered broker/dealer. For the majority of Vancouver issues, he would have to go through one or two middlemen in order to make the transaction for you. There are a number of Vancouver stocks (90 out of 20,000), however, that trade in the U. S. Over the Counter market. U.S. market makers own an inventory of these stocks and buy and sell them for their own accounts.

In closing this brief discussion of the Vancouver Stock Exchange, it's good to remember one Northwestern broker's comments. Mark Lang of Dillon Securities cautions, "There are really some wild stocks up there. You have to be careful with whom you trade." But on the positive side, Lang said in closing, "There are [also] some very, very good situations."[5]

MINING BOOM

The two other exchanges also enjoying robust, renewed activity are the Intermountain Stock Exchange and the Spokane Mining Exchange. Salt Lake City, known for its rampant mining speculation, already has played host to several penny stock booms, including the current one. In the 1950s and again in the early 1970s, the town proved a wellspring of venture capital for mining firms and others.

One pamphlet on Utah stock ventures explained the reason behind the century-old interest in mining and mining stocks. "There is a unique thrill and fascination that comes with speculating in low-priced natural resource stocks that cannot be found in any other investment . . . And when the risk-reward ratio is appetizing, men will dig into their jeans to come up with venture capital 'to speak to the earth,' to find these treasures . . . Of course, the risks are great, but the Intermountain West remains one of the few places where a speculator of small means can still dream realistically of 'hitting it big.' "[6]

The Intermountain Exchange was founded in 1888 as the Salt Lake City Stock and Mining Exchange. Back then as now, miners came to venture capitalists in search of funding. Today the Intermountain Exchange also hosts trading of energy shares as well as various other industries. Its primary interest, though, remains in mining.

Mining is also the mainstay of the Spokane Mining Exchange of eastern Washington, which first began conducting transactions in 1897. Founded primarily to finance mining ventures, the exchange has expanded along with the Coeur d'Alene Mining District of Shoshone County, Idaho. Since the 1880s, the district has produced about $2.7 billion worth of metals and today provides 40% of the nation's newly mined silver.[7] The securities of thirty-three mining companies are traded on the Spokane Exchange. Richard Fudge, president of the exchange, boasts that his exchange enjoys greater volume and greater consistent volume than does the Intermountain Exchange. Transactions of shares in 1980, a record year, totaled more than 29 million, with a market value of $42.5 million. Fast-moving stocks included Little Squaw Gold, Silver Butte, Silver Ledge, and Allied Silver.[8]

To trade stocks in either of these exchanges, you have several choices. The first option is to find a brokerage house that is a member of the exchange in question. To execute an order, you would simply contact your broker, who would in turn contact the firm's floor agent.

Many of these shares also trade in the Over the Counter market. Accordingly, dealers across the country make markets for these select securities, so the trade could be executed just as it would be for other OTC securities.

The action on these exchanges is tremendously volatile and directly tied to the price direction of precious metals. You'll remember from the discussion of mining stocks how the price of the metal influences the price of OTC mining shares. When interest is strong in metals (i.e., the price is rising), volume on these exchanges reaches a frenetic pace. Of course, the same holds true on the downside as well.

These three exchanges offer other means of profiting from the current explosion in venture capitalism. The methods of analysis for companies in these markets are the same as those described for OTC stocks. To invest successfully, it is wise to locate a regional broker. The reason is simple: he, more than others, will be on top of the current situation. Outside of these areas, interest on the part of brokerage houses may be marginal at best.

NOTES

1. James Fortune, interview conducted by the author in Colorado Springs, August 1981.

2. "Canada's Oils: How Much Is Hype?" *Business Week,* June 8, 1981, p. 102.

3. Henry Huber, "Buying on Mystery—Sell on History," *Vancouver Uptrend,* September 1981, p. 1.

4. Frank Underhill, telephone interview conducted by the author in Vancouver, October 1981.

5. Mark Lang, telephone interview conducted by the author in Spokane, September 1981.

6. John Potter, "1980 Digest of Stocks Listed on the Intermountain Stock Exchange," quoted in *One Cent Utah* (North Salt Lake City: Ghost Town Publishing, 1980), p. 5.

7. Art Johnson, "The Coeur d'Alene—Rich in Silver and Penny Stocks," *The Penny Stock News,* November 2–15, 1981, p. 1.

8. Sherie Winston, "Spokane Exchange," *The Penny Stock News,* November 2–15, 1981, p. 13.

14

Venture Stocks: The Future

America is in a period of transition. We're shifting gears, and whether or not the country will slip back into low gear is anybody's guess. The election of Ronald Reagan in 1980 certainly seems to indicate that Americans want their country to move into high gear.

Part and parcel of Mr. Reagan's election victory, of course, was the promise and the hope that the economy would be revived from its inflation-sickened doldrums. In actual programmatic terms, this meant easing onerous taxes, slashing the voracious federal budget, and lessening the stranglehold of regulation.

While the final verdict on the success of the economic program probably won't be in for a decade or longer, we can still discern some of the current economic trends and postulate what the future of the venture stock market might look like.

The deepest tax cuts in history have been legislated, along with the largest cuts in the growth of the federal budget. If the economy doesn't wither away (which, of course, is highly unlikely), further moves will be made to tighten it up. The federal government will steer away from its role as provider of last resort, which will leave a void in the economy. The private sector and, in particular, small business will pick up the ball and run (we hope).

Tax rates, especially those relating to investments, will continue to be eased. The maximum effective rate on capital gains has already been reduced. It's possible that the holding period for long-term capital gains will be reduced to six months, as it was up until the latter half of the 1970s. Further, there are proposals floating around that would lessen capital gains taxes on investments made in small business. Only time and the state of the economy will tell whether or not investment taxes will be reduced further. Nonetheless, the outlook for such measures is certainly good, as it is for venture stock investments.

BOOM TIMES

Time magazine, that preeminent interpreter of popular culture, has already proclaimed the 1980s to be a boom time for venture capitalism. Backing this claim, *Time* estimated that private venture capital investment amounted to $1.1 billion in 1981, almost a fourfold increase since 1979. The magazine, though, only discussed well-heeled capitalists willing to put up more than $1 million in a start-up firm on the cutting edge of "micro electronics, genetics, and robotics."[1]

Time completely overlooked venture stocks. The reason is obvious, though not completely forgivable. Mr. and Mrs. Small Town America, investing a mere $500 in Big Shot Oil, aren't nearly as glamorous as Mr. Slick Businessman, betting a cool million in a robotics start-up. Nevertheless, the venture stock market plays a very important role in the financing of young companies. Hundreds of millions of dollars have been raised there through low-priced equity offerings. As the market matures, it will continue to play an even greater role in the functioning of American capital markets.

An entire industry has sprung up to serve the needs of small venture capital companies and their investors. In response, the number of periodicals reporting on this subject has also expanded considerably. Both *Venture*, which calls itself "the magazine for entrepreneurs," and *Inc.*, which calls itself the "magazine for growing companies," have been around only since 1977. These magazines focus on the latest innovations in the entrepreneurial world as well as on creative financing techniques for small businesses. *Inc.* has hailed the 1980s as "the decade of the entrepreneur."[2] *Money* magazine, a growing national publication, also concerns itself with small business and with the ways in which small investors can stay ahead. While these journals cover the entire spectrum of venture capitalism, specialized periodicals reporting on the venture OTC market have also appeared. Some of the more prominent publications include *The Penny Stock*

News and *The National OTC Stock Journal.* A list of many of the magazines and newspapers directly related to the market is included in Appendix B. If the number of periodicals focusing on a specific subject is any guide, the venture capital stock market will do quite well in the coming years.

The venture stock market has also spawned an entire service industry. Countless new brokerage houses have opened to satisfy the growing demand for venture stocks. Colorado, the *de facto* headquarters of the industry, houses the most venture stock brokerages in the country. In addition, many older houses already specializing in OTC stocks have begun servicing the lower-priced market. (Appendix A includes a comprehensive list of those broker/dealers that have underwritten at least one low-priced new stock issue.) This phenomenon further confirms the proposition that the 1980s are, in fact, a boom time for venture capitalism.

THE PENNIES' ROLE

The number of stock offerings has grown dramatically over the last five years. This is a result of double-digit inflation and of the small investor's desire to get ahead. The overwhelming majority of these issues have been priced under $5. In late 1981, Joel S. Lawson, publisher of *Going Public,* a new issues periodical, claimed that "more equity capital will be raised by companies making their public debut [in 1981] than ever before. The old record of $2.7 billion [raised in the national market] in 1972 should be [easily] surpassed."[8] The venture stock market will continue to play a crucial role in funding entrepreneurial visions and dreams.

Chris S. Metos, Salt Lake City venture stock historian, says of this market and its *raison d'être:*

> Inflation, engulfing not only the United States, but the entire world, will unquestionably remain the most serious problem facing our generation. The severity of inflation, which in the United States averages about 12% yearly, threatens to reduce our society into financial income classes—the financial "haves"—those who have the ability to cope with inflation—and the financial "have nots," who are being driven further down the economic scale. Investments in real estate and big board stocks, which once were

havens of security, are no longer within the financial capability of the younger generation.

The low-priced market represents financial hope for those who need it the most.[4]

In short, there are many reasons for the venture stock market to thrive well into the 1980s: small companies need money, small investors need low-priced investments, and the country needs reindustrialization. But despite all of these compelling incentives, the venture stock market faltered during much of 1981. Why?

VENTURE STOCKS: BARGAINS, OR WORTHLESS SCRAPS OF PAPER?

In late 1980, the venture stock market got overheated. It had happened several times before, over the last decade, and undoubtedly will happen again. The 1980 blaze of activity broke many old records, however. Neophyte investors in the market, lacking background or understanding, bought almost any low-priced stock. These investors knew nothing about the companies or the makeup of the market; all they knew was that their friends were making incredible profits. It was a little like buying the last tickets to the most popular show in town.

Then, in January 1981, something happened. Joe Granville made his infamous pronouncement: "Sell all." Interest rates were hovering in the upper teens. Meanwhile, Ronald Reagan had just been inaugurated. It was against this mixed backdrop that the venture market, for no apparent reason, began sliding. Shortly thereafter, the market took a nose dive. Positive developments on the economic front didn't seem to have any impact: the market held its kamikaze course.

For new and inexperienced investors, it was as if someone in a theater had yelled "Fire." Many investors—new and old alike—sold out their positions and bolted for the doors. The new investors who held onto their stocks grew edgy and wondered whether or not they could make it out unscathed. When they looked, they didn't see any fire, but the rest of the audience was obviously becoming more and more nervous. Many fled, sold out their positions at a loss, and swore they would never go in again.

The alleged fire in this case was the oil glut. Because the venture market is composed of many start-up oil and gas companies, the stabilization of world oil prices caused these stocks' prices to tumble.

Another reason for the decline was an oversupply of new stock issues. Because such tremendous gains were made earlier on new stock offerings, more and more issues were introduced. More than $200 million was raised in Colorado in public offerings during the first six months of 1981, as compared with $280 million for all of 1980. Consequently, the demand just wasn't there to propel the issues upward on their first few days of public trading.

The final explanation of the decline lies in the market's feverish condition itself. By January 1981, many relatively seasoned investors showed incredible profits. They began selling out of these stocks in order to take advantage of the high prices. Remember Dick Regan, the MBA? He contemplated taking out a second mortgage on his house to fuel his venture stock market appetite. But then he thought, "That's crazy" and became a seller, rather than a buyer.

New investors, who had essentially pushed the market to its record levels, saw others selling out. Market makers dropped their bid and asked prices because they were unwilling to buy stock but more than happy to sell it.

Rumor of the fire, then, became a self-fulfilling prophecy. The strange mythology of doom and gloom, which periodically takes hold, overcame investors. Many new investors were left holding stocks bought at high premiums that suddenly became depressed, almost undervalued.

When the venture market drops, it stays low for a long time. Possibly, it is still depressed. Does this mean that the stocks are a bargain? Or instead, does it mean that the market is dead and you've wasted your money and time buying and reading this book? Let's return to our theater analogy to answer this question.

As all of the patrons run out, the theater manager is in a panic. He knows that there is no fire; nevertheless, his patrons can't get out fast enough. Those still standing in line ask nervously, "What's going on?" The cashier is flustered. The manager tries to coax patrons into the theater by marking down the ticket price from $10 to $5 and then down to $2.

You were all set to buy a ticket to what you believed to be the hottest show in town. But people continue running out and the price of entry keeps dropping. Making matters worse, you see the people who have been trampled while trying to get out. You decide to go stand on the curb, away from the rush, to determine your next step. Others follow your lead; now, there's a whole crowd on the curb.

You hear the fire engines racing down the street. You're sure by now that there's a fire and you begin searching for your car keys to go home. The price is down to $1. The manager comes over to explain that the show's great and that there is no fire. "Popcorn's free," he says.

Then, to your surprise, the fire engines race past you to another building that's on fire down the street. The ticket price is down to 50 cents. Do you buy a seat to catch the best show in town or do you go home to watch TV? Do you invest in the venture stock market or do you put the money back in a money market fund? It's up to you.

THE FUTURE

This kind of panic infected the venture stock market during most of 1981. Stocks dropped to new lows, but the market has gone through similar corrections, though not quite as severe. But it's not dead and will thrive well in the 1980s. Here's why.

In the first chapter, I described the various reasons behind the emergence of the market in the first place. If those conditions still hold, which I believe they do, there's no reason to believe that the market won't react in a similar fashion again.

First, let's look at the market from the company's perspective. As we know, many of these companies cannot qualify for a loan and come to the market for equity financing. Start-up companies are as risky as ever.

These companies also come to the public market because interest rates are too prohibitive. Is there any reason to believe that borrowing charges will drop back down to reasonable levels any time soon? I think not.

But there's still a need for rambunctious young companies in the high-tech, energy, and mining fields. And these companies still need money. High-tech firms, carving out niches in the electronics industry, will thirst for more and more venture capital. Energy firms will also need money for risky exploratory efforts. The prospects for this industry, however, seem to have diminished because of stabilized world oil prices. But have they really?

"The United States appears to be on the brink of winning the war it began in the 1970s for control of its energy destiny," trumpeted the New York *Times* in late 1981. The perceptive reader would have learned, though, that this declaration was premature. Buried deep within the article was the fact that the surplus was more a result of stagnant business conditions than of any stepped-up domestic energy production. Indeed, William B. Nobles, Jr., deputy manager of planning of Exxon, said that he sees "only a temporary surplus that is more likely to shrink than to grow."[5] The energy war hasn't been won and, accordingly, the outlook for small venture stock energy firms is still good.

Similarly, mining firms will need risk capital in order to exploit the resources of the earth. The question here is whether or not the price of a given metal will warrant its extraction. Modern-day prospectors will find the precious ore that can be mined at the going price, but they'll still need money to get the ball rolling. The dramatic resurgence of the Spokane and Intermountain exchanges is evidence of this growing necessity.

Let us now consider the market from the investor's point of view. Originally, investors came to this market as a means of easing the pressure of inflation. The superior gains achieved in the market presented a monetary escape hatch that investors could use without investing huge sums. While small investors can now take advantage of money market funds, those instruments are a bit like a treadmill: it's possible to stay even, but what about getting ahead? Inflation has decelerated, but there is considerable uncertainty whether the inflationary cycle will renew itself once the current recession ends. The venture market still offers small investors superior, inflation-beating rewards.

The venture stock market has become an integral part of this nation's financial structure. These stocks play a unique role in the financing of unproven companies. The young companies discussed in this book, along with other similar firms, will be the ones leading the reindustrialization charge. If you accept these assumptions, then the venture stock market may be for you. But I urge you to invest intelligently. It will require a lot of work but should pay off handsomely.

Your first step, once again, should be to find a broker whom you can trust and work with comfortably. Even then, always check the facts concerning any potential investment yourself. Obtain annual reports and quarterly financial statements. Call the firm you're researching and ask them to send sales brochures and any recent press releases. Talk with others about the prospects for the company and for the industry.

If, after all of this work, you decide a company is worthy of investment, look at its price and trading volume history. After all, you don't want to buy a stock at its peak. Look at the quarterly highs and lows to get a feel for where the stock could go. Based on this analysis, you can make a fairly wise decision whether or not this is the right time to buy. A good company today will probably be a good company tomorrow or six months hence. You have time.

On the other side of the coin, after you have invested in a company, you'll receive quarterly and annual reports. Read through them. Is the quality company that you bought two years ago still a quality concern? Is there consistent revenue and asset growth?

When a stock sprints upward, don't be afraid to take a profit (i.e., sell out). You should realize that your chances of selling at the top are very slim; even if you do sell out and the stock moves up a few more notches, you've still made money.

Before you close this book and begin your venture stock market career, I would like to leave you with a thought presented by David Lewis, veteran market watcher.

"This game is fun, exciting, and rewarding. It's a little like poker—the better players usually win. What kind of player are you?"[6]

NOTES

1. Alexander L. Taylor III, "Boom Time in Venture Capital," *Time,* August 10, 1981), p. 46.

2. Christopher A. Leach, "The Billion Dollar Gamble," *Inc.,* September 1981, p. 57.

3. Joel S. Lawson, quoted in David Lewis, "Denver's Penny Stock Bonanza," *Town and Country,* November 1981, p. 73.

4. Chris S. Metos, *The OTC Penny Stock Digest,* Mark Scharmann, ed. (Salt Lake City: Chris S. Metos Publishing, 1981), p. 9.

5. Robert D. Hershey, Jr., "Winning the War on Energy," New York *Times,* October 11, 1981, Sec. 3, p. 1.

6. Lewis, p. 82.

APPENDIXES

Appendix A

Penny Stock Brokerage Houses
The following is a list of brokerage firms that have underwritten at least one new stock issue selling for five dollars or less since 1978. Other firms emphasizing penny OTC stocks are also included. While attempts have been made to include all brokerage houses concentrating in the penny stock market, no assurance is given to its completeness. Toll-free telephone numbers are listed for those firms that have them.

Adams, James, Foor & Co.
1140 N.W. 63rd St., Suite 104
Oklahoma City, Okla. 73116

2261 N.E. 36th St., Suite 4
Lighthouse Point, Fla. 33064

Alexander (Joseph) & Co.
3129 S. Farmcrest Dr.
Cincinnati, Ohio 45213
(Mailing address: P.O. Box 37391
Cincinnati, Ohio 45222)

Alta Investment Co.
410 17th St., Suite 570
Denver, Colo. 80202

American Venture Securities
115 Broadway, Suite 1200
New York, N.Y. 10006
800-221-3411

Balogh Securities
3564 N. Ocean Blvd.
Fort Lauderdale, Fla. 33308

Blair (D.H.) & Co.
44 Wall St., 19th Fl.
New York, N.Y. 10005
800-221-4278

B&L Capital
7300 S. Alton Way, Suite 1
Englewood, Colo. 80112
800-525-7678

Blinder, Robinson & Co.
500 N. Circle
East Bank Bldg. No. 205
Colorado Springs, Colo. 80909

1860 Lincoln St., Suite 803
Denver, Colo. 80203

1385 S. Colorado, Suite 306
Denver, Colo. 80222

6455 South Yosemite
Englewood, Colo. 80111

2000 S. College Ave., Suite 208
Fort Collins, Colo. 80522

4403 Beach Blvd.
Jacksonville, Fla. 32207

12550 Biscayne Blvd., Suite 705
North Miami, Fla. 33181

Lochmann's Plaza at Palm Aire
  Shopping Center
5 S. Pompano Parkway
Pompano Beach, Fla. 33060

4004 Carlisle Blvd., N.E.,
  Suite D
Albuquerque, N.M. 87110

Home Office Plaza
2403 San Mateo, N.E., Suite W-4
Albuquerque, N.M. 87110

4245 Union Rd.
Buffalo, N.Y. 14226

98 Cuttermill Rd.
Great Neck, N.Y. 11021

40 Exchange Place
New York, N.Y. 10004

55 Post Ave.
Westbury, N.Y. 11590
800-525-7678

Bond, Richman & Co.
115 Broadway, Rm. 1815
New York, N.Y. 10006

Brodis Securities
One Great Neck Rd.
Great Neck, N.Y. 11021

Brooks, Hamburger, Satnick
80 Broad St.
New York, N.Y. 10004

Bunker Securities
98 Cutter Mill Rd.
Great Neck, N.Y. 11021

Carm Industries, Ltd.
98 Cuttermill Rd.
Great Neck, N.Y. 11021

Centennial State Security
5990 S. Syracuse, Suite 200
Denver, Colo. 80111
800-645-8278

Chesley & Dunn
Colorado Center
1777 S. Harrison St.
Denver, Colo. 80210
800-525-8539

1111 Camino Del Rio
Durango, Colo. 81301

Columbine Securities
1050 17th St.
2020 Prudential Plaza
Denver, Colo. 80265

Covey & Co.
29 E. 2nd St.
Salt Lake City, Utah 84111
800-321-6404

Craig-Hallum
133 S. 7th St.
Minneapolis, Minn. 55402
800-328-4559

Creative Securities
32 Broadway
New York, N.Y. 10004

Delaney-Christiansen
718 Kearns Bldg.
Salt Lake City, Utah 84101

2144 Washington Blvd.
Ogden, Utah 84401

49 N. University
Provo, Utah 84601
800-453-9466

Devanney (S.W.) & Co.
10200 E. Girard, Suite C-150
Denver, Colo. 80231

2965 Broadmoor Valley Rd.
Colorado Springs, Colo. 80906

121 E. 1st St.
Casper, Wyo. 82601

510 E. Main St.
P. O. Box 549
Riverton, Wyo. 82501
800-525-3711

Dillon Securities
N. 10 Post St., Suite 243
Spokane, Wash. 99201
800-541-0857

Donald & Co. Securities
30 Montgomery St.
Jersey City, N.J. 07302
800-526-3193

Engler & Budd Co.
930 Midwest Plaza Bldg.
801 Nicollet Mall
Minneapolis, Minn. 55402

4905 North Union, Suite 201
Colorado Springs, Colo. 80907

7860 E. Berry Pl., Suite 200
Denver, Colo. 80111

4660 West 77th St., Suite 150
Minneapolis, Minn. 55435
800-525-7342

Faherty & Faherty
11 Broadway
New York, N.Y. 10004
800-221-5729

Financial America Securities
1148 Euclid Ave., Suite 301
Cleveland, Ohio 44115

7232 Pearl Rd.
Middleburg Heights, Ohio 44130

4135 Erie St.
Willoughby, Ohio 44094
800-321-0550

1340 N. 16th St.
Yakima, Wash. 98901

1142 Main St.
Green Bay, Wis. 54301

411 E. Mason St., Suite 226
Milwaukee, Wis. 53202

507 6th St.
Racine, Wis. 53403
800-854-2175

*First Colorado Investments &
Securities*
621 17th St.
First National Bank Bldg., Suite
1801
Denver, Colo. 80293

1830 E. Sahara Ave.
Las Vegas, Nev. 89104
800-525-3537

First Equities Corp.
10 W. First South, Suite 309
Salt Lake City, Utah 84101
800-453-9497

First Financial Securities
2851 S. Parker Rd., 11th Fl.
Aurora, Colo. 80014

The Financial Park
5055 E. Broadway, Suite D208
Tucson, Ariz. 85711

Prentice Office Bldg.
7950 E. Prentice Ave., Suite 100
Englewood, Colo. 80111

300 West Oak St., Suite 1000
Fort Collins, Colo. 80521

Village Center, Suite 10
Lamar, Colo. 81052
800-525-6107
800-821-9191

*First New England Securities
Corp.*
1 Federal St., 34th Fl.
Boston, Mass. 02110

(Mailing address: P. O. Box 2238
Boston, Mass. 02107)

First Southeastern Co.
134 Peachtree St., N.W.,
Suite 810
Atlanta, Ga. 30303

1300 N. Westshore Blvd.,
Suite 100
Tampa, Fla. 33622

711 Green St., Suite 119
Gainesville, Ga. 30501

5454 Wisconsin Ave., Suite 1125
Chevy Chase, Md. 20015

1104 Hamilton Bldg.
Gay St.
Knoxville, Tenn. 37902
800-241-3823

*First Western Securities of
Wyoming*
120 N. Center, Suite 101
Casper, Wyo. 82601
800-443-3343

First United Securities
1900 Wayzata Blvd.
Minnetonka, Minn. 55343

Fittin, Cunningham & Lauzon
833 Belmar Plaza
Belmar, N.J. 07719

211 Morristown Rd.
P. O. Box 187
Bernardsville, N.J. 07924

192 Paterson Plank Rd.
Carlstadt, N.J. 07072

400 Kinderkamack Road
Oradell, N.J. 07649

1500 Central Ave.
Albany, N.Y. 12205

120 Delaware Ave.
Buffalo, N.Y. 14202

Banco de Ponce, Suite 1104A,
Hato Rey
San Juan, Puerto Rico 00918

Fitzgerald, DeArman & Roberts
3005 E. Skelly Dr.
Tulsa, Okla. 74105
(Mailing address: P. O. Box 3094
Tulsa, Okla. 74101)

First National Bank Bldg.
1200 Main St., Suite 410
Hays, Kans. 67601

Wolcott Bldg.
Hutchinson, Kans. 67501

Home State Bank Bldg.
P. O. Box 633
Russell, Kans. 67665

908 W. Park
Enid, Okla. 73701

117 N. 4th St.
Henryetta, Okla. 74437

6401 N.W. Grand Blvd., Suite
100
Oklahoma City, Okla. 73112

140 S. Main
Stillwater, Okla. 74074

Frederick & Company
Cudahy Tower
925 E. Wells St.
Milwaukee, Wis. 53202
(Mailing address: P. O. Box 453
Milwaukee, Wis. 53201)

818 St. Clair St.
P. O. Box 752
Manitowoc, Wis. 54220

Friedman, Manger & Co.
30 Howe Ave.
Passaic, N.J. 07055

64½ Main St.
Little Falls, N.J. 07424

J. W. Gant & Company
7600 E. Orchard Rd., No. 160
Englewood, Colo. 80111

T. Geimer Securities
2955 E. 1st Ave., Suite 400
Denver, Colo. 80206

Hackert & Modesett
5675 S. Tamarac Pkwy.,
Suite 180
Englewood, Colo. 80011
800-433-6930

Hanifen, Imhoff
1125 17th St.
Denver National Bank Bldg.
Denver, Colo. 80202

University Tower Bldg., Suite
1100
University Ave. at 12th St.
Little Rock, Ark. 72204

344 E. Foothills Parkway, Suite
1-E
Fort Collins, Colo. 80525

Village Plaza, No. 203
106 6th Ave.
P. O. Box 324
Glenwood Springs, Colo. 81601

Union Colony Bank Bldg., Suite
F.
Cottonwood Square
1701 23rd Ave.
Greeley, Colo. 80631

328 Main St., Suite 300
Wichita, Kans. 67202
800-525-2136

Helfer Broughton, Inc.
4 World Trade Center, Suite 7178
New York, N.Y. 10048

Hereth Orr & Jones
200 Union, Suite 213
Lakewood, Colo. 80228
800-524-6704

Hyder & Company
214 Gold S.W.
Albuquerque, N.M. 87102

Johnson-Bowles Co.
Continental Bank Bldg., Suite 420
200 S. Main St.
Salt Lake City, Utah 84101
(Mailing address: 418 Douglas St.
Salt Lake City, Utah 84102)
800-453-4549

Kaufmann (Jay W.) & Co.
111 Broadway
New York, N.Y. 10006
800-221-7015

*Kivlan (William C. M.), Stabb &
Montagu, Ltd.*
230 E. 73rd St.
New York, N.Y. 10021

Kobrin Securities
415 Rt. 18
East Brunswick, N.J. 08816
800-526-2455

Larmer-Sykes Co.
600 Bitting Bldg.
107 N. Market
Wichita, Kans. 67202

7611 E. 46th Pl.
Tulsa, Okla. 74145
800-835-3105

Leonard (B. J.) and Co.
Greenwood Plaza
5600 S. Syracuse Circle
Englewood, Colo. 80111
(Mailing address: P. O. Box 1109
Denver, Colo. 80201)

2871 Sky Harbor Blvd.
Phoenix, Ariz. 85034

5353 W. Dartmouth, No. 405
Denver, Colo. 80227

5325 S. Valentia Way
Englewood, Colo. 80111

660 Rood Rd.
Centennial Bldg.
Grand Junction, Colo. 81501

1109 10th Ave.
Sidney, Nebr. 69162

1515 E. Tropicana Ave., Bldg.
 C., Suite 670
Las Vegas, Nev. 89109

1035 12th St.
P. O. Box 486
Cody, Wyo. 82414

207 Grand Ave.
Laramie, Wyo. 82070

P. O. Box 951
Rawlins, Wyo. 82301
800-525-7497

MacDonald, Krieger & Bowyer
356 N. Camden Dr.
Beverly Hills, Calif. 90210

4530 Waikui St.
Honolulu, Hawaii 96821

Main Street Securities
50 South Main St., No. 400
Salt Lake City, Utah 84114
800-426-3076

Malone & Associates
817 17th St., Suite 610
Denver, Colo. 80202
800-221-7700

R. B. Marich, Inc.
999 18th St., Suite 201
Denver, Colo. 80202

Meyerson (M.H.) & Co.
15 Exchange Place
Jersey City, N.J. 07302

2800 E. Commercial Blvd., Rm.
 210
Fort Lauderdale, Fla. 33308
800-526-3166

(Colorado) 800-525-0303
800-327-8875

Monarch Funding Corp.
79 Wall St., Rm. 502
New York, N.Y. 10005

Moore & Schley, Cameron & Co.
2 Broadway
New York, N.Y. 10004

18 The Plaza
Styertowne Shopping Center
Clifton, N.J. 07012

26 Broadway
New York, N.Y. 10004

Muller and Co.
25 Broad St., 20th Fl.
New York, N.Y. 10005

1100 17th St., N.W.
Washington, D.C. 20036

811 Church Rd.
Cherry Hill, N.J. 08002

111 Broadway
New York, N.Y. 10006
800-221-3525

Multi-Vest Corp. of Kansas
4004 E. Kellog
Wichita, Kan. 67218

Neidiger, Tucker, Bruner
1675 Larimer St., Suite 300
Denver, Colo. 80202

1628 Market St., Suite 304
Denver, Colo. 80202

125 E. 8th St.
Casper, Wyo. 82601

300 S. Gillette, Suite B-1
Gillette, Wyo. 82716
800-525-3086

Noble Securities Co.
21 Water St.
Excelsior, Minn. 55331
800-328-8688

Norbay Securities
39-02 Bell Blvd.
Bayside, N.Y. 11361
800-221-0646

North Hills Investors
98 Cutter Mill Rd.
Great Neck, N.Y. 11021

Olsen & Co.
175 S. West Temple
Salt Lake City, Utah 84101
800 363 6771

Omega Securities
Main Lobby, Boise Cascade Bldg.
1600 S.W. 4th Ave.
Portland, Ore. 97201

Patten Securities Corp.
306 Main St.
Millburn, N.J. 07041

170 Summerhill Rd.
East Brunswick, N.J. 08816

Paulson Investment Co.
729 S.W. Alder, Suite 450
Portland, Ore. 97205
800-547-8999

Peterson, Diehl, Quirk & Co.
1201 Dove St., Suite 570
Newport Beach, Calif. 92660

Pittock (E. J.) & Co.
7951 E. Maplewood St., Suite 230
Englewood, Colo. 80111

1212 Pine St.
Boulder, Colo. 80302

817 17th St., Suite 600
Denver, Colo. 80202

5347 S. Valencia
Englewood, Colo. 80111

1 Drake Park, Suite 111
333 W. Drake Rd.
Fort Collins, Colo. 80521

124 N. 4th St.
Grand Junction, Colo. 81501

Valley Federal Plaza, Suite 205
Grand Junction, Colo. 81501

1022 11th St.
Greeley, Colo. 80631

Powell & Associates
2670 Union Ave., Executive Suite 1012
Memphis, Tenn. 38112

Putnam (F.L.) & Co.
50 Congress St.
Boston, Mass. 02109

111 Founders Plaza
East Hartford, Conn. 06108
(Mailing address: P. O. Box 1891
Hartford, Conn. 06101)

1 Steamboat Wharf
Mystic, Conn. 06355

2929 E. Commercial Blvd., Suite 800
Fort Lauderdale, Fla. 33308

Windham Professional Center, Suite 302
North Windham, Me. 04062
(Mailing address: P. O. Box 1390
North Windham, Me. 04062)

228 E. Lothrop St.
Beverly, Mass. 01915

938 Main St.
Chatham, Mass. 02633

First Safety Fund Bldg., Suite 422
470 Main St.
Fitchburg, Mass. 01420

52 Franklin St.
Framingham, Mass. 01701

189 Main St.
Milford, Mass. 01757

32 Pilgrim St.
P. O. Box 84
North Andover, Mass. 01845

69 Main St.
Rockport, Mass. 01966

12 Orchard Hill Rd.
Bedford, N.H. 03102

1 Manor Parkway
P. O. Box 663
Salem, N.H. 03079

300 Powers Bldg.
Rochester, N.Y. 14614

434 State St.
Phillips Bldg., 8th Fl.
Schenectady, N.Y. 12305

3180 Bellevue Ave.
Syracuse, N.Y. 13219

P. O. Box 275
21 Peterboro St.
Vernon, N.Y. 13476

508 Park Bldg.
Cleveland, Ohio 44114

39 Bellevue Ave.
Newport, R.I. 02840

50 S. Main St.
Providence, R.I. 02903

1104 Turks Head Bldg.
Providence, R.I. 02903

157 River St.
Rutland, Vt. 05701

Quinn & Co.
301 Central Ave., N.W.
Albuquerque, N.M. 87103

11001 N. 99th Ave., Suite 120
Peoria, Ariz. 85345

Richey Frankel & Co.
1745 Stout St., No. 500
Denver, Colo. 80202

Rigel Securities
16231 E. Alabama Dr.
Aurora, Colo. 80017
800-831-4751

RLR Securities
7539 W. Oakland Park
Lauderhill, Fla. 33319
800-327-9193

Robertson Securities Corp.
32 Broadway
New York, N.Y. 10004

25-40 Old Kings Highway N.
Darien, Conn. 06820

*Rockey Mountain Securities &
Investments*
909 17th St., Suite 200
Denver, Colo. 80201
(Mailing address: P. O. Box 237
Denver, Colo. 80202)

1007 9th Ave., Suite 206
Greeley, Colo. 80631

Rooney, Pace
11 Broadway
New York, N.Y. 10004

4500 Biscayne Blvd.
Miami, Fla. 33137

182 Middle St.
Portland, Me. 04112

98 Cuttermill Rd.
Great Neck, N.Y. 11021
800-221-4138

Securities Clearing of Colorado
700 Broadway, Suite 1021
Denver, Colo. 80203

2006 Broadway, Suite 201
Boulder, Colo. 80302

411 Lakewood Circle, Suite 103B
Colorado Springs, Colo. 80910

5225 S. Valentia Way, Suite 220
Englewood, Colo. 80111

1007 Lemay St.
Fort Collins, Colo. 80524

1333 N. 13th St., Suite 1
Grand Junction, Colo. 81501

4220 Maryland Parkway, Suite
204
Las Vegas, Nev. 89109
800-525-3562

R. L. Smith & Associates
24 E. Broadway
Salt Lake City, Utah 84111
800-453-3059

Southwest Securities of Florida
5 Marineview Plaza
Hoboken, N.J. 07030
800-526-6057

Michael C. Talley & Company
820 Paulsen Blvd.
Spokane, Wash. 99201
800-247-7011

Underhill Associates
12 Broad St.
Red Bank, N.J. 07701

Unified Securities Corp.
120 Broadway, 30th Fl.
New York, N.Y. 10271
800-221-8584

Vantage Securities
7000 E. Belleview, No. 307
Englewood, Colo. 80111

Venhu Securities
3760 Highland Dr., Suite 303
Salt Lake City, Utah 84106
800-453-0412

Wachtel & Co.
Wire Bldg., Suite 700
1000 Vermont Ave., N.W.
Washington, D.C. 20005

Walford & De Maret
1512 Larimer St., Suite 300
Denver, Colo. 80202

Wall Street West
5340 S. Quebec, Suite 100
Englewood, Colo. 80111

1 California St., Suite 945
San Francisco, Calif. 94111

1702 E. Pikes Peak
Colorado Springs, Colo. 80909

5125 N. Union Blvd.
Colorado Springs, Colo. 80918

3575 Cherry Creek North Dr.
Denver, Colo. 80209

1630 Welton St., Suite 240
Denver, Colo. 80202

2004 N. 12th St., Suite 5
Grand Junction, Colo. 81501

1117 8th Ave.
P. O. Box 1468
Greeley, Colo. 80631

3770 Citadel Dr.
North Colorado Springs, Colo.
80909
800-525-7598

Wegard (L. C.) & Co.
U. S. Highway 130 and Levitt
Parkway
Willingboro, N.J. 08046

Weller (J. W.) & Co.
230 Broad St.
Bloomfield, N.J. 07003

26 Broadway
New York, N.Y. 10004
800-526-1367

Werbel-Roth Securities
5560 W. Oakland Park Blvd.
Fort Lauderdale, Fla. 33313

Western Capital and Securities
1527 S. 1500 East
Salt Lake City, Utah 84105
800-382-3851

White Investment Company
155 S. 300 West, Suite 103
Salt Lake City, Utah 84101

Williamson (A. L.) & Co.
1129 Bloomfield Ave.
West Caldwell, N.J. 07006

Wilson-Davis & Co.
79 W. 1st South
Salt Lake City, Utah 84111

1100 E. Sahara, Suite 1-D
Las Vegas, Nev. 89104
800-453-5735

Wood Gundy
100 Wall St.
New York, N.Y. 10005
800-221-4929

Appendix B

Sources of Penny Stock Information

GENERAL

The Bowser Report
P. O. Box 6278
Newport News, Va. 23606
Monthly; $36 annually

Informally written newsletter concerning minipriced stocks selling for $3 or less in the OTC market as well as on the New York and American Stock Exchanges.

The Ground Floor
6 Deere Trail
Old Tappan, N.J. 07675
Bimonthly; $144 annually

The National OTC Stock Journal
1650 S. Colorado Blvd.
Denver, Colo. 80222
800-824-7888, op. 588
Weekly; $40 annually

Newspaper specifically covers OTC stocks selling for under $10; provides in-depth profiles on penny companies; presents information concerning new issues; discusses trends within the penny market.

The OTC Review
P. O. Box 110
Jenkintown, Pa. 19046
Monthly; $36 annually

Extensive magazine, reporting on OTC and penny stock market.

The Penny Stock Journal
595 5th Avenue
New York, N.Y. 10017
Monthly; $25 annually

Newspaper provides news about penny stock companies, includes extensive quotes.

Penny Stock News
P. O. Box 86
Columbia, Md. 21045
Semimonthly; $45 annually

Comprehensive reports on penny stock companies.

Penny Stocks Newsletter
31731 Outer Highway 10
Redlands, Ca. 92373
Monthly; $240 annually

Penny stock newsletter containing recommendations.

Penny Stock Performance Digest
10076 Boca Entrada Blvd.
Boca Raton, Fla. 33433
Monthly; $39 annually

Summarizes articles from other penny stock periodicals into concise reports.

Penny Stock Ventures
108 Columbus Drive
Jersey City, N.J. 07302
Bi-monthly; $90 annually

Presents penny stock buy recommendations, provides rating service, and tracks new issues.

Profit Strategy Newsletter
Kogerama Building
Koger Office Center
Charlotte, N.C. 28212
Periodic; fee

Newsletter geared toward well-heeled investors interested in venture capital and tax deferral situations.

CHARTING SERVICES

The Denver OTC Stockline
P. O. Box 4202
Boulder, Colo. 80306
Monthly; $175 annually
Quarterly; $125 annually

Stock price chartering service for over 350 penny stocks and others in the energy, mining, high tech, medical, and financial industries; provides daily prices, moving averages, and five-year earnings history; also includes shares outstanding and two-year weekly price ranges.

NEW ISSUES

Going Public: The Initial Public Offering Reporter
1528 Walnut St.
Philadelphia, Pa. 19102
Weekly; $500 annually

Comprehensive summary of all new public offerings—penny stock offerings and others; provides special reports.

Investment Traders
461 Beach 124 St.
Belle Harbor, N.Y. 11694
Monthly; $100 annually

Magazine devoted to the new issues field and recent aftermarket issues; provides short summaries of new issues and recently gone-public companies.

New Issues: The Investor's Guide To Initial Public Offerings
3471 N. Federal Highway
Fort Lauderdale, Fla. 33306
Monthly; $100 annually

Newsletter providing short summaries of new issues; detailed new issues calendar.

EARTH RESOURCES

California Mining Journal
P. O. Drawer 628
Santa Cruz, Calif. 95061
Monthly; $9 annually

Comprehensive journal covering mining industry in the West.

Energy Sources
P. O. Box 1917
Denver, Colo. 80201
Annual; $15.95 annually

Annual reference book that includes financial summaries of small energy companies.

The Mining Record
311 Steele St.
Suite 208
Denver, Colo. 80206
Weekly; $18 annually

Weekly paper covering mining industry and mining securities.

Sundex: The Solar Energy Newsletter
P. O. Box 1699
Grand Central Station
New York, N.Y. 10163
Monthly; $130 annually

Newsletter devoted to business aspects of solar industry; follows approximately 50 OTC companies devoted strictly to solar as well as larger companies with a solar division.

The Wallace Miner
506 6th St.
Wallace, Idaho 83873
Weekly; $17.50 annually

Newspaper devoted to current developments in mining industry in Northwest; Spokane Stock Exchange quotes included.

Western Mining News
N. 3019 Argonne Rd.
Spokane, Wash. 99206
Weekly; $55 annually

Newspaper covering gold, silver, and strategic metals mining and markets. Contains selected quotes from Vancouver and Spokane Stock exchanges as well as from the U.S. OTC market.

VANCOUVER STOCK EXCHANGE

Canadian Market News
P. O. Box 159
Colorado Springs, Colo. 80901
Weekly; $80 annually

Multi-page newsletter providing short descriptions of companies and stock price movement of Canadian energy and mining stocks.

George Cross News Letter
404–750 W. Pender St.
Vancouver, B.C. Canada V6C 1H7
Daily; $225 annually.

Provides concise synopses of companies trading on the Vancouver Stock Exchange.

Uptrend: The Canadian Penny Stock Newsletter
600–789 W. Pender St.
Vancouver, B.C. Canada V6C 1H7
Semimonthly; $200 annually

Two-page newsletter providing short company summaries and stock price activities for Vancouver stocks.

Appendix C

Glossary

AFTERMARKET—Trading of security by public; typically in context of trading new issues after close of offer.

AGENCY TRADE—Security trade made between brokerage houses in which customer incurs commission free.

ALLOTMENT—Portion of new issue allocated to brokerage house, registered representative, or customer.

ASKED PRICE—Price paid by investor to obtain security; also termed offer price.

ASSETS—Those items that give a company worth, including sums owed to the firm, property, plant, and equipment, etc.; can be found on balance sheet.

BACKDOORING—Immediate sale of new stock issue through a broker who did not sell client the issue in the first place.

BALANCE SHEET—Financial statement depicting all of a firm's assets and liabilities and equities.

BASE METALS—All metals except for precious metals.

BID PRICE—Price paid to investor selling an OTC security before mark-up or commission.

BEST EFFORTS—The sale of a new stock issue where underwriter agrees to use its "best efforts" to sell out the issue; contrast with firm commitment offering.

BLUE SKY LAWS—Refers to state securities regulations.

BOOK VALUE—Value of firm's assets on the books attributed to shareholders; synonymous with stockholder's equity. Book value per share determined by dividing stockholder's equity by number of shares outstanding.

BROKER—Refers to one engaged in the buying and selling of securities for others; also informal name for registered repesentatives working for brokerage house.

BROKERAGE HOUSE—Firm engaged in the buying and selling of securities for customers.

CARRIED WORKING INTEREST—Working interest in an oil or gas prospect retained by firm even though another partner carries the costs.

CASING POINT—When oil or gas well has been drilled to targeted depth.

COMMISSION—Sales fee paid by investors in an agency trade.

COMPLETION—Procedure used to alter hole in the ground into one capable of producing oil or gas.

CORE DRILLING—Procedure to obtain ore sample from ore body.

DEALER—Refers to firm that buys and sells securities for its own account; typically, broker/dealers are referred to as brokerage houses.

DEVELOPED ACREAGE—Lease acreage with productive wells.

DEVELOPMENT WELL—Well drilled within the same stratigraphic area as another producing well.

DILUTION—Difference between offering price of new issue and net tangible book value of share.

DRY HOLE—Well drilled for oil or gas that did not prove to contain commercially exploitable resources; also called "duster."

DUE DILIGENCE—Procedure by which underwriter and members of selling syndicate obtain pertinent facts relevant to new stock issue.

EQUITY—Refers to stockholder's interest in company. Common stocks are called "equities."

EXPLORATORY WELL—Well drilled to find oil or gas in previously unproven region; also called "wildcat."

FACE—Exposed portion of mine where work is underway.

FARM-OUT (or FARM-IN)—Agreement whereby an interest holder in a lease assigns portion of that interest in exchange for contribution to development of property. The interest holder is said to farm-out a share of his interest. The other participant(s) are said to farm-in to the acreage.

FIRM COMMITMENT OFFERING—New stock issue whereby the underwriter buys out the stock from the issuing company and then resells it to the public.

GROSS ACRE—An acre in which an interest is owned.

GROSS VALUE OF ORE—The ore content of the ore body multiplied by the current selling price of the metal.

GROSS WELL—A well in which an interest is owned.

HEADS—The value or metal content of an ore before milling.

HOT ISSUES—A new stock issue with widespread interest.

INDICATION OF INTEREST—Expression of desire to buy new stock issue that has not been cleared by the SEC for public sale.

INITIAL OFFERING PRICE—Original price of new stock issue.

JOINT VENTURE—Agreement by two or more parties to conduct business together in a single venture; usually for short duration.

LANDHOLDER'S ROYALTY—Interest paid to a landowner for production of minerals or energy resources; usually a percentage of gross revenues.

LEASE—Rental agreement between landowner and company for potential oil and gas producing acreage. The landowner receives rental fees, bonus fees, and an overriding royalty on any resource revenues generated from the land.

LISTED SECURITIES—Securities that trade on organized exchanges; as such, OTC securities are not deemed listed securities.

MCF—1,000 cubic feet of natural gas; standard measure of gas reserve volume. MMCF is $1,000 \times 1,000$ cubic feet, or one million cubic feet.

MARK-DOWN—Difference between current market bid price and price paid by customers of market-making brokers in a principle trade.

MARK-UP—Difference between current market asked price and price paid by customer of market-making brokers in a principle trade.

MARKET MAKER—A dealer who agrees always to buy and sell certain securities and carries inventory of particular securities.

MINERALIZATION—Precious metal or base metal showings in ore body.

NASD—National Association of Securities Dealers; self-regulating watchdog of the OTC market.

NASDAQ—National Association of Securities Dealers Automated Quotation system; electronic system displaying current bid and asked prices of selected OTC securities.

NET ACRE—The interest in one gross acre owned by party.

NET INCOME—Revenue less costs and taxes; profit.

NET REVENUE INTEREST—Interest in oil or gas revenues attributable to working interest after any royalties and overriding royalties have been paid.

NET WELL—Interest owned in one gross well.

OFFERED PRICE—Synonymous with asked price.

OFFERING CIRCULAR—Abbreviated prospectus used with smaller Regulation A public stock offerings.

OFFSET WELL—Well drilled near an already producing well.

OPEN PIT—Ore body that can be mined directly from surface without need of mine shaft.

OPERATOR—Direct supervisor of oil or gas well drilling activity.

ORE BODY—A mineral mass of earth believed to contain desirable metals.

OVERRIDING ROYALTY—An interest in production revenues over landholder's royalty that is not encumbered with any of the expenses incurred to develop resource.

PAR VALUE—Face value assigned to shares of company; no longer meaningful.

PATENTED MINING CLAIMS—Right to explore for minerals in a certain section of land, secured from federal government.

PAYOUT—That time when gross production revenues cover previous costs to develop well.

PRELIMINARY PROSPECTUS—A draft prospectus for a new stock offer not cleared by the SEC; also called "red herring."

PRECIOUS METALS—Refers primarily to gold and silver.

PRO FORMA ADJUSTMENT—Adjustment of financial data to take into account changes in the company's structure, e.g., pro forma adjustment to earnings statements due to acquisition of another firm.

PROSPECT—A lease to acreage on which company plans to drill well.

PROVED DEVELOPED RESERVES—Oil and gas reserves that are recoverable through existing wells.

PROVED RESERVES—Oil and gas reserves believed to be recoverable under existing economic and regulatory constraints.

PROVED UNDEVELOPED RESERVES—Lease to acreage with potential for producing oil and gas even though no wells have been drilled.

PROSPECTUS—SEC-cleared offering document for the sale of new security issue; must be delivered to original and subsequent buyers for 90 days after clearance.

PRINCIPAL TRADE—Security sale to one's own broker/dealer, i.e., the brokerage house sells the stock to you or buys it from you.

QUIET PERIOD—Usually 90 days after the new stock issue has been cleared for public sale by the SEC. During this time, the company is required to send a new prospectus to owners for any material change in the company's financial outlook.

RED HERRING—Street name for preliminary propectus; called such because of red print advising investors that it is not the final prospectus.

REGISTERED REPRESENTATIVE—Official title of those working for broker companies; in street parlance, called the "broker."

REGISTRATION STATEMENT—The formal document submitted to the SEC to register a securities offering. The statement includes the prospectus for the offer as well as additional information.

REGULATION A—A conditional exemption from full registration for certain public offerings, not exceeding $1.5 million; requires less information to be included in offering circular than for full registration.

RESERVE RECOGNITION ACCOUNTING—Accounting method which attempts to evaluate oil and gas reserves for companies' financial statements.

RESERVOIR—Underground trap of oil and/or gas.

RESTRICTED SHARES—Stock that cannot be sold to the public because it has not been registered with the SEC.

RULE 144 STOCK—Restricted shares sold through registration exemption from the SEC. Restricted shares equal to either 1% of the total outstanding shares or to the average weekly trading volume for the four weeks prior to the sale (whichever is greater) may be sold once in any three-month period; shares cannot be sold until two years after purchase date.

SEC—*See* SECURITIES AND EXCHANGE COMMISSION.

SECONDARY OFFER—Sale of securities by shareholders; in common usage, refers to second and subsequent public sales of stock by company.

SECURITIES AND EXCHANGE COMMISSION (SEC)—Federal watchdog over the entire securities industry.

SECURITY—A negotiable or redeemable instrument representing ownership of, or debt of, or interest in another party.

SELLING GROUP—Typically, refers to broker/dealers assisting the underwriter in dispersing a new stock issue.

SIPC—The Securities Investors Protection Corporation; organized in 1971 to protect investors' accounts at broker/dealers.

SPREAD—Difference between bid and asked price of OTC stock.

STEP-OUT WELL—Oil or gas well drilled to define parameters of already-proven field.

STICKER—Amendment added to already-cleared prospectus indicating changes in material financial condition of firm; process of distributing amendments is known as "stickering."

STOCK DIVIDEND—Distribution of additional shares of security to shareholders relative to number of shares owned.

STOCK IN STREET (NAME)—Securities held in the name of brokerage house even though a customer owns it; facilitates transfer of shares.

STOCK SPLIT—Division of already outstanding shares; e.g., a ten-for-one stock split (10:1) results in nine additional shares being issued, a reverse one-for-ten stock split (1:10) results in ten shares being considered one.

STOPE—Vertical or inclined large ore vein.

SYNDICATE—Joint venture agreement between broker/dealers to sell new stock issue; also called selling syndicate.

TOMBSTONE—Advertisement of new security issue; may contain only limited information.

UNDEVELOPED ACREAGE—Leased acres on which no commercially producing wells have been drilled.

UNDERGROUND MINE—Ore body that can only be developed through the use of underground mine shafts.

UNDERWRITER—Firm that agrees to sell new stock issue.

WARRANT—Security enabling the holder to buy a security during a certain time at a preestablished price.

WORKING INTEREST—Interest in oil and gas lease allowing holder to conduct operations on property, paying all costs associated with portion of interest held, and to receive net revenues attributable to interest, exclusive of royalties and overriding royalties.

The above was compiled with the assistance of Chris S. Metos, *The OTC Penny Stock Digest* (Salt Lake City: Chris S. Metos Publishing Company, 1981), pp. 777–82.

Index

KEEP YOURSELF UP-TO-DATE

WHERE TO PUT YOUR MONEY
Peter Passell

Not long ago, the small investor had few choices—and he didn't make much money on his savings. He could open a passbook account at the bank, buy a government savings bond, or perhaps, get life insurance. Now the savings rules have changed, increasing both the opportunities and the risks. If you have time to read half a dozen newspapers and investment magazines every week you can sort out your optimum choices, but here's a simple, clear guide that will help you to zero in on what's best for you. Written by a former professor of economics at Columbia University, who is also a *New York Times* expert journalist and author of THE BEST, it is soundly based, comprehensive information.

Available in quality paperback   (K37-954, $3.95, U.S.A.)
                                              (K37-955, $4.75, Canada)

MEGATRENDS
John Naisbitt

In this book, John Naisbitt presents a new way of looking at America's future and a new way of understanding the jumble of the present. It shows you the coming decade as a period of great changes and transitions in which America will shift from industrial production to providing service and information. From it you can learn where you should live and how you should target your energies. MEGATRENDS is a primer for the eighties that outlines where our sophisticated technology is taking us, how we will be governed, and how our social structures will change. It is a must for everyone who cares about tomorrow.

Available in pocket-size paperback   (K90-991, $3.95, U.S.A.)
                                              (K32-035, $4.95, Canada)

MORE ABOUT MONEY FROM WARNER BOOKS